The Voice of Nations

Recent Titles in
Contributions to the Study of Music and Dance

Philosophy and the Analysis of Music: Bridges to Musical Sound, Form, and Reference
Lawrence Ferrara

Alfred Einstein on Music: Selected Music Criticisms
Catherine Dower

Salsiology: Afro-Cuban Music and the Evolution of Salsa in New York City
Vernon W. Boggs

Dancing Till Dawn: A Century of Exhibition Ballroom Dance
Julie Malnig

Mainstream Music of Early Twentieth Century America: The Composers, Their Times, and Their Works
Nicholas E. Tawa

Televising the Performing Arts: Interviews with Merrill Brockway, Kirk Browning, and Roger Englander
Brian Rose

Johann Sebastian: A Tercentenary Celebration
Seymour L. Benstock, editor

An Outward Show: Music for Shakespeare on the London Stage, 1660–1830
Randy L. Neighbarger

The Musical Image: A Theory of Content
Laurence D. Berman

Opera Odyssey: Toward a History of Opera in Nineteenth-Century America
June C. Ottenberg

Passport to Jewish Music: Its History, Traditions, and Culture
Irene Heskes

Music of the Repressed Russian Avant-Garde, 1900–1929
Larry Sitsky

THE VOICE OF NATIONS
European National Anthems
and Their Authors

F. Gunther Eyck

Contributions to the Study of Music and Dance,
Number 34

Greenwood Press
Westport, Connecticut • London

Library of Congress Cataloging-in-Publication Data

Eyck, F. Gunther.
  The voice of nations : European national anthems and their authors
/ F. Gunther Eyck.
     p.   cm.—(Contributions to the study of music and dance,
  ISSN 0193–9041 ; no. 34)
  Includes bibliographical references and index.
  ISBN 0-313-29320-1 (alk. paper)
  1. National songs—Europe—History and criticism.   I. Title.
  II. Series.
  ML3580.E93   1995
  782.42'1599'094—dc20   94–13235

British Library Cataloguing in Publication Data is available.

Library of Congress Catalog Card Number: 94–13235
ISBN: 0-313-29320-1
ISSN: 0193–9041

First published in 1995

Greenwood Press, 88 Post Road West, Westport, CT 06881
An imprint of Greenwood Publishing Group, Inc.

Printed in the United States of America

The paper used in this book complies with the
Permanent Paper Standard issued by the National
Information Standards Organization (Z39.48–1984).

10 9 8 7 6 5 4 3 2 1

Copyright Acknowledgments

The author and publisher gratefully acknowledge permission for use of the following
material:

Percy A. Scholes, *God Save the Queen: The History and Romance of the World's First
National Anthem*. Copyright © 1954 by Oxford University Press. Reprinted by permission
of Oxford University Press.

Dionysios Solomos' epigram, *To Psara*, is reprinted, with slight change, in English
translation by M. Byron Raizis from his book, *Dionysios Solomos*. Copyright © 1972 by
Twayne Publishers, Inc. Used by permission of Twayne Publishers, an imprint of
Macmillan Publishing Company.

To Diane,
who made it possible

Contents

Acknowledgments

This pioneering study could not have been completed without the generous help of old and new friends in both the old and the new world. They are so numerous that, regrettably, only the briefest individual acknowledgment can be recorded here. Worse still, those many who have taken an interest in the project and sampled a chapter without a detailed comment or who helped with the logistics of supplying research materials have to remain unmentioned.

Collectively, this book owes its existence in the first place to European embassies in Washington, D.C., and to national libraries or archives in various European capitals. Thanks must also go to my colleagues at The American University. Last but not least, I am indebted to members of the Library of Congress.

Among the individuals who have done so much to enhance the quality of this book there are two who have read the whole manuscript and made many substantive and stylistic improvements: Mrs. Diane Bendahmane, and Professor Carl Gustav Anthon, retired chairman of American University's department of history. Professors Richard Breitman and Terence Murphy of the same department perused several chapters each and strengthened them immensely. The help of other colleagues at The American University will be acknowledged in conjunction with individual chapters.

At the Library of Congress, two persons in particular never failed to render essential assistance throughout the seven years that this manuscript was in the making: Elizabeth Jenkins-Jaffe persistently found elusive bibliographical items, and Wayne D. Shirley of the Music Division provided essential information on and interpretation of musical terminology in a most cooperative manner.

Andreas te Boekhorst and Peter Theunissen at the Dutch embassy rendered valuable support for the Dutch chapter. Among the Danes, the DCM Niels Dyrlund graciously secured much-needed research materials; Ivan Boserup of the *Kongelige Bibliotek* supplied several of these. Dr. Erik Dal, secretary of the Danish Academy of Sciences and Letters, kindly reviewed the chapter, and Mrs. Marianne Borg-Hansen proved to be a most competent translator. Ward Thompson generously provided useful materials and some translations.

The French chapter benefitted from reviews by Professor George A. Carbone and Ariel de Pontet. The Polish chapter could not have been written without the invaluable help of Dr. Stanislaw T. Skrzypek. The chapter also owes much to the thoughtful comments of my colleagues Professors Jim Malloy and Jack Piotrow. The Portuguese chapter received much-appreciated support from members of the embassy of Portugal; foremost among them are Mrs. Rita Varela Silva of the cultural section, the press councillor Luis de Sousa, and Lt. Col. Americo Henriques, the military attaché. The comments of Professor Jorge Borges de Macedo, Director of the National Archives, were most helpful. The Irish chapter had the good fortune of similar help from Denis Sheehan at the embassy here. Dr. Patricia Donlon, Director of the Irish National Library, and Dr. Dónall Ó Luanaigh, Keeper of Printed Books, not only provided materials but carefully reviewed the draft chapter. Thanks are also due to Mr. and Mrs. Thomas F. Troy.

Professor István Deak of Columbia University and Dr. István Csicsery-Ronay helped in shaping the Hungarian chapter, as did Gabor Szentivanyi of the Hungarian embassy. The late Madeleine Wilkins rendered thoughtful translation. Among the several readers of the Greek draft chapter, Professor M. Byron Raizis, chairman of the English Department at Athens University, offered essential advice. Bernard Huys, head of the music section of the *Bibliothèque Royale* in Brussels, proved to be a constant support and appreciated reviewer of the Belgian chapter. Mme. Bernadette Goovaerts at the Belgian embassy kindly assisted with some translation and useful reference. The Norwegian chapter owes its improvements primarily to Professor Harold Naess, University of Wisconsin Scandinavian Studies Department.

The German anthem, the most controversial among the anthems presented in this book, drew surprisingly little critical comment from the readers of the draft chapter; perhaps adequate proof of its objectivity. Those readers included Professor Hans-Adolf Jacobsen, emeritus at Bonn University; Dr. Barthold C. Witte, retired head of the Cultural Bureau in the German Foreign Ministry; Professors William C. Cromwell of The American University and Walter R. Roberts of George Washington University; and Dr. Bowman H. Miller of the Department of State. Professor George Carbone and Dr. Douglas Wertman, both experts on Italy, offered useful comments on the Italian chapter, as did Mrs. Margaret Anthon.

The Swedish one greatly benefitted from the much appreciated support and advice of Lars Olsson in the Reference Division of the *Kungl. Biblioteket* in Stockholm. Professor and Mrs. Albert Mott commented helpfully on the draft chapter. Mrs. Eva Dunhem supplied several needed translations. Completion of the Luxembourg chapter was made possible by the unfailing help of Dr. Jul Christophory, Director of the *Bibliothèque nationale*, who also reviewed the piece. Ambassador André Philippe took an early interest in its preparation.

This very appreciative acknowledgment must also include those ladies who made the manuscript take final form or converted it into a book. Mrs. Martha Murphy, with steadfast determination and professional skill, converted old-fashioned typescript into a high-tech disk, the initial typescript being the work of Mrs. Mary Henderson. Mrs. Murphy was also instrumental in drawing up the bulk of the index, an essential service to readers of this book. Mrs. Mildred Graham Vasan, senior editor for Social and Behavioral Sciences at Greenwood Press, took an interest in the manuscript after sampling a few chapters. Its acceptance for publication is largely due to her initiative, and through long months of preliminaries she has shown a much appreciated understanding and cooperation. Ms. Emily Okenquist as the production editor has been equally helpful in the extended process of giving the book its final form.

Thanks also must be rendered to members of the School of International Service faculty support staff. Laurie A. Walsh and Ramin Tabib in particular gave unstintingly of their time and have done so with much patience throughout the numerous revisions of the manuscript.

Last but not least, two members of my family have to be thanked specifically. My wife not only put up with all the inconveniences caused by a preoccupied husband but uncomplainingly settled all the expenses incurred in the preparation of this book. Our son, on his part, followed the slow progress toward completion with unflagging attention. His advice and encouragement alike proved to be welcome boosters along the rough road to a challenging goal.

The Setting

The nineteenth century provided the most propitious breeding grounds for the conception of national anthems in the western world. The very term *national anthem* came into being in the early decades of that century. And the evolution of the nation-state, growing out of the American and French revolutions, proved inseparable from the creation of most European anthems, with the latter sometimes even preceding or hastening the establishment of these states.

All of the seventeen anthems included in this book were nourished in the fertile seedbeds of nationalism, romanticism, and liberalism. They were driven by a fervent patriotism that had, in some cases, an assertive but rarely aggressive nationalist pitch. A majority of the anthems dealt with here came into being in the heyday of romanticism, between the 1820s and 1850s. About one-half of them were created by men with strong liberal proclivities.

Nationalism, a new and dynamic phenomenon, had been honed in the fires of the French Revolution and spread throughout Europe in the wake of Napoleonic conquests. In itself, nationalism was a complex phenomenon with multiple cultural, economic, social, and political layers. But its incandescent core was psychological in nature, a spontaneous association with the concerns and hopes of countless compatriots. Giving voice to their aspirations or frustrations constituted the basic stimulus in the creation of national anthems.

Romanticism, next to nationalism, often acted as a major influence in the conception of future anthems. They reflected the main components of the romantic movement: emphasis on native tradition and folklore, glorification of a distant past, the search for symbols, religious revivalism, and an emotional rather than a rational approach to contemporary issues.

Liberalism, in turn, grew out of the fundamental transformation of an agrarian and feudal society into an industrial and commercial one. The drive to free ever more people from economic, social, and political disabilities gave an emancipatory ambiance to much of nineteenth-century Europe. The forward momentum of liberalization spread its benefits to a steadily growing number of citizens. And it was the citizenry who formed the nation. Its freedom was theirs. A free country was also the country of the free. For the anthem authors nation–hope–freedom were interrelated concepts and the core of their creations.

Most of the anthems originally were conceived as poems. They ran in length from the two stanzas of the Swedish through the fifteen of the Dutch, up to the one hundred fifty-eight of the Greek anthem. Their literary qualities ranged just as widely from the beautiful to the banal. Their overall stance varied from martial assertion through buoyant affirmation of patriotism to pleas for redemption by the grace of God. But each anthem reflected a specific national culture at sometimes two widely separated points in time: creation of the poem and its acceptance or reacceptance as the national anthem.

Both poem and anthem mirrored that culture. The poem invariably was a spontaneous creation, an outlet of the pent-up hopes or concerns of its creator. Emanating from deep personal emotions, such poetry nevertheless contained elements of a collective if not already a national experience. Like rivulets welling up from native soil, the anthems-to-be meandered in their often long and uncertain course, until broadening to wider use and official recognition.

Such recognition might come quickly, as in the case of the *Marseillaise*, prototype of the modern national anthem, or be delayed anywhere from exactly one hundred years for the Italian anthem to nearly four centuries for the Dutch. Sooner or later, a poem that emerged from an individual mood was cast into a national mold as an anthem. That transformation took the most varied forms, ranging from popular preference to governmental fiat or constitutional embodiment, from serendipitous to deliberate choice, from the fluid state of public opinion to the fixed opinion of the leaders of the state. But however diverse the selection process, public acceptance or reacceptance of a song as anthem constitutes, next to the initial creation of the poem, the second indicator of a national culture.

The musical score gave wing to the body of the chosen poem, and sometimes the melody became better known than many of the anthem's verses. Yet only in a few instances did the melodies act as true indicators of a national identity. Music by definition is transnational, and tunes are interchangeable. Thus, that of *God Save the King* also served at one time or another as the score for more than a half-dozen continental anthems. The tune of the German anthem was borrowed from that of imperial Austria.

But even when melodies were not simply interchanged, they often resembled one another. Many anthems were provided with marching tempi, varying in movement from allegretto to allegro, indicative of martial attitudes and the new spirit of national assertiveness. Others, such as the Hungarian and Norwegian compositions, reflected the influence of romanticism. And all of the anthems created since the *Marseillaise* differed from the solemn adagio tempo of their predecessors, such as the British or Dutch.

In almost every case, musical composition postdated the creation of the stanzas, and therefore the tunes were accompaniments rather than core creations. Rarely were authors also the composers. In only three instances, the Dutch, French, and Polish anthems, could authors claim credit for the composition of the melodies. Invariably, such claims have been challenged with more or less justification. Certainly, even the most evocative of lines such as *Aux armes, citoyens*; *Deutschland, Deutschland über alles*; or *God Save the King* are carried to their ultimate effect by the accompanying melodies. But the notes would be empty shells without the words to which they resound. Thus, verbalization rather than vocalization bestows the national imprint upon an anthem.

Perhaps the most convincing proof that music per se does not make an anthem is provided by the British and German anthems, respectively. Franz Joseph Haydn's masterful melody did not guarantee acceptance of a German poem, commonly known as the *Deutschlandlied*, for some eighty years after its creation. The melody of *God Save the King* antedated the words by at least a century and a half; without them the Elizabethan "Ayre" would have remained forever an insignificant tune. And *A Portuguesa* needed verses to convert a march into an anthem.

In only one case, that of the British anthem, is the author unknown, and in that of the Dutch there is no certainty as to authorship. Yet it was the author's life that gave life to a poem destined for anthem status, and the triangular relationship of author to poem, poem to anthem, and anthem to nation encapsulates national identity and culture. The life stories of both author and anthem represent phases in the kaleidoscopic life of nations. In some cases these stories are analogous while in others they differ, but they always reflect the matrix in which a nation is cast.

Nowhere is the relationship of the lives of author and anthem and their reflection of national history more strikingly demonstrated than in the *Marseillaise*. For much of its author's long and troubled life, acclaim and rejection followed one another in bewildering sequence. But that sequence continued after his death in the 1830s, into the middle of this century, and mirrored the dramatic changes in France's political structure and fortunes. The author of the *Deutschlandlied* was chased as a liberal from one German state to another while his life and poem were dedicated to the vision of bringing these states together. And his *Lied* suffered a similar fate when torn asunder, one stanza alone allowed by the Nazi Third Reich and another one by the German Federal Republic. The evolution of the present Belgian state was reflected in three different poems, held together only by the title *La Brabançonne*, by three different authors in three different time periods.

Whatever the diversities among the writers of the anthems presented here, they had some features in common. Perhaps not surprisingly, all were male. Many had written the future anthems as young men whose idealism and passion were at their peak. A majority had university training and came from middle-class backgrounds, with the exception of a few aristocrats, some but recently titled. There was only one working-class man among them.

None of the authors wrote their anthems-to-be with such purpose in mind. That specific poetry derived spontaneously from moments of a public crisis or an incisive personal experience. What separated the anthems, not only chronologically but conceptually, was the great divide of the French Revolution. The three anthems preceding it—the Dutch, British, and Danish—centered on the sovereign prince. It was he who protected his people from foreign or domestic enemies; in turn, his subjects not only depended on him but sang his praise. By contrast, not the popular sovereign but the sovereignty of the populace constituted the core of new anthems ushered in by the *Marseillaise*, and the divine right of kings was replaced by the Rights of Man and the Citizen.

Unlike these two types of anthem, with their instinctive and passionate origins, rising like effervescence from the depth of common feelings, commissioned anthems were handed down to the people from way on high by imperial or princely ordinance. Only four of these anthems came into being between 1792, birthyear of the *Marseillaise*, and 1914: the Austrian, Russian, Romanian, and Bulgarian. They are excluded from this book because they fail to meet two of its criteria for inclusion: spontaneous creation and current use.

A third determinant excludes all European anthems composed as a result of World War I. Many of them, much like those after World War II in the new states in Africa or Asia, were government ordained and some were little more than a conventional adjunct to newly proclaimed independence. Unlike the pre–1914 anthems, they often did not rise from the same wellsprings of a nationalism tempered by liberalism and of a commitment to national freedom that also implied individual freedom. And if they did, as in the cases of Czechoslovakia or Finland, these countries had never before existed as independent states, the final criterion for inclusion.

The anthems covered here have a number of common themes; most noteworthy among them independence, liberty, unity, praise of country and countrymen, and hopes for future blessings. Independence either had to be maintained or else to be attained. Its corollary, liberty, had equal salience and could best be secured by unity. To arouse the nation—in many cases yet to be formed or freed—anthems might recall past glories, praise the beauty of the country, the quality of accomplishments, or the valor of its people. And these assets had to be preserved for a rewarding future.

If such themes were common, they did vary in emphasis. Apart from the pre-revolutionary anthems, all others can be grouped into four categories: resistance, independence, unification, and contentment. Resistance is undeniably the keynote in the *Marseillaise* and the Polish *Dąbrowski Mazurka*, followed a century later by *A Portuguesa* and the Irish *Soldier's Song*.

The independence theme is most pronounced in the Greek *Hymn to Liberty*, the initial version of the *Brabançonne*, and the Norwegian *Sang for Norge*. While the first two anthems called for militant action to secure independence, Norway's anthem expressed relief that such action could be avoided. The Hungarian *Himnusz*, whose *leitmotif* is lament, provided nevertheless a rallying cry for later generations fighting for Hungary's independence.

The theme of unification found its strongest expression in the German and Italian anthems. Where they differed, perhaps surprisingly, was in the fervent appeal to arms and armed conflict. That appeal resounded passionately in the Italian *Inno di Mameli*, while it was conspicuously absent in the often misquoted or misunderstood German anthem. A final category includes the Swedish and Luxembourg anthems. Free from defiance or demands, they express quiet pride in the stability and beauty of their countries. This section ought to include the Danish national anthem, a perfect specimen of contentment. But for the sake of comparison and contrast with the Danish royal anthem, a just as typical example of the ancien regime anthems, both have been grouped together in the first chapter. Although a world apart in character as well as time, it would have been more confusing to present them in widely separate parts of this book than to show them back-to-back in the same chapter.

Most of the poems raised to anthem status had close competitors, quite often of superior literary quality. Why, then, did one poem gain the place of honor and hold it, albeit sometimes with interruptions, up to the present day? Some poems-turned-anthems doubtless benefitted from political circumstances and considerations; others from the call for decisive action; still others gained preeminence because of their visions of a better future. But in the last analysis, selection of the anthem-to-be was conditioned by spontaneous public use and the degree of popularity. As once observed by an Irish legislator in a debate over that country's anthem, "The national anthem is, and must be by its nature, the song which the people of the country regard as their national anthem."

Notwithstanding the continued use of an anthem by successive generations, specific criticism of certain verses or even whole stanzas has not been absent. And almost always it is the text rather than the music that has come under review. In some cases the literary quality has been the subject of critique and not without reason. There is just one Nobel prizewinner in literature among the authors presented here, while less than a handful are major literary figures in their respective countries.

More often, however, the relevance of certain stanzas has been questioned. Certainly, there are obvious oddities. The loyalty to the king of Spain proclaimed in the first stanza of the Dutch anthem seems nowadays entirely out of place. After all, the Netherlands secured independence from Spain in 1648! The appeal in the first stanza of Italy's anthem to Italians as "the slave of Rome" must strike everyone nowadays singing the lines as wholly irrelevant, since Rome has been the capital of a united and secular Italy since 1870. And there appears to be little likelihood of an invasion of France, except by hordes of tourists.

Public debate on how to revise or even replace an existing anthem has taken place in several countries, sometimes for decades. Current arguments offered by both sides do not basically differ from earlier ones. Traditionalists uphold existing anthems, whatever their conceded flaws, as a venerable part of the nation's history. Denying that part would be tantamount to the obfuscation either of a proud moment in the nation's history or of momentous developments in that nation. The reformers, in turn, assert with no less emphasis that it would be in the country's best interest to discard anachronistic verses which no longer benefit it and could only distort its image abroad.

Pressures to revise or replace existing anthems have been exerted generally either through state-appointed commissions, legislative measures, or prize competition. Thus far, a few anthems have been supplanted in their entirety. The traditional anthem of Switzerland, dating to 1811, was replaced, not without opposition from a half-dozen cantons, in 1961. Yet the cause for that replacement was not the text but the tune! Apparently, the Swiss had tired of using a foreign melody—that of *God Save the King*! Austria has changed anthems nearly a half-dozen times with every change in statehood or regime. The original Spanish anthem, created on the model of the *Marseillaise* in 1812, was suppressed a decade later by a reactionary monarchy. The anthem, known after its author as the *Himno del Ciudadano Riego* (Hymn of the Citizen Riego), made another brief appearance during the ill-fated Spanish republic between 1931 and 1939. The victorious Franco regime then replaced it with the *Marcha Real* (the Royal March), dating back to 1770. In the post-Franco era the *Himno Nacional Español*, which unlike the *Marcha Real* has a text, took the latter's place, except for military ceremonies.

Elsewhere, however, efforts to displace existing anthems have failed spectacularly. The most striking example of such a failure has occurred in the German Federal Republic. Its first president, recent horrors of the Nazi regime and misuse of the anthem fresh in his mind, commissioned a new anthem in 1950. A respected author provided a creditable piece, but it fell literally on deaf ears. And the well-meant attempt at a replacement of the controversial *Deutschlandlied* was forthwith abandoned. In 1952, a communist-sponsored proposal to substitute the Hungarian *Himnusz* failed to find even an author.

More common but equally unsuccessful were the commissions called for by legislatures in Belgium, Ireland, and Poland; either these commissions never got going or failed to make progress in the quest for new anthems. Prize competition, as in Great Britain, did not lack in entries, but none of them proved acceptable, not even for revamping a single stanza.

It is often far easier to adduce reasons for the failure to disestablish existing European anthems than to fathom the causes for their acceptance in the first place. The most obvious cause underlying all abortive efforts at change is that these anthems, however irrelevant certain of their passages, are part of the national matrix. Quite possibly, collective conventionalism and inertia may also explain why existing anthems are retained. Many who join in singing them hardly know more than a few lines or at most the whole first stanza, and not so few hum only the melody. In periods of great national or personal tragedy, trials, or triumph, however, the verses come back to mind and may acquire a renewed meaning.

The Marseillois, marching into Paris on that last day in July 1792, eager to battle the oppressive invaders, probably did not miss a single verse of that stirring new song soon to be identified with the volunteers from Marseille. The Norwegians, gathered on their national holiday in 1864, did not need sheet music to sing *Yes, We Love This Land of Ours*. Hungarians intoned their *Himnusz* when they secured independence in November 1918 and when they struggled to regain it in the revolution of 1956. And the German parliament struck up the *Deutschlandlied* on the morrow of German reunification in October 1990.

Nor did individuals fail to recite emphatically lines that would be simultaneously their last words and their ultimate identification with the nation. A Belgian resistance fighter facing a German firing squad in 1916 instructed his family to break into the *Brabançonne* at the moment of his execution. Facing a similar execution detachment in 1939, a young Polish woman sang her national anthem—in German so that her executioners would understand word for word what valor and patriotism meant to the Poles!

In all these cases of individual or collective spontaneity, the words counted as much as the melody, if not more so. Even if a country, after prolonged search and deliberation, were to accept a new anthem, regardless of its artistic qualities and relevance to a new era, it would resemble a hothouse plant rather than one that grew naturally out of the national experience. Replacements can be created and promoted by every possible means, but they still would lack the patina of tradition and the ring of familiarity of long-existing anthems.

This would hold equally true for any efforts to substitute in their place a supranational European anthem. Such an anthem is already available, albeit in an informal capacity. It may well be heard increasingly at the numerous high-level meetings and other supranational functions of the European Union. And it can lay claim to be the greatest of anthems in terms of the music, taken from Beethoven's majestic Ninth Symphony. Nor are the words, taken from Friedrich von Schiller's *Ode to Joy*, of a less illustrious parentage. Yet, such qualities notwithstanding, the European anthem does not have the two essentials of the anthems included here: national tradition and popular usage.

However high-minded the sponsors of either the European or any revised or new national anthem, the upshot is the same. Existing anthems will prove hard to displace. Such is the magnetic pull and power of these anthems that they draw together the past, present, and future; different generations; people of various creeds and social backgrounds. Anthem authors are not always readily identified; some stanzas may be forgotten or only vaguely remembered, and the tunes are sometimes difficult to sing. But as long as there are national states, the prism of their national anthems will retain the reflections of salient events of the past and at the same time fully reflect current moods. And if the primacy of the national state in Europe should fade further, that would be all the more reason to have a record of the history of its most vital and viable symbol.

Anthems may be heard less often nowadays, except on national holidays or at international sports events in countries that are members of the European Union or about to join it. By contrast, national anthems not only retain their primary political functions in many East European countries; as some of these have split up additional anthems are likely to proliferate with the advent of new states. But in one case or the other, East or West, anthems will continue to be heard, either routinely or spontaneously. In peace as in war, defiance or hope, triumph or tragedy, nostalgia or celebration, reaffirmation or revolution, anthems are likely to remain the collective voice of their respective nations.

Ancien Regime Anthems

1

The Netherlands

Wilhelmus van Nassouwe
(Philip Marnix van St. Aldegonde[?])

The sonorous sound and solemn stanzas of the Dutch anthem have echoed through five centuries. At times these echoes faded away, only to reverberate all the more strongly later on. Even though the Dutch anthem antedates the *Marseillaise*—progenitor of modern anthems—by nearly two and a half centuries, it contained some of the very themes of these anthems: resistance to foreign domination, the struggle against tyranny, and an imperishable love for the home country and its people.

But in other respects the *Wilhelmus*, together with the British and Danish anthems, belonged to the pre-revolutionary age that ended in 1789. These three anthems focus on the sovereign prince rather than the sovereign nation, hallmark of European anthems since the *Marseillaise*. It is not happenstance that the prince himself speaks the fifteen stanzas of the *Wilhelmus*. After all, his name runs through each of their first lines as an acrostic, spelling Willem van Nassov. And it was he who became, however hesitatingly, the leader of the rising opposition to misgovernment in the Spanish Netherlands.

Its territory, the Low Countries, reached from the French border in the south to the Frisian coast in the north and from the Channel to the Rhine. Since the mid-fifteenth century the region had been part of the Habsburg empire, an empire so large that Emperor Charles V divided it between his brother Ferdinand of Austria and his son Philip in October 1555. Philip inherited the crown of Spain with all of its vast possessions overseas, much of Italy, and the seventeen provinces of the Low Countries where his father had been born.[1]

The new ruler, however, showed little personal interest and less understanding for that part of his inheritance. What he wanted to do was to integrate these provinces, long since accustomed to a measure of autonomy, into the absolutist and uniform structure of the Spanish-ruled world. For a decade after his enthronement, Philip II had increased pressures to fit the Low Countries into the Hispanic mold. In this attempt Spanish officials had violated ancient liberties and privileges, alienating much of the population, most significantly among them nobles and burghers who felt their interests and institutions endangered by the ongoing Hispanization.

Spanish policies had still another dimension fraught with fateful consequences. Orthodox Roman Catholicism, which Philip so ardently promoted, reasserted itself against a hardly less rigid and belligerent Protestant sectarianism. The great religious schism that had affected, with ever-increasing vehemence, most of Europe since the Reformation was bound to engulf the seventeen provinces. In the summer of 1566, long-smoldering Protestant extremism flared up in the wholesale destruction of Roman Catholic churches and other properties by the iconoclasts. They were as much agitated by an anti-Spanish as by an anti-Catholic frenzy.

To rein in extremism, yet safeguard religious freedom as well as regional interests, proved a daunting task. If anyone could measure up to it that man would be William of Nassau. Born into a minor German count's family, he inherited in early youth vast foreign possessions. Some of the holdings had given him a substantial foothold in Brabant and Flanders, the two richest provinces in the Spanish Netherlands. And as a newly established prince of the Holy Roman Empire, he had gained the favor of Emperor Charles V, a favor which William requited with a strong loyalty to the Habsburg dynasty.

When he finally and reluctantly raised the banner of resistance to further Hispanization, it was more in defense of local institutions and privileges than against the Spanish king; more against the Duke of Alva, Philip's iron hand in the Low Countries, than against Spanish officialdom as such. The first campaign, launched by William in 1567 in the hope of freeing some of the region from Alva's harsh rule, ended in disaster. Prince William soon ran out of money, his mercenary troops ran out on him, and many of his supporters ran out of hope.

Yet out of that failure there arose, phoenix-like, a song of endurance and fortitude. Sometime between 1569 and 1572, someone vented not only the frustrations but also the perseverance of those who stood against the Hispanization of their lands. A solemn, even pious, poem expressed both chagrin at current failure and a fervent belief in a better future. Once set to music the poem sounded like a church hymn.

Of the fifteen stanzas the first and the sixth—the only ones to be sung nowadays on official occasions—represent the two major themes: religious and patriotic commitment.

William of Nassau, scion
Of a Dutch and ancient line,
I dedicate undying
Faith to this land of mine.
A prince I am, undaunted,
Of Orange ever free.
To the king of Spain I've granted
A lifelong loyalty.

A shield and my reliance
O God, Thou ever wert.
I'll trust unto thy guidance,
O leave me not ungirt.
That I may stay a pious
Servant of Thine for aye
And drive the plagues that try us
And tyranny away.[2]

While the verses left little doubt as to William's trust and resolve, the author who puts the words into his mouth disappears behind the prince. The creation of the *Wilhelmus* by an anonymous writer has touched off a quest for his identity that has lasted to the present day. A composite picture of the author's characteristics, as drawn in a recent study, reveals the following traits. "A deep insight into the Bible; a Calvinist who does not play carelessly with revolutionary thought; in all probability somebody from the entourage of the Prince, a genuine poet . . . and likely to be a nobleman."[3]

Of the half-dozen possible authors, only one comes close to fitting that "wanted author" description: Philip Marnix van St. Aldegonde. Born into a noble family from the Hainault province, he was raised a Roman Catholic. But in 1560, as a student of law at Geneva, he had come under the influence of Calvin, the dominant personality in that city. Not surprisingly, young Marnix left Geneva as a thoroughly committed Calvinist. Having hitherto used his facile pen to write French poetry, he turned it now to purely political purposes and Calvinist propaganda.

In early 1566, he had a hand in drawing up a petition by leading noblemen in the Low Countries who requested affirmation of their privileges, restraints on the Inquisition, and greater religious toleration. The presentation of that petition led to an open confrontation with the authorities in Brussels, capital of the Spanish Netherlands. But it also gave the opposition a name: *Geux*, the Beggars. Meant as an opprobrium, that designation soon became a mark of honor for those rallying against the Spaniards.[4]

The challenge thus posed elicited a forceful response from the Spanish king. To avoid arrest, Marnix fled to the court of the Calvinist Elector Palatine in the Rhenish Palatinate. Quite possibly, he composed the *Wilhelmus* while in exile.

He had known Prince William since the early 1560s and entered his service in 1571, to become not only William's confidant but his political alter ego. Marnix knew the prince more intimately than any other man and may have indeed spoken for him in the *Wilhelmus*, as he was commissioned to do on many a later occasion.[5]

What joined the two men in friendship was their determination to resist Hispanization by diplomacy if possible, by force if unavoidable. The struggle against the Spaniards in the field oscillated between disheartening losses and hard-won successes, a sequence often repeated in a conflict that was to last on and off for eighty years. William's ultimate goal to preserve the union of the seventeen provinces, regardless of any religious division, proved unattainable.

The *Wilhelmus*, however, was sung in north and south alike. As has been remarked rightly, "A cause which was to find such a voice . . . disposed of greater reserves than guessed by Alva."[6] There was, however, another reserve power equal to that of poetic eloquence: water. The age-old challenger of the Dutch proved their most dependable ally in the hour of greatest need. Several towns flushed out their Spanish besiegers by opening the dikes.

More offensive but no less dependent on water were the operations of the *Watergeuzen*. They, a mix of adventurers, exiles, and Calvinist diehards, had become quite literally the sheet anchor of Dutch resistance. With their small ships, they cut Spanish supply lines, ran weapons into outlying ports, and raided hostile garrisons. When they first gained a foothold on Dutch soil, entering the small port of Ten Briel on April 1, 1572, they lustily sang the *Wilhelmus*. It was heard in an equally triumphant rendition in January 1578, when William entered Brussels at the peak of his successes. And some three years later, the song found its way into Dutch print for the first time. Suitably, it appeared in a songbook of the *Geuzen*.[7]

Ultimate victory and the achievement of independence, however, were by no means assured. On July 10, 1584, William of Nassau—the champion of self-government for the seventeen provinces—fell under the pistol shots of a Catholic fanatic in Spanish pay. Ironically, the most tolerant statesman in this era of intolerance became its most illustrious victim. It is even more ironic that he, a German nobleman, should become fortuitously as Prince of Orange—title to his holdings in southern France—a great magnate in the Low Countries and, subsequently, the prime mover of Dutch liberation from Spanish control. Yet, most ironic of all, he never failed to proclaim his loyalty to the king of Spain and most emphatically so in the *Wilhelmus*, while fighting much of his adult life against Spanish officialdom and influence.

With the passing of William of Orange-Nassau, founder of the Orange dynasty of the Netherlands and still the ruling family today, the song bearing his name fell into gradual disuse. Small wonder, since the *Wilhelmus* had been cast into the first person singular; now that the singular person of "Vader Willem" was no more, his song seemed to lack its full meaning. It did survive, however, in various songbooks of the seventeenth century, most notably in the *Neder-*

landtsche Gedenck-Clanck, a collection of Dutch national songs published in 1626. Its compiler observed that in the 1570s the *Wilhelmus* had "caused great stirring among the people and . . . brought with it the Prince's name."[8] Yet the same commentator had nothing to say about the popularity of the song a half century later.

For more than two centuries it was the melody rather than the words which gave the *Wilhelmus* prominence. Such composers as Johann Sebastian Bach and Wolfgang Amadeus Mozart used the original score, which probably antedated the text,[9] in variations on its main theme. All the same, a Dutch commentator in the mid-eighteenth century could remark that the *Wilhelmus* was mainly known by its title.

The principal cause for this near-oblivion was that the Seven Provinces which formed the original Dutch republic had gradually assumed the structure of an oligarchy. "Their High Mighty Lords of the States General"—according to the official appellation—constituted the ultimate executive and legislative authority in the Netherlands. The rival power rested with the *Stadhouder*—or governors— of the several provinces, who acted since Spanish times as the principal regional officials. Command of the armed forces of the republic from its beginnings had devolved upon the preeminent *Stadhouder* family, that of Orange, if only because Prince William had led the resistance movement in its first phase. Before long the civilian and military top authorities were bound to lock horns.

Wisely, Prince William and his immediate successors had avoided the conflict over ultimate authority by proclaiming themselves servants of the States General and refusing the lures of a crown. In turn, the Orange *Stadhouders*, following one another through five generations, were not a true or fully accepted monarchical dynasty, and there was no apparent need for a royal anthem.

The constitutional clash between the two power centers ran its zigzag course through much of the time, reaching a climax at the end of the eighteenth century. William V naggingly insisted on strengthened prerogatives for himself and his successors, and the States General just as persistently opposed such claims. The resulting impasse deeply divided the Dutch into "Orangists" and "Patriots." In 1787 the indecisive William was left with a Hobson's choice: foreign intervention or exile. The first proved of short duration and the second, some eight years later, never ended for him.[10] The Patriots, driven out with the help of Prussian bayonets, returned in 1795 with the support of French bayonets, and it was the turn of William to become an exile.

Neither of the two interventions by foreign troops redounded to the benefit of the *Wilhelmus*. If anything, it was parodied during the two decades of Orange exile and discredit.[11] Not until December 1813 could the tune be heard again in its traditional form and dignity when sung at a thanksgiving service in The Hague. Appropriately, Prince William VI, son of the exiled prince, was present, having returned from England a month earlier to reassert his family's hereditary rights and assume leadership of the nation. Recognition came in the form of kingship. It seemed fitting for King William I as first crowned head of the newly created kingdom of the Netherlands to revive the stately hymn of his famous ancestor.

But was it in keeping with the monarchical aspirations and obligations of the new king, with secular nationalism sweeping through Europe at the end of the Napoleonic wars, and with the activist spirit of an expanding bourgeois influence? What the new kingdom needed to unite monarch and people was an anthem befitting the era.

It did not take long to find a suitable poem and accompanying melody. A prize had been offered in 1816, and among the numerous entries was a poem with the attractive motto "Prince and Fatherland." Its author, Hendrik Tollens, combined all the desired features of both the new kingdom and the new age: nationalist, bourgeois, romantic, and royalist. There was no public event or issue that Tollens could not conveniently commemorate or grace with rhymes at once banal, sentimental, and easy on both ear and tongue.[12]

His prize entry was no exception. Its eight stanzas differed little in their sentimentalism and parochialism. But the good cause was served: the dynasty and the nation were interlaced. A German-born composer quickly furnished the score, and within a decade the *Volkslied* of Tollens became informally the Dutch anthem. It did not, however, displace the older hymn altogether, which mainly survived in songbooks, historical tomes, and learned journals that devoted reams of arcane argument to the quest for the real author of the *Wilhelmus*.[13] Even its sonorous melody had to give way to a martial rhythm which, as the *Prinsen marsch,* served military functions.

But before the end of the nineteenth century the original *Wilhelmus* acquired a new lease on public life. The urge for its restoration to prominence came from a most influential quarter. Queen Wilhelmina, who had assumed the throne in 1898, took a personal interest, not least because of the strong affinity she felt for the progenitor of the Orange dynasty, whose name was so similar to her own. She agreed readily with the observation of the minister of war that the *Wilhelmus* was far more beautiful with its chorale character than any newer version.

But it was one thing to be moved by sentiment and quite another to move toward the acceptance of the old hymn as the national anthem. Tollens' piece, however trite, remained popular. On the eve of Wilhelmina's accession to the throne, a crowd had intoned the *Volkslied* outside her palace at The Hague. She heard it again in the hour of crisis in August 1914 from hastily mobilized soldiers.

Nevertheless, the partisans of the *Wilhelmus* did not lose faith. Comparisons drawn between it and the Tollens piece invariably pointed out that by age and character alike the older song should be the preeminent one. Tollens' creation, the argument ran, was not very different from some other anthems and could be readily used in other constitutional monarchies. The *Wilhelmus*, by contrast, "is solely for our people."[14] And its proponents never failed to stress that it was synonymous with Dutch independence and fortitude.

In May 1932, fourteen months after the *Star-Spangled Banner* finally received the accolade as national anthem, the *Wilhelmus* was elevated to the same status. There were reasons for that decision by the Dutch cabinet. The 400th anniversary of the founding father of both country and dynasty was approaching. Queen Wilhelmina pointed out with pride that her likely successor, Princess Juliana, had been named after the mother of "the founder of our independence."[15]

There may have been other motivations underlying the cabinet's decision. Emphasis on "Dutch blood free from foreign stains," as the *Volkslied* had it, could prove rather embarrassing for a nation taking pride in its long history of tolerance, especially at a time when in neighboring Germany the Aryan blood myth was propagated. Moreover, the middle part of the *Volkslied* melody resembled, probably not by chance, the German nationalist song "Watch on the Rhine."

Whatever the reasons for the long-delayed official status, the *Wilhelmus* did not need much promotion as the national anthem. In September 1932, when the queen made her annual speech from the throne to the Dutch parliament, a couple of communist deputies voiced dissent to the traditional call of "Long live the queen." Immediately, all other members rose in a show of loyalty and unity while singing the anthem.[16] Within a year it reverberated at a large public gathering in honor of the queen's thirty-fifth jubilee. But there were dark days ahead for monarch and people alike. In early 1940, no time was left for even one rendering of the anthem as the Germans swept through the country. And within a couple of days, Wilhelmina and her government had to take refuge in England.

Almost five long years went by before the queen could set foot again on her homeland. As she crossed from liberated Belgium onto Dutch soil on March 13, 1945, the crowd assembled at the border broke into the ancient yet curiously relevant stanzas. Two months later the queen made her entry into the capital. And again the *Wilhelmus* resounded triumphantly in the streets. None of its verses carried more meaning for the returning monarch than the second stanza.

> I've ever tried to live in
> The fear of God's command,
> And therefore I've been driven
> From people, home, and land.
> But God, I trust, will rate me
> His willing instrument,
> And one day reinstate me
> Into my government.[17]

In the half century that has followed, the *Wilhelmus* has kept its place of honor unchanged and even unchallenged. However hoary with age some of the lines may appear, to say nothing of the obvious irrelevancy "to the king of Spain I have sworn lifelong loyalty," there has been no known demand for any changes. The measured cadencies, the quiet determination, the stolid fortitude, and the unostentatious dignity of words and tune alike appear to fit most readily the Dutch psyche.[18] Probably the best explanation of the survival of the *Wilhelmus* may be found in its very antiquity. By the same token, it has become a veritable time capsule whose contents are viewed with respect if not with awe. Sacrosanct by its words, it would be nothing short of sacrilege for many Dutch people to change any part of the *Wilhelmus*.

NOTES

1. The seventeen provinces comprised what is now known as the Benelux countries. Charles V was born in Ghent.

2. The commonly accepted English translation is that by Professor Adriaan J. Barnouw which has been reprinted often, most recently in a press release by the Dutch foreign ministry, and distributed by the Dutch embassy in Washington, D.C.

3. Ad den Besten, *Wilhelmus van Nassouwe: Het Gedicht en zijn Dichter* (Wilhelmus van Nassouwe: The poem and its author) (Leiden: Universitaire Press, 1983), 67.

4. This petition became known as the *Compromis des nobles*. When it was handed to the regent of the Spanish Netherlands, Margaret of Parma, she shook visibly. One of her councillors opined that she could not possibly be afraid of *ces Gueux*. The next day, the nobles involved in the remonstrance sported beggar bowls around their necks, occasionally rattling the wooden containers.

5. Marnix stood in for Prince William on several occasions, such as when he presided at the meeting of delegates from all Dutch cities in open revolt at Dordrecht in July 1572, or acted as William's substitute in the governing council chosen by the States General in 1578.

6. Pieter Geyl, *The Revolt of the Netherlands* (New York: Barnes & Noble, 1958), 108.

7. Curiously, the *Wilhelmus* first appeared in print in a German songbook of 1580.

8. Adrianus Valerius, *Nederlandtsche Gedenck-Clanck* (Haarlem, 1626; reissued, Amsterdam: Facsimile Uitgaven Nederland, 1968), 45.

9. The origins of the hymn-like melody are hardly more certain than the authorship. The most common assumption is that the melody was a variation of a somewhat earlier French song occasioned by the failure of the Huguenots to take Chartres in 1567.

10. Prussian intervention for which William V had not asked but which favored the Orangist cause ended quickly; not so the French, which forced the last *Stadhouder* into exile in 1795, when he sought refuge in England. He died there in 1806.

11. One of the parodies ran as follows:

> Wilhelmus of Nassau
> Ar'st thou of Dutch blood?
> The elbow through the sleeve,
> The hair through the hat.
> Is that thou, Wilhelmus?

Quoted by Anon., *Het origineele Volkslied Wilhelmus van Nassouwen* (Leyden: J. van Thoir, 1813), 2. The translation was kindly provided by Mr. Peter Theunissen of the Dutch embassy in Washington.

12. Tollens' poetry alone fills six volumes. His most original work is an epic in praise of a Dutch expedition to the Arctic island of Novaya Zemlya in 1596, which won for him a gold medal from the Dutch Academy of Arts and Sciences.

13. More than eighty articles and monographs were written on the *Wilhelmus* in the last one hundred years, showing both the continued interest and uncertainties regarding the piece. S. J. Lenselinck, "Het Wilhelmus, en andere interpretatie," in *De Nieuwe Taalgids* 57 (1964): 140.

14. S. S. Mensonides, *Het Wilhelmus*, 2d ed. (Groningen: J. W. Wolters–Uitgevers-Maatschappij, 1940), 11.

15. H. R. H. Wilhelmina, *Lonely But Not Alone*, trans. from the Dutch by John Peereboom (New York: McGraw-Hill, 1959), 76.

16. Adriaan J. Barnouw, *The Dutch: A Portrait Study of the People of Holland* (New York: Columbia University Press, 1940), 273.

17. This is the second stanza in the Barnouw translation.

18. Putting it another way, one commentator pointed out with obvious pride: "There is nothing of a narrow-minded nationalism, highfaluting patriotism or romantic heroism in our *Wilhelmus*." Lenselinck, loc. cit., 140.

2

The United Kingdom

God Save the King/Queen
(author unknown)

No other anthem except, possibly, the *Marseillaise* enjoys a wider recognition than the British, known as much by its first line as by its melody. The stately tune was adopted at one time or another by almost a dozen countries as their anthem's melody. Great composers were not only impressed but influenced by it. Franz Joseph Haydn, who had heard *God Save the King* during his London sojourns in the 1790s, thought that his beloved Austria and equally beloved emperor should have an anthem of like magnificence. He eagerly accepted a commission in 1797 to set the words of an inferior versifier to a magnificent score. No less a master than Beethoven commented in 1813, "I would like to make clear to the English people just a little bit what a blessing they have in *God Save the King*."[1] In the same year, he worked the melody into his *Battle of Vittoria*, celebrating the victory of the Duke of Wellington in Spain. A decade later, Carl Maria von Weber included that music in his *Jubilee Overture*, and the theme subsequently reappeared in compositions by Brahms, Meyerbeer, and Gounod.

Yet, while widely known and readily identified, the anthem is an orphan of uncertain parentage. The author, if there was one, remains unknown; nor is the identity of the composer established beyond all doubt. As it is, *God Save the King* has drifted into British public life, like so much else in Britain, on a wave of tradition.

The hymn made its debut on September 28, 1745, when it was elaborately and simultaneously performed at the two most famous London stages: Drury

Lane and Covent Garden. There were good reasons for that timing. On September 21, rebellious Scots, flocking to the cause and standard of Charles Edward, the Young Pretender, had defeated an English force at Prestonpans, some ten miles south of Edinburgh. They now threatened to cross into England and challenge King George II, his government, and even his dynasty.

That threat had triggered an outpouring of English patriotism. The very same actors who staged the original presentation of the anthem had volunteered a couple of days earlier for military service "in defence of His Majesty's person."[2] As an earnest of their commitment to king and country, they now offered a less demanding though more spectacular display of loyalty in the form of three well-known soloists, backed by the full ensemble, to render the new royal anthem.

Arranged by Dr. Thomas Arne, music director at Drury Lane and composer of *Rule Britannia,* the presentation elicited a resounding response. A couple of days later, a newspaper reported, "the anthem of God save our noble King . . . being encored with repeated Huzzas [which] sufficiently denoted in how just an Abhorrence they hold . . . our invidious Enemies and detest the despotick Attempts of Papal Power."[3]

A similar enthusiastic reaction greeted the song at other London theaters, and in November it could be heard in cities like Bath. While the Scottish rebellion petered out within a year, the anthem remained in its preeminent position. But then it did have deeper roots and a longer past than realized by those who sang it so loudly and proudly in "forty-five."

The origins of *God Save the King* have been contested as sharply as the quest for its authorship. Dr. Arne, somewhat of a slick promoter, was also the first to admit that he had no knowledge of who the author or the composer were. Arne himself may well have contributed the third stanza, since it was not part of a previous printing. The first two stanzas had appeared anonymously in a collection of songs titled either *Harmonia Anglicana* or *Thesaurus Musicus*, a subject of much learned if somewhat esoteric argument.[4] What really matters is that the stanzas did exist before 1745 and that some of the lines were altered for very obvious reasons at the latter date. As originally printed, these two stanzas are the familiar ones:

> God save our Lord the King,
> Long live our noble King,
> God save the King!
> Happy and glorious,
> Long to reign over us,
> God save the King!
>
> O Lord our God arise,
> Scatter his enemies,
> And make them fall.
> Confound their politicks,

Frustrate their knavish tricks,
On Him our hopes are fix'd,
O save us all.[5]

In a second printing of these artless and undramatic verses in the *Thesaurus Musicus* that appeared toward the end of 1745 there was, however, a noteworthy change. The innocuous heading "A Song for Two Voices" had been replaced by the far more meaningful title "A Loyal Song." More significantly still, the first line of the opening stanza now read "God save great George, our King." And thereby hangs a tale. Someone had tampered with the earlier text, adjusting it to the prevailing political situation. The Jacobite rebellion, as yet not quelled, had temporarily bifurcated the union of England and Scotland, existing since 1707. The supporters of Bonnie Prince Charlie had opted out of allegiance to the Hanoverian dynasty established just thirty short years earlier in London; hence they had excluded themselves from the pale of the anthem. It stood to reason that they would avoid praising any king George, let alone pray for the divine protection of any Hanoverian king or queen.

Some invisible hand had interposed itself between the first and second printing of the royal stanzas but had done so for a very visible purpose: to fortify and glorify the standing of the challenged dynasty. A claim by the son of Henry Carey that his father, a prolific rhymester and musician, had composed the stanzas in 1740 found little acceptance; not least because that claim was made fifty years later and in a barely hidden attempt to secure a pension for the claimant. His claim, however, touched off a lively and continuing controversy as to the real sire of the anthem.[6]

In that quest one name turned up more and more often. Such was its fame and association that the name seemed not only a natural but a preordained selection befitting the creator of the British national anthem: John Bull. He did, indeed, not only exist but also had made quite a name for himself as a composer with special skills in keyboard composition during the Elizabethan era. But Dr. Bull, who acquired that degree at Oxford University, was hardly a model gentleman and probably not much of a patriot. Somewhat of a rake, he ran afoul of the Church of England and had to migrate to the Low Countries.

Long before, he had composed a virginal titled "God Save the King" which, in the words of one later musicologist, was "no more like the anthem than a frog is like to an ox."[7] There was, however, a greater similarity in an "Ayre" that Bull had composed and that has been often referred to as the likely model for the anthem's tune.

Yet words and melody had other potential forbears. The very expression "God save the King" was deeply embedded in English tradition. That time-honored exclamation validated royal proclamations, opened or ended parliamentary sessions, and recurred throughout the centuries in variegated forms ranging from fleet orders through prayers and pamphlets to songs and inscriptions.[8] Above all, it was a collective plea for the safety of the sovereign and connoted the identification of the people with the crown.

If there were predecessors of certain lines in the anthem, this held equally true for parts of the melody. Tunes similar to that of the anthem had made their appearance throughout the seventeenth century. They included folk songs, carols, and compositions by men of such renown as Henry Purcell and Georg Philipp Telemann. The anthem's rhythm traced back to the sixteenth-century *Galliard* dance.[9]

Quite possibly, the anthem's basic form could date to the late 1680s. If so, there is irony in the possibility that it would have thus been composed for James II, last Stuart king and a Roman Catholic to boot. He certainly stood in need of all divine and human help to hold onto his throne that soon was to slip from under him, regardless of any invocation. The anthem, which was heard nearly sixty years later, by contrast served the opposite cause: the backing of a Protestant dynasty asserting itself against an attempt at Stuart restoration.

But if such intriguing assumptions as to the origins of *God Save the King* cannot be sufficiently documented, there remains the plausible contention that the stanzas have been formed serendipitously over the centuries. Picking up a line here, a phrase there, the verses are said to have come into existence gradually, much like folk songs. However uncertain in its antecedents, the anthem's forward course from 1745 on is incontrovertibly delineated. The most salient feature of that evolution is the minimal mutation that both the text and the status of the anthem have undergone in two and a half centuries.

The three stanzas have remained intact, with some minor semantic and gender changes. The stability of the British governmental system and freedom from foreign invasions, so different from the traumatic convulsions in many continental countries, have lent strength to the British national anthem. Once established by popular acclaim, *God Save the King* (or *Queen*) has stayed in its place of honor, even though only the first stanza is nowadays sung on official occasions.

Not that the anthem lacked imitators, parodists, or would-be improvers. The very periodical which first had made it available in October 1745 to the reading public asked a mere two months later for a thorough revision on the defensible grounds that "the former words [are] having no merit but their loyalty."[10] Alas, the new stanza proposed by the *Gentleman's Magazine* hardly could be called an improvement, since it reeked of jingoism. Britain's epochal struggle against Napoleon that started half a century later and was to last for twenty years spawned a dozen similar creations.

In the post-Napoleonic era, however, variations to the anthem carried another theme—that of social and political reform. No less an author than Percy Bysshe Shelley penned his *New National Anthem* with its dramatic plea for the return of liberty. His song ended with "God save the Queen" but his queen was the goddess of liberty worshipped by so many romanticists, not the least among them several of the anthem authors.

In the 1830s, during the prolonged controversy over "cheap bread"—the famed Corn Laws conflict—"God save the people" rather than the monarch could be heard for the first time.[11] And before the end of that century, the country was put ahead of the monarch in yet another "new anthem" whose stanzas ended in "God save our land."[12]

But whether of greater literary value or a more timely political appeal, neither of these poems could displace the existing anthem. British traditionalism, seemingly unbroken and certainly unique, underlay that rejection. After all, the anthem, since its creation, had linked crown and country, monarch and people into a remarkable polity. If that was the basic motivation for both creation and initial acceptance of *God Save the King*, then that motivation has not changed throughout the centuries.

Nevertheless, the anthem was used on occasion to demonstrate against a ruling sovereign. The long reign of George III offered opportunities for acclaim as well as attack. After he had recovered from his first bout with mental disorders in 1789, pleased crowds saluted the king on his way to Bath by singing the anthem. It was parodied, however, within a couple of years by sympathizers of the French Revolution, the verses leaving no doubt where the sympathies lay.

> Long live great Guillotine
> Who shaves the head so clean
> of Queen or King.
>
> Whose power is so great
> That every Tool of State
> Dreadeth its mighty weight
> Wonderful thing![13]

In May 1800, an abortive attempt on the life of George III, while he attended a theater performance, caused the shocked audience to break into *God Save the King* and repeat it for good measure no less than three times. Yet after the king's renewed schizophrenic seizures in 1811, the anthem lost popularity, along with the king, among those who wanted his son to act as regent.

When that son finally succeeded to the throne in 1820 as George IV, he immediately encountered substantial hostility by his unseemly efforts to rid himself of his wife, Caroline. Her numerous supporters deliberately substituted on several occasions the traditional salutation of *God Save the King* with *God Save the Queen*. Less than a year later, however, there was no such challenge mounted at the coronation ceremonies for George IV—the first coronation at which the anthem formed part of these ceremonies—Queen Caroline having providently died.

At the coronation of Queen Victoria on June 28, 1838, the anthem "swelled forth gloriously after the recognition."[14] It certainly swelled to unparalleled proportions during the queen's seemingly endless reign, the ebullient expansionism of the Victorian age having a large share in the manifold use of the anthem.

Not everywhere in the steadily expanding empire, however, was the anthem equally welcome. In March 1894, the Montreal orchestra did not respond to calls for *God Save the Queen*, and Dublin University graduates prevented the playing of the anthem in connection with their graduation in 1905.[15] Yet the balance tipped heavily in favor of the anthem, ever more popular as the queen's reign became identified with a whole era. Underlying the anthem's popularity was an emotive attachment, partly romantic and partly chivalresque, to a queen regnant who over the decades had become the incarnation of grandeur.

Her successors did not quite reflect that mystique; nor were they quite as fond as Queen Victoria of hearing the anthem excessively. King Edward VII, bon vivant that he was, thought that it sounded like a dirge! Conversely, to his successor, the pedestrian George V, the tune seemed a jig. And the anthem did have critics other than these crowned heads. Such criticism ran the gamut from the assertion that the verses were mere doggerel, through concern that they focused exclusively on the crown rather than the country, to the contention that the second stanza was "un-Christian" in its emphasis on bringing down the enemies of crown and country.

Yet most of the critics were only too well aware of the fact that the anthem would be hard to replace for two reasons: its popularity of long standing and British aversion to break with tradition. Even the sharp-witted and sharp-tongued George Bernard Shaw conceded in 1914 that "its direct and passionate invocation" could hardly be done away with.[16] For the selfsame reasons, revision efforts in the interbellum period came to naught. In view of the empire's invaluable help in World War I, attempts were made to include a stanza of imperial dimension. A selection from some four hundred entries was duly made and grafted onto the familiar verses, only to wither away rapidly.

In 1931, a lengthy controversy ensued in the form of readers' letters to the London *Times* as to the quality of the somewhat dusty anthem. Among those who came gallantly to its defense was a former custodian of the highly respected Tate Gallery. His comments concluded laconically, *"God Save the King* is a sturdy John Bullish strain, set to a Dr. John Bullish tune."[17]

The supreme arbiter of the British print media, after having given quite a bit of time and space to the controversy, closed it with these editorial lines of unchallenged authority and incontestable finality: "We did not choose our national anthem but it has somehow adopted us; and there it is. Some day perhaps . . . a miraculous accident will produce a wholly new National Anthem. Meanwhile the old remains impregnable, and for all its long date alive and expressive."[18]

Such judgment was borne out in the mid-1930s when a National Anthem Amendment competition drew over one thousand entries. After careful examination the judges declared that "nothing was found . . . to put forth as alternative or supplementary verses."[19] And so the almost two hundred-year-old veteran stayed in service. Within half a decade World War II offered plentiful opportunity for frontline duty.

As in August 1914, the nation was called again to arms in September 1939. Not only was the mood different—a sense of high adventure had given way to grim determination now—but also the mode of the anthem's presentation. In 1914, enthusiastic crowds had intoned *God Save the King*, along with *Rule Britannia* and the *Marseillaise*, outside Buckingham Palace after the proclamation of a state of war with the German empire. On that first Sunday morning in September 1939, the reassuring sounds of the anthem had reached the bulk of the British people in their homes in the form of a BBC broadcast carrying Prime Minister Neville Chamberlain's somber announcement of yet another war with Germany.

That fateful moment was well remembered in such later comments as the following: "When the national anthem was played on the radio we all stood up. That was how the war began for my family and for millions of other families throughout Great Britain."[20] If people stood up in their homes it was not only because custom required them to do so when hearing the anthem, but they felt anew its magnetic pull drawing together crown and country, monarch and people, past and present at a crucial juncture in British public life.

Some six years and many bitter experiences later, the anthem rang out once more, its lines and functions unchanged in contrast to attitudes and times. Twenty-five thousand internees, just released from Stanley Camp in Hong Kong after the collapse of imperial Japan, intoned *God Save the King* with as much pride as relief. But in the home country such pride and relief were voiced in different songs. Those who had gathered around Buckingham Palace, as their parents might have done on November 11, 1918, acclaimed King George VI and the royal family as well as victory in Europe on May 9, 1945 with the informal *For he is a jolly good fellow*, rather than with the anthem. As for the principal architect of that victory, Mr. Winston Churchill, he was greeted at 10 Downing Street with *Land of Hope and Glory*.[21]

In the half-century since the end of World War II, the British empire has gone the way of all empires and with it the imperial use of the anthem. Countries like Australia and Canada have adopted their own anthems. In the home islands, however, *God Save the Queen* continues to be heard, though occasions for singing it jubilantly have sharply diminished.

The reassuring and stalwart tune is no longer played routinely at the end of cinema shows. Its use in schools is optional. In keeping with British tradition in general and the spontaneous origins of the anthem in particular, the secretaries of education and science repeatedly issued statements that, while they favored the singing of the anthem in schools, there would be no intervention or regulation on the subject by Her Majesty's Government.[22]

Still, the anthem was heard on special occasions such as the coronation of Queen Elizabeth II in 1953 and, again, on her silver jubilee. Appropriately, the solemn melody rises to a crescendo at such military ceremonies as the annual

Trooping of the Colours. It is played nightly at the end of BBC television programs. And, most fittingly, the anthem can be heard at the very place where it originated: Covent Garden. There it opens the annual opera season.

Whatever the recent troubles and tribulations of the royal family, it appears unlikely—given British traditionalism and the nearly sacrosanct institution of the Crown—that the anthem will give way altogether. It is rather safe to predict its culminating role in Westminster Abbey at the coronation of the Queen's successor—whenever that may come. And it is even safer to anticipate that Britain would be the last member country in the European Union to replace its time-honored anthem with a European one, however more commensurate with the times such an anthem may be.

NOTES

1. Quoted by Percy A. Scholes, *God Save the Queen! The History and Romance of the World's First National Anthem* (London and New York: Oxford University Press, 1954), on the title page. The author is the most authoritative source on the evolution of the British anthem.

2. Ibid., 6.

3. *The Daily Advertiser* (London), September 30, 1745.

4. The arguments that the anthem was first printed in the *Harmonia Anglicana* have been summed up by Donald W. Krummel, "God Save the King," in *The Musical Times* (London, March 1962): 159 et seq. But Professor Scholes (306–7) has flatly stated that this erroneous assumption, generally accepted for nearly a century, dated back to William Chappell, *Popular Music of the Olden Time*, 2 vols. (London, 1855–59). An erudite and much quoted German essay also categorically declared that the anthem was first printed in the *Thesaurus Musicus*. See *Jahrbücher für musikalische Wissenschaft*, ed. Friedrich Chrysander (Leipzig: Breitkopf & Härtel, 1863), 1:381.

5. The well-known stanzas have been often reprinted. They were reissued together with a brief sketch of the history and use of the anthem in *Fact Sheet on Britain: The British National Anthem*, by the reference division of the Central Office of Information (London, 1981).

6. Richard Clark, a rather dubious commentator who rose to become choir master at St. Paul's, asserted in 1814 that Henry Carey was the author of the anthem. Less than a decade later he made a volte-face and attempted to prove that the anthem's origins date to 1607, when King James I was feted by the Merchants Tailors' guild. Clark strongly suggested that Ben Jonson may have been the author of the anthem. Richard Clark, *An Account of the National Anthem Entitled God Save the King!* (London: W. Wright, Fleet Street, 1822).

7. William H. Cummings, *God Save the King: The Origins and Words of the National Anthem* (London: Novello & Company, 1902), 10, quoting the nineteenth-century musicologist Dr. William Kitchiner.

8. F. S. Boas in *Report* by Education Officer, London County Council on the national anthem (London: London County Council Education Offices, 1916), 14. Fleet Orders for August 10, 1545 read: "The watch wourde . . . shall be this. 'God save the King Henrye'; the other [side] shall answer 'And long to raign over us.' " Since the accession of Queen

Elizabeth I, royal proclamations routinely ended with the statement, "God save the King" (or Queen).

9. The Galliard rhythm had two uneven halves, of which the first had three and the second four measures. The uneven melody fitted the anthem's verses since they, too, had a sequence of six and seven lines, respectively.

10. *The Gentleman's Magazine* 15 (London): 662.

11. Ebenezer Elliott, *Poems*, 3 vols. (London: B. Steill, 1833–1835). See especially *Corn-Law Hymn* #1 in 3:171.

12. William Watson, *Odes and Other Poems* (New York and London: Macmillan & Co., 1894), 76–78. Watson was a prolific poet who was ultimately raised to the peerage.

13. Quoted in Scholes, 163; requoted here by permission of Oxford University Press.

14. Harriet Martineau, *Autobiography*, ed. Maria Weston Chapman, 2 vols. (Boston: James R. Osgood & Company, 1877), 1:422.

15. These incidents are referred to by Scholes, 221–24.

16. Ibid., 134.

17. *The Times* (London), February 17, 1931.

18. Ibid., September 5, 1931.

19. Scholes, 144.

20. Norman Longmate, *How We Lived Then: A History of Everyday Life During the Second World War* (London: Hutchinson, 1971), 1.

21. *The Times* (London), May 9, 1945. The same paper had reported on Armistice Day 1918 that as soon as the Guards band had struck up the anthem in the forecourt of Buckingham Palace, the crowds gathered nearby joined in singing it.

22. In 1960 the then minister for education stated: "I certainly hope that all children do learn the National Anthem. How and when they do that is best left with parents and teachers." A similar statement was made some twenty years later and concluded that the anthem was not "a suitable subject for central Government guidance." *Hansard Parliamentary Debates*, House of Commons, 5th ser., vol. 622 (1959–60), p. 95, and 6th ser., vol. 24 (1981–82), p. 90.

3

Denmark

Kong Christian
(Johannes Ewald)

Der er et yndigt land
(Adam G. Oehlenschläger)

KONG CHRISTIAN/JOHANNES EWALD

The Danes do not face the difficulties of the British or the Dutch in identifying the author of their national anthem. In fact, they have to do so twice since Denmark is the only country among those dealt with here to have two officially recognized anthems.[1] One of them is intoned in the presence of Danish or foreign royalty, during state visits and other official gatherings at home or abroad, and at military reviews. The second anthem is heard on less formal occasions or at international sports events. Thus, the two anthems are conveniently separated into the royal and national anthem, respectively.

More substantial differences than those of protocol, however, underlie this separation. The contrasting nature of the two anthems is so antithetical that they seem to represent two different countries: one forceful and warlike, the other peaceful and placid. The two future anthems were written in two different centuries, divided by the French Revolution. In the intervening forty years, the western world had changed dramatically. Monarchical absolutism reigned supreme in 1780; in 1820 it had been irreversibly undercut by a swelling tide of nationalism that put the nation rather than the monarch first. Thus, either poem represented the spirit and values of a different era.

Kong Christian, as the royal anthem is known, glorifies martial triumphs and is a paean to a particular monarch and to Danish naval heroes who, like him, led the country to heroic deeds. By contrast, *Faedrelandssang*, generally known from its first line as *Der er et yndigt land* (There is a lovely country), praises the pacific achievements of the Danish people even though the monarch is still duly and honorably mentioned. There were but two spiritual links that joined the two authors: patriotism and romanticism.

The Denmark in which *Kong Christian* had come into being had just undergone a traumatic experience. The Enlightenment had reached Denmark by a circuitous route. The reigning king, Christian VII, was hardly the person to initiate much needed reforms let alone to evoke an outpouring of literary homage. To the contrary! His disastrous reign shook the solid foundations of the Danish monarchy, one of the oldest and most stable in Europe. King Christian's *dementia praecox* made him into an unpredictable ruler, much different from some of his fellow monarchs who methodically advanced reforms in their respective countries. The Enlightenment, with its rational approach to public and intellectual life, might have bypassed Denmark altogether had it not been for the entry of a foreigner into that very life.

The severe mental affliction of the king had brought to his court Dr. Johann Struensee, a physician, who first treated the king not unsuccessfully; then treated himself to the queen, a sister of King George III of Great Britain; and finally treated the host country to a whirl of overdue reforms. He held sway for a brief but eventful time in 1770 and 1771. Challenged by resentful Danish noblemen as a usurper, he was arrested, tried, and executed in one fell swoop. While most of his reforms were forthwith invalidated, his disappearance from the royal court led to further complications for the royal couple.[2]

Elsewhere in the country a patriotic backlash resulted from the Struensee episode. That backlash not only found expression in measures such as the exclusion of foreigners from all government positions; it also affected the intellectual and artistic elite. One of its most prominent members had already satirized Struensee's newly proclaimed freedom of the press in the comedy *Harlequin Patriot*. Its author, Johannes Ewald, however, was neither a narrow-minded conservative nor a member of the privileged class.

His brief and erratic life rested on the shakiest of conventional foundations. But whatever the vagaries of Ewald's troubled life, his patriotism could be doubted as little as his literary genius or his pioneering role in opening up a new era in Danish literature. In 1770 he had written the first national tragedy, *Hrolf Krake*, based on the life of the almost legendary Danish tribal king who had first brought the Danes together in the sixth century A.D.

Ewald's second tragedy, *Death of Baldur*, drew heavily on Scandinavian mythology. In yet another verse drama, set to music, the author in a lighter mood turned to a more contemporary subject. The libretto of the operetta (or *Singspiel*) *Fiskerne* (The Fishermen) had as heroes neither a mystical chieftain nor a young god but the common people of Denmark, a new subject in Danish literature. The story involved hardy fishermen and their womenfolk, the men braving storm and sea in a daring rescue. It ended dramatically with the saving of the sole survivor of a stranded brig.[3]

The appeal of that local event could best be enhanced by poetic embellishment and patriotic exultation. Ewald was not loath to use both to optimum effect. Why not raise the level of emotion and that of example from the local to the national level? And why not take the occasion to remind the Danish people of their proud and impressive naval tradition?

He found a suitable outlet for his efforts in a four-stanza "Romance," one of several lyric insertions into the *Singspiel*.[4] This particular Romance had some of the characteristics of a tableau vivant: historical inaccuracies, colorful contrasts, set-piece positions, and sentimental appeal. Yet, in its entirety, the robust poem radiated both the power of and the pride in the Danish navy, whose titular head, the king, rarely saw action with that navy.

One such exception was Christian IV, a king who had always stood out among the long line of Danish kings, if not for his diplomatic and military successes then at least for his personal vitality. What Ewald wanted to commemorate above all was the raw courage shown by Christian IV in a naval battle with the Swedes which, though indecisive, set an example to be emulated by later Danish naval heroes.[5]

Ewald's tribute to these leaders provided the core of what would one day become his most famous poem and the anthem of the Danish monarchy.

> Kong Christian stood by the lofty mast
> In mist and smoke,
> His sword was hammering so fast,
> Through Gothic helm and brain it passed.
> Then sank each hostile hulk and mast
> In mist and smoke.
> "Fly!," shouted they,
> "Fly who can,
> Who braves of Denmark's Christian . . . the stroke?[6]

The other three stanzas were cast in similar turn of pithy phrase, and all were set either against stormy seas, darkened skies, or daring deeds of Danish naval chiefs. For that very reason, however, the Romance had to be severely curtailed on opening night of *Fiskerne*, January 31, 1780. The director and actors of the Royal Theater raised strong objections to the martial verses. How could these verses, so the objectors reasoned not unconvincingly, be squared with the peaceful habits of fisherfolk whose only motivation for action was to rescue fellow men in utter distress?[7] Apparently, they could not and subsequently only the last stanza was heard that January evening and during the following performances.

> Path of the Dane to fame and might!
> Dark-rolling wave.
> Receive thy friend, who scorning flight,
> Goes to meet danger with despite.

Proudly as thou the tempest's might,
Dark-rolling wave!
And amid pleasures and alarms
And war and victory, be thine arms
My grave!

It is unrecorded whether this remnant triggered specific applause, but it is known that the premiere of *Fiskerne* was received with somewhat less than stormy enthusiasm.[8] And certainly none in the audience, which included the royal family as well as the author, could foresee that the stanzas of this Romance would one day attain anthem honors. Ewald had to be propped up in his box while he watched the performance, since his ravaged body was failing him. But he knew that his reputation as Denmark's first great romantic author was secure. Above all, he had accomplished his principal goal of "standing out from among the crowd and having fingers pointed at me."[9]

There were plenty of opportunities in his turbulent life for finger-pointing. Born to incompatible parents, the father was a melancholic chaplain and the mother of dubious character, with little interest in her son. Small wonder that after his father's early death young Ewald felt homeless. At thirteen he ran away from home and an uncle's supervision. His hope for a Robinson Crusoe life ended precipitously four miles out of town.

Yearning for care and comfort, he became infatuated with a girl when barely in his teens. She remained uncommitted and Ewald ran off for a second time to prove himself. He wanted to become a missionary, but instead took service with the Prussian army, which was then fighting halfway through the Seven Years' War. Full of adventurism and dreams of glory, he had wished to become a hussar.

Like so many aspiring wartime volunteers before and after him, he was put, instead, into a far less glamorous unit of infantry. Such were his disappointment and resentment that he deserted at the first opportunity, in 1759. Having scanty respect for either convention or responsibility but an undiminished desire for adventure, he forthwith joined the Austrian army, Prussia's major opponent. If this move seemingly made him into a turncoat, he hardly could be called a traitor. With fine disregard for partisanship, he soon deserted anew, this time resentful that he could not as a Lutheran hold an officer's commission with the Austrians.

Fortunately, he escaped the gallows, or at the very least the gauntlet, for a second time and made his way back to Denmark. Unfortunately, however, his homecoming soured almost at once when renewed wooing of his adolescent love was decisively rejected. In his despair he all but threw himself away, avowing that "henceforth I shall saunter through life."[10]

He did so with a vengeance, contracting consumption and possibly syphilis. A fall from a horse crippled him further and made him an invalid, dependent on the good or ill graces of others. Worse still, a second love affair ended even more tragically than the first.[11] What sustained Ewald throughout mounting adversity and failing health were his literary creativity, a mordant wit, and his vicarious experience of heroic acts of determined men. Fourteen months after the debut of the *Fiskerne* he died, just thirty-seven years old.

The dead poet was duly honored in eulogies and memorials, but his last play, much like the brave fishermen, gradually faded away and with it the stanzas of *Kong Christian*. They briefly resurged in the first decade of the nineteenth century, when Denmark was drawn into the Napoleonic wars on the side of the French. The determined sound of *Kong Christian* could be heard from marching and singing Danish marines.[12] Yet the destruction of the Danish navy in two British raids on Copenhagen in 1801 and 1807 put a damper on the song of Danish naval heroes and victories. The loss of Norway, which had been joined to Denmark for over four hundred years, further deflated Danish power and pride. Not surprisingly, *Kong Christian* failed to be entered in a prize competition for a national anthem that got under way in 1818. But it was not solely the apparent irrelevance of an assertive nationalism that caused the song's near oblivion in a period of patriotic contraction and material expansion. As yet the virile Romance was embedded in a seasonal operetta; to stand out on its own it would have to be broken out, much like a pearl from an oyster.[13]

A first step to greater prominence occurred in 1828 when the melody gained a new attractiveness, having been previously reworked several times without much improvement. Through a stroke of good luck that melody was now recast by a skillful composer into the finale of an overture.[14] This overture happened to introduce a very popular Danish operetta, *Elverhøj* (*Elves' Hill*), remaining the most often performed piece on the Danish stage. Thus, *Kong Christian*'s restyled melody was assured a permanent as well as a prominent place in the public mind.

In the 1840s, *Kong Christian* at last came into its own as a Danish national song. Two political developments proved a boost to the revival of nationalist sentiments. The ethnic and intellectual movement of Scandinavianism had gathered momentum for almost two decades. Initially artistic and social in orientation, Scandinavianism now acquired a political dimension. Danish, Norwegian, and Swedish students joined in demonstrative gatherings advocating Nordic solidarity which, in turn, infused a sense of collective patriotism into their respective compatriots.

In the case of the Danes, this sense manifested itself above all in a hardening opposition, as yet mainly cultural, to expanding German pressures in the contested border area of North Slesvig.[15] A series of public rallies in favor of the Danish language and culture brought together an ever-larger number of demonstrators. From 1843 on, they assembled annually near the Danish-German linguistic border at the elevations of Himmelbjerget and Skamlingsbanken. There the Danish patriots were treated to rousing speeches, the drafting of strongly worded resolutions, and not least to patriotic music.

Among the patriotic songs, the two that were to attain anthem honors took wing at this time, though they were not as yet in a class by themselves. Several other songs had at least the same emotive appeal and could be heard as often. And all patriotic tunes rose to their peak of popularity in 1848. In March of that dramatic year Danish political activism and excitement crested, as did the wave of patriotism when the army was mobilized to ensure full governmental control of the duchy of Slesvig. Its German majority resisted that effort with arms and with the support of the sister duchy of Holstein. Agitated crowds in Copenhagen "hurrahed for Denmark to the Eider,"[16] the river that separated the two duchies, and broke into patriotic songs. They were often intoned during the three years of that war, which the Danes fought to a successful conclusion. Denmark, however, was not victorious in a second Danish-German war. National pride and self-assurance suffered considerably from the quick and thorough defeat in 1864. Yet *Kong Christian* remained the most frequently printed tune in Danish songbooks, as it had been for the preceding thirty years.[17]

DER ER ET YNDIGT LAND/ADAM G. OEHLENSCHLÄGER

Denmark's other anthem did not quite match that frequency, though the circumstances of its creation and the fame of its creator made the poem a likely contender for national status. After all, Adam Oehlenschläger had written his twelve stanzas of *Der er et yndigt land* with some such purpose in mind. Was he not Denmark's foremost author, its most widely respected literary arbiter, and known not only throughout Scandinavia but on the European continent as well! He owed this patriotic creation as much to his compatriots as to his own reputation.

Born the year that Ewald had started work on his *Fiskerne,* in 1778, Oehlenschläger was in every respect the antithesis to Ewald, though he never failed to laud him. Growing up in the comfortable milieu of a solid, middle-class home and enjoying an agreeable childhood and good education, his life at no stage was exposed to the tribulations to which Ewald had been subjected.

Before reaching middle age, Oehlenschäger had already reached the pinnacle of his professional life. Endowed with numerous honors as well as an *embonpoint* derived from good living, he projected an image of bourgeois stability and respectability, both woven into his future anthem. Ultimate recognition came with the crowning as poet laureate of Scandinavia in 1827, a distinction never gained before or after by any other writer.

Yet he could not quite shake off the shadows of Ewald, stating repeatedly that he might equal but not surpass him. Such self-serving modesty notwithstanding, Oehlenschläger could hardly disguise his underlying confidence that he was able to surpass his potential rival in the undeclared competition for preeminence among Danish men of letters.[18]

His nominal rival for the authorship of Denmark's national anthem, however, was not the *Kong Christian* of Ewald but a surprise winner of the prize competition held in 1818. The commander of the Danish occupation forces in post-Napoleonic France had requested that a national song be furnished, since his men had no tune similar "to the British *God Save the King* or the French *Henri Quatre.*"[19] Officers in his command, he pointed out, already had collected a substantial sum to sponsor a competition whose winner would give Danish soldiers a proud and tangible association with their country. A learned society in Copenhagen readily endorsed that request and organized the competition with additional funding. Of the sixty entries submitted, that of an elderly and sickly spinster took the prize, making her in fact the only woman author of a potential European anthem.

Unfortunately, her *Denmark, Denmark–Sacred Sound* lacked ab initio in popular appeal, probably because it overflowed with sentimentalism and hyperbole, neither of them a noted Danish trait. Moreover, when a melody was at last supplied a couple of years later, the Danish troops in France had been withdrawn and the military need for an anthem no longer existed.[20] The rapid disappearance of Miss Jensen's *Sacred Sound* in a vortex of parodies provided incontrovertible proof that a national anthem may be proclaimed by fiat but its survival can be guaranteed only by the seal of popular choice.

The void existing both before and after the competition for a Danish anthem gave the Olympian Oehlenschläger the opportunity to make *his* bid for a national song. He did so with a dozen weighty, if also wordy, stanzas which reflected both the satiation and self-satisfaction of a middle-class and middle-aged author, basking in the glow of acclaim and achievement.

But the stanzas also mirrored quite accurately the views and values of his fellow-citizens. They had their fill of glory and gore, of heroics and hardiness. For them Denmark had other assets of a far more peaceable nature. And Denmark's leading author was neither slow in enumerating nor shy in lauding such assets.

In fact, he seemed not to have missed a single one: the beauty of the seagirt land, the peace now enjoyed throughout that land, the "noble women, lovely maidens, brave men, and fearless boys" who inhabited it, the freedom they enjoyed and the work they engaged in, the achievements in arts and sciences. Nor did the author, patriotic and royalist as he was, fail to praise the ruling monarch, the ancient national flag—oldest in Europe—or the continued existence of "Old Denmark."

Having praised all this and more, it may not surprise that Oehlenschläger's paean, first printed in 1823—a year when several future anthems came into being—subsequently underwent a continued contraction as if to deliberately reduce its effulgence. By mid-century the poem, as portly as its creator, had shrunk in most songbooks to the first three stanzas. In more recent times the final stanza has often been added. Both it and the first stanza are nowadays rendered on public occasions as the national anthem.

There is a lovely country
Where the mighty beech trees grow
Along the salty shores of the Baltic.
It undulates with hills and valleys,
Its name is Old Denmark
And it is the hall of Freia.

Hail King and Fatherland!
Hail every Dane,
Who works as best he can!
Our Old Denmark will last
As long as the crown of the beech trees
Is reflected in the blue sea.[21]

The *Faedrelandssang* was suffused by pleasurable tranquillity and cheerful imagery symbolized by the hall of Freia, the Nordic goddess of love, and the reassuring concept of "Old Denmark." By the same token, the poem, much like the Danish scenery, while pleasing, lacked in spectacular let alone dramatic features; nor did it have to rally the people to action. Not surprisingly, therefore, that poem went pretty much unnoticed for some twenty years in a somnolent Denmark.

In the mid-1830s, however, the magisterial paean, which read more like a glossy travel prospectus than a rousing summons, was set to music by a part-time composer. The chromatic melody matched the lumbering stateliness of the poem but, probably for that reason, did little to enliven its immediate appeal.

Not until the patriotic recrudescence that brought *Kong Christian* to national attention in the 1840s did Oehlenschläger's panoramic account of Denmark's attainments and blessings reach a larger public. At the Skamlingsbanken demonstrations, culminating in that of July 4, 1844,[22] a student choir first struck up *Der er et yndigt land.* It was heard again four years later during the first Dano-German war. By 1849 the song had gained such popularity that Hans Christian Andersen recorded hearing it on several occasions while visiting Sweden.[23] Yet after the debacle of the short war in 1864, the opportunity for proudly intoning national songs became rather rare, all the more so since the people's main concern was henceforth with domestic reform.

Denmark remained without a recognized anthem until the early twentieth century. When the Scandinavian neighbors acquired their anthems,[24] the time had come for Denmark to do likewise. *Kong Christian* was proclaimed the anthem of the monarchy upon the coronation of Frederick VIII in 1906. Anti-Swedish memories had long since faded, but what remained alive was the respect of the Danes for their past.

They now had an officially established anthem, to be played at state occasions. But was that song the people's choice, best representing their aspirations and attitudes? Not that they were antimonarchical. If anything, the monarchy became ever more popular in the course of the twentieth century.

The narrow focus and martial timbre of *Kong Christian* left space for a potential national anthem of vastly different dimensions. Oehlenschläger's panoramic poem was a natural candidate, not only because of its glowing account of Denmark's peaceful attainments, but because of the author's eminence in the country's cultural life. In the early 1920s, his much abbreviated *There is a lovely country* received the accolade as national anthem, for good reasons.

It almost seemed a necessity for a country with as tranquil a record as modern Denmark to have as its anthem a song that corresponded to that record and reputation. Moreover, the poem's last stanza praised every Dane, whatever his or her station in life, for work performed. Thus, the anthem fully reflected the social democracy into which Denmark evolved in the twentieth century. Most important, however, the Oehlenschläger piece was the psychological antidote to Ewald's gory and forceful one.

The rise to national prominence of both poems can be explained readily, but it is more difficult to understand how they have coexisted comfortably, in spite of their contrasting character, ever since the 1920s. The laid-back attitude of many Danes, noted inter alia by an expert on the use and popularity of the two anthems, may well account for their frictionless, side-by-side existence.[25] Each anthem represented a different facet of Danish mentality and a different aspect of Danish history; yet both were complementing one another much like the obverse and reverse of the same coin.

If theme and thrust of both anthems are widely apart, so are their functions. Instructions of the Danish foreign service clearly stipulate on what occasions the one or the other anthem may be played and, if played back-to-back, which must be heard first. Partisanship, a common feature of the debate over quality and relevance of many an anthem, has not been lacking in Denmark, all the more so because of the coexistence of both anthems. The warlike character of *Kong Christian* has elicited criticism culminating in statements such as "many Danes consider the martial nature uncharacteristic" of Danish mentality.[26] Sure enough, the socialist minister of education attempted to exclude the song from presentation at the Royal Theater in October 1924, to no avail! The audience rose to its feet when the king entered and heartily greeted him with the royal anthem.[27]

In the years of Nazi occupation it still was heard when the popular King Christian X celebrated his seventieth birthday in September 1940. And in 1943, the author of a new biography of Ewald could write that "when we sing *Kong Christian* . . . we are imbued with the proud feeling of being Danish."[28] During much of the occupation period, however, the rousing song was rarely heard. For one thing, its martialism seemed somehow irrelevant as long as the majority of Danes preferred passive to active resistance. For another, why remind anyone of almost-forgotten Danish-Swedish conflicts at the very time when many Danes looked for support from Sweden? Moreover, *Kong Christian* had found its way into the songbooks of the small but despised pro-Nazi "Frikorps." By contrast, the royal anthem did not appear in a collection of songs of the resistance movement. During the large strikes of June 1944, demonstrators struck up the *Internationale* rather than *Kong Christian*.[29]

In the postwar era, the anthem embellished such ceremonies as the monarch's birthday or the silver jubilee of the currently reigning Queen Margrethe II. Quite apart from such official occasions, the song retained its popularity with individual Danes both at home and abroad. Perhaps the most moving example of such individual use came with the solo recitation by an octogenarian lady. She sang the four stanzas at a service on St. Thomas, commemorating the seventy-fifth anniversary of the transfer of the Virgin Islands to the United States in 1917. And she remembered the tune lovingly from her school years on the then Danish St. Thomas.

Judgment and use of *Der er et yndigt land* have likewise fluctuated. Some of those most emphatic in their praise of the "magnificent" *Kong Christian* have been sharply critical of the national anthem. One expert has bluntly labelled it "one of the world's ugliest."[30] Another commentator thought it "little suited for a national anthem."[31] Yet several Danish comments have been more charitable, and at least one foreigner with a unique expertise in Danish songs has unequivocally stated that "the Danes have reason to be proud of having made it their national anthem."[32]

Oehlenschläger's stanzas proved popular in World War II when the song was included in communal singing, the *Alsang*, as a noncontroversial expression of national identification vis-à-vis the German occupation authorities. They evinced no objections, since the verses were inoffensive and unchallenging. The poem appeared in several new editions, and it even found its way into communist songbooks.

Still, in moments of great tension or excitement, Danish crowds avoided singing that anthem because of its peaceful character. *Kong Christian* was thought unsuitable for the very opposite reason. That peculiar situation appeared to leave the Danes without any anthem whatsoever. But on occasions of angry demonstrations or patriotic outpourings they had recourse to a common song; alas, a borrowed one. The Norwegian anthem, deeply patriotic but not excessively belligerent,[33] was intoned by Danish crowds objecting to their government's signature of the fascist Anti-Comintern Pact in November 1941. The same anthem was used by Danes attending their national soccer team's matches abroad. The prime reason for such vicariousness was the admiration many Danes felt for the kindred Norwegians in offering militant resistance to the German invaders.

Much like the royal anthem, the national anthem retained its standing in postwar Denmark. It remains a familiar tune that is sung annually on Constitution Day (June 5) and can be heard every New Year's eve in broadcasting programs. Among the younger generation the gentle lines about the "lovely country where the mighty beech trees grow" and "the hall of Freia," offering love, predictably have more appeal than the grim ferocity of split skulls, hoarse battle cries, and heavy gun smoke. Yet the Danes continue to use both anthems as appropriate, and there has been no known controversy as to whether one anthem should be given up in favor of the other. If one represents Danish civil achievements and comforts, the other recalls Danish history and glory.

For well over a century now, the Danish image abroad is one of an eminently peaceful and progressive people, open and hospitable to the world at large. Shortly after Oehlenschläger's song became the recognized national anthem, a commentator could justifiably remark that "the song conformed to the Danish people's character in our time."[34] Still, there are Danes who recall—and sometimes with nostalgia—the earlier centuries of Danish power and preeminence in Scandinavia, so strikingly depicted in *Kong Christian.*

Willing as most Danes are to cooperate on the international level, they are certainly not unwilling to assert their national interest and identity. Their negative vote in the first referendum on the Maastricht Treaty of European Union in June 1992 and the subsequent and successful insistence on exemptions from major obligations under that treaty herald a continuous national self-assertion and self-confidence so clearly apparent: the former very marked in the royal anthem and the latter in the national anthem.

NOTES

1. Sweden also has two anthems, but neither one has been formally recognized. See Chapter 14. Norway, too, has a royal anthem.

2. Queen Caroline had to leave the country and died in exile, while her husband's recurrent mental illness made it necessary to establish a regency under the crown prince in 1784.

3. In November 1774, this small vessel had run aground within sight of a Danish fishing village near Helsingør during a raging winter storm. For several days Hornbaek fishermen attempted vainly to rescue the crew who perished one after the other, except for the captain. He, too, was near drowning in the mountainous seas when five of the intrepid fishermen succeeded in taking him off the wreck. Ewald heard of that episode in the spring of 1775, while seeking to recuperate near Hornbaek. He was immediately fascinated by this story, not least because of his quest for heroes.

4. The *Kong Christian* Romance was inserted into Act II, Scene 5.

5. Although not directly referred to by Ewald, the battle was that off Kolberger Heide, fought on July 1, 1644. The Danish navy engaged that of the Swedes in an inconclusive contest. During the battle, Christian IV was severely wounded by fragments from an exploding gun aboard his flagship. Nothing daunted, he wrapped a kerchief around an eye just lost and continued to fight. Remembrance of such toughness inspired legends, painting, and poetry. The bloodied kerchief is still on display in a Copenhagen museum.

6. The translation is that of Henry Wadsworth Longfellow, who was much taken by Ewald's evocative poem. It is contained in the Cambridge edition of Longfellow's poetical works (Boston-New York: Houghton Mifflin Company, 1893), 607.

7. Some of the fishermen who had partaken in the rescue were invited to attend opening night of the *Fiskerne.* When asked for their opinion on the presentation, one of them replied that it was quite realistic but added "only we didn't sing." Kai Flor,

Johannes Ewald: vor nationalsangs Digter (J.E.: Our national anthem's author) (København: Gyldendalske Boghandel, 1943), 44.

8. Article on Ewald in *Encyclopaedia Britannica*, 11th ed., 29 vols. (New York: Encyclopaedia Britannica Company, 1910–1911), 10:39.

9. Quoted by William Morton Payne in his comments on Ewald, in John W. Cunliffe and Ashley H. Thorndike, eds., *The World's Best Literature*, 30 vols. (New York: University Edition of The Warner Library, 1917), 9:5614.

10. Louis Theodor Bobé, *Johannes Ewald, Biografiske Studier* (København: H. Hagerup, 1943), 37.

11. Placed in the care of the Jacobsen family, he fell in love with their daughter Anna Hedevig. Her parents strongly objected to a possible marriage and removed the crippled poet from her care.

12. Leif Ludvig Albertsen, *Sang og Slagkraft* (Song and power) (København: Privattryk, 1975), 30.

13. The only other anthem that originally was part of an opera or operetta was the Czech *Kde domov muj* (Where my home is). The libretto of the operetta *Fidlovacka* (The Fair) originated with Jan K. Tyl and was set to music by Frantisek Skroup in 1831.

14. Friedrich Kühlau, a German-born music director at the Royal Theater in Copenhagen, gave Ewald's stanzas their final tune. It had previously undergone various revisions. The music to the *Fiskerne* operetta was provided by Johann Ernst Hartmann who, however, did not score *Kong Christian*. The composer of that song listed most often is D. L. Rogert, an amateur musician and friend of Ewald.

15. The complicated Schleswig-Holstein issue bedeviled European diplomacy for generations, especially throughout much of the nineteenth century. In the 1840s, constitutional and legal problems as to the future of the two duchies were further tangled by nationalist pressures from both the Danish and the German side. Germans constituted a large majority except for the northern part of Schleswig (Slesvig in Danish), but the two duchies had been under Danish sovereignty since 1460 when the newly elected King Christian I of Denmark had solemnly sworn that they could never be separated.

16. Jens Peter Trap, *Fra fire kongers tid* (From the times of four kings), 3 vols. (København: G.E.C. Gad, 1966–1967), 2:38.

17. Hans Kuhn, *Defining a Nation in Songs: Danish Patriotic Songs in Songbooks of the Period 1832–1870* (København: C. A. Reitzels Forlag, 1990), 68. This pioneering and valuable study of Danish national songs in the mid-nineteenth century is a unique contribution to the subject field. I am indebted to Dr. Erik Dal for a timely reference to that monograph.

18. Curiously, Oehlenschläger used some of the same themes as Ewald, such as Hrolf Krake or Baldur, as if he wanted to prove that he could not only match his predecessor but even outdistance him.

19. The reference to *Henri Quatre* is hardly surprising, since the *Marseillaise* had been all but banned in post-Napoleonic France. See Chapter 4 on the evolution of the French national anthem.

20. The history of Denmark's first and aborted national anthem has been treated fully by Flemming Conrad, *Konkurrencen 1818 om en dansk nationalsang* (Competition for a Danish national anthem in 1818), in *Dansk identitetshistorie*, ed. Ole Feldbaek, 4 vols. (København: Glydendalske Boghandel, 1991), 2:150–252.

21. This translation was rendered by Mrs. Marianne Borg-Hansen, whose gracious help throughout this chapter is gratefully acknowledged here.

22. July 4 was deliberately chosen by the organizers of the meeting to symbolize the striving for national self-determination. It is still annually celebrated by Dano-Americans at Rebilt in Jutland as a token of close relations between Denmark and the United States.

23. Helga Vang Lauridsen and Tue Gad, eds., *H.C. Andersens Dagbøger 1845–1850* (H. C. Andersen's diaries), 3 vols. (København: G.E.C. Gads Forlag, 1974), 3:314 passim.

24. See Chapters 11 and 14.

25. Johan Borup, "Kong Christian og andre Sange" (King Christian and other songs), in *Litteraere udkast* (København og Kristiania: Gyldendalske Boghandel, 1910), 105–6.

26. Flemming Lundgreen-Nielsen, ed., *På sporet af dansk identitet* (On the trail of a Danish identity) (København: Spektrum, 1992), 120.

27. This episode has been referred to by Kuhn, 73.

28. Flor, 1.

29. Richard Petrow, *The Bitter Years: The Invasion and Occupation of Denmark and Norway: April 1940–May 1945* (New York: William Morrow, 1974), 283.

30. Leif Ludvig Albertsen, *Lyrik der synges* (Lyric as sung) (København: Berlingske Forlag, 1978), 48.

31. Birger Isaksen, *Sangen i Danmark* (Songs of Denmark) (Odense: Fyns Boghandels Forlag, 1941), 76. On the next page, however, the author calls the Oehlenschläger poem "our most beloved and finest patriotic poem."

32. Kuhn, 129.

33. See Chapter 11.

34. That statement was contained in a brief article on H. E. Krøyer, the composer of *Der er et yndigt land*, in *Dansk Biografisk Haandeleksikon*, 3 vols. (København: Gyldendal, 1920–1926), 2:411. Later and more famous Danish composers such as Carl Nielsen and Thomas Laub have tried new scores for the anthem but failed to gain general acceptance for a replacement.

Resistance Anthems

4

France

La Marseillaise
(Claude-Joseph Rouget de Lisle)

Among the national anthems of the world, none has attained such widespread renown, triggered such vibrant emotions, become the model for such a variety of other anthems as the *Marseillaise*. Its pulsating tune and fiery verses have stirred up deep passions in more than two centuries and served as a clarion call for those many who have struggled defiantly, if at times unsuccessfully, for liberty and progress. Created at a crucial juncture of occidental history when national self-determination, a new phenomenon since the American Revolution, was challenged by foreign intervention, the French anthem breathed nationalist assertiveness, defiance, and pride.

But since the mid-nineteenth century, the *Marseillaise* has also been used to express the yearning for social justice. As such, it became the rallying song of the underprivileged and revolutionaries throughout the world. Arguably the most nationalist of all European anthems, the *Marseillaise* thus acquired an international dimension. This dual function of articulating both national and international proclivities has marked the evolution of the French anthem as it was pulled left or right by conflicting political movements. Dichotomy has been the hallmark not only of the *Marseillaise* but also of the fate of its creator. He had cast his best-known song in the crucible of a revolutionary nationalism while holding traditionalist and royalist views.

Yet he had welcomed the epochal early measures of the French Revolution: the establishment of a national legislature, the storming of the Bastille, the Declaration of the Rights of Man and the Citizen, the abolition of feudalism, and not least the growing awareness of nationhood—as symbolized by the *fête de la nation* on July 14, 1790; henceforth, Auvergnats and Normands, Alsatiens and Provençals would be Frenchmen first and proud of it. A fledgling constitutional monarchy had come into being by 1791. The real threat to its survival appeared to emanate from abroad rather than from within the country.

Since August 1791, the possibility of foreign intervention had loomed ominously. The Declaration of Pillnitz, issued that month by the Austrian and Prussian monarchs, had served notice on the French government that they stood ready to use force to ensure the full liberty of person and action of their fellow sovereign, King Louis XVI of France.

If that interventionist threat seemed to materialize in the spring of 1792, what more opportune occasion than to challenge the would-be invaders of French soil and despoilers of the newly proclaimed sovereignty of the French nation! Their "mercenary" troops would prove no match for the citizen-soldiers of France. And as for the despised emigré aristocrats, gathering strength and hope on the right bank of the Rhine, they soon would find out that such traitors had neither place nor part in the new national community of free Frenchmen. Now was the moment to challenge the arrogant foreign despots and their lackeys.

The news of the declaration of war on Austria, followed shortly by that on Prussia, reached Strasbourg after midnight on April 24, 1792. It had taken four days since issuance by the national assembly in Paris, but anticipation of war had preceded it for some time. In Strasbourg, the French city most exposed to the impending war, exultation matched excitement when word spread that the Paris government had at last thrown down the gauntlet.

All of the next day, volunteers and regulars belonging to *l'armée du Rhin* marched out to their assembly points. The thud of heavy boots mingled with the steady roll of drums and the raucous voices of the marching soldiers. They lustily sang the revolutionary and popular *Carmagnole* and the catchy *Ça ira* that mocked the old order and its privileged supporters.

At dusk these provocative tunes still reverberated through the streets of Strasbourg. They could be clearly heard in the mansion of Frédéric de Dietrich, mayor of the city. He and his wife Louise hosted a party that evening to celebrate the declaration of war. Many of the guests were frequent visitors at the Dietrich's salon. This April evening most of them wore uniforms.

The future and fate of those present was to differ greatly. For now, however, everybody at the mayor's table shared the same feelings and had one overriding interest: winning the war for France. Conversation centered on that subject. As the evening wore on and wine and champagne flowed freely, expressions of patriotism became effusive. The flippant tunes and irreverent lines of popular revolutionary songs still could be heard through the open windows, and irked the mayor. He complained that from Paris had come only tunes such as the *Ça ira* and *Carmagnole*, "base examples . . . unworthy of the new nation and of posterity."[1]

Then he turned to one of his guests, a captain in the royal corps of engineers.

The mayor had known Rouget de Lisle since his posting to Strasbourg a year ago, and he soon came to like him for his artistic talents. Captain Rouget not only had been in regular attendance at the mayoral soirées but joined in their musical presentations with his violin. Better still, he had successfully assisted the mayor in staging an elaborate ceremony to celebrate the new constitution of September 1791 under which France had become a constitutional monarchy.

Mayor Dietrich remembered that occasion with pleasure as he turned to his collaborator. "Look here, Captain; you who are both a musician and a poet should compose a new marching song for the soldiers which would also become the true song of the nation."[2] Rouget, in a show of modesty, declined at first but the evening had not as yet run its course. As he was to record many years later, "the news of war together with the plentiful champagne enhanced the exultation in each of us."[3]

The words "patrie," "aux armes," "libre" dominated the conversation. But these stirring words not only expressed the sentiments of those gathered at the mayor's mansion; they also could be heard in the streets. Posters, put up there, proclaimed: "To arms, citizens! The banner of war has been unfurled . . . .To be free it will be necessary to fight, conquer, or die."[4]

Such fervent exhortations echoed in Rouget's agitated mind as he made his way through excited crowds back to his lodgings. Once there, he picked up the violin, a prized possession that accompanied him on all his assignments. He recalled, over two decades later, "in my first strokes I found the tune that I desired. The words came with the melody; the melody came with the words."[5] And soon his emotions reached a high intensity as if "I were consumed by an intense fever . . . .The next morning when awakening from a slumber no less agitated than my condition before I had finally fallen asleep, I was almost surprised to find on my desk the stanzas of my hymn."[6]

Arise, children of the native land,
The day of glory has arrived,
Tyranny is upon us
Its bloodstained banner raised.
Do you hear in the fields
Those ferocious soldiers roar?
They are coming right into our midst
To slaughter your sons, your companions,

To arms, oh citizens,
Form your battalions;
March, March!
So that their impure blood
Will drench our furrows!

Sacred love of our native land,
Guide, sustain our avenging arms!
Liberty, oh dearest liberty,

Do fight along your defenders!
With our banners there lies victory
Flock to their virile appeal;
So that our dying enemies
Witness your triumph and our glory

[Refrain][7]

These, the first and the last stanzas—now most frequently sung—are shot through with a fiery vehemence. And the vibrant refrain, with its martial appeal, carries that note to its climax. While the opening stanza conjures up the threatening specter of invaders bringing tyranny, the concluding stanza, with its thrilling invocation of devotion to the country and to liberty, depicts France's ultimate triumph and glory.

The four middle stanzas are suffused by the same manichaean contrast, pitting the dark forces of the invader and their still darker designs against the heroic defenders of the home country. All the verses breathed a truculent defiance; their stark language did neither shade contrasts nor offer literary finesse. A streak of nationalist assertiveness ran through every one of the stanzas and carried over into anthems modelled on them.[8]

To be sure, Rouget was an officer on active service and created his piece at a moment of high national tension. If that creation sounded warlike, even gory, it did not follow, however, that he was a martinet. Rather, he articulated emotions running both widely and deeply among the population. That was evident from the moment Mayor Dietrich himself rendered the verses for the first time at his mansion on the evening of April 26, 1792. Words and music alike triggered an enthusiastic acclaim from the same guests as the night before.

Within a day the gripping song spread like wildfire through the city. Handwritten copies appeared, and the new tune could be heard in cafés and inns around Strasbourg. Within a month the city's official printer had a first printing in circulation—leaving the author's name conveniently off the title page, perhaps to save on royalties.

Known as the *Chant de guerre de l'armée du Rhin*, Rouget dedicated it to the commander of that army. Marshal Nicholas Luckner was soon removed for incompetence, but the song succeeded beyond all expectations. Four days after its creation Rouget's composition was officially played for the first time at a Strasbourg troop review. The Army of the Rhine quickly and proudly adopted the song that bore its name. In mid-June the thrilling stanzas could be heard in Montpellier—far to the south—where the Rouget family had originated, and on June 22, a member of the Montpellier section of the *Société des amis de la Constitution* in Marseilles introduced the tune to that city. As yet it carried its original title.

The Rhine was far away for the Marseillois volunteers gathering in response to an urgent request from Paris "for six hundred men who knew how to die." When they marched out on July 2, 1792, the song went with them. It not only cheered the volunteers on their long way to the capital but also the villagers and townspeople who heard the fanfare-like cadencies as the marchers passed.

At noon on July 30, the Marseillois lustily sang all the stanzas as they marched to great applause through the St. Antoine quarter of Paris. It was here that the revolution had its most active and resolute supporters, and it was here that a new title was bestowed on the marching song with its clarion-call refrain: *La Marseillaise.*

Whatever the title, it was the song that mattered. It not only called to arms; it seemed to guarantee victory. And like the new blue-white-red tricolore, the song carried with it the impetus of the revolution. At Valmy, where the soldiers of that revolution stood off the Austrian and Prussian invaders on September 20, 1792, it could be heard from some sectors of the extended French lines. A week later the legislature of the newly proclaimed republic bestowed on Rouget's composition the status of an official hymn, making it the first in history to be declared a national anthem by legislative fiat.

Commanders and troops alike made effective use of the new song. One general reported that he had won a battle "because the *Marseillaise* commanded together with me." Another general asked for an additional ten thousand men and "an edition of the *Marseillaise.*" And General Charles François Dumouriez, whose troops had won the first French victory abroad, issued an order of the day on March 4, 1793: "If the enemy crosses the Meuse close ranks . . . fix bayonets, strike up the Marseillois [*sic*] and you will win."[9]

While the new revolutionary armies first rallied and then conquered to the tune of the *Marseillaise,* its author in a sharp contrast turned antirevolutionary. In April 1792, he had struck off his hymn in a moment of patriotic rapture. He had done so as an officer in the king's army and a supporter of the constitutional monarchy that had emerged from the first phase of the revolution. Yet as the heady days of that spring faded into the hotter ones of summer, the foreign invaders and the Parisian radicals alike gained ground. In view of the rapidly changing situation, Rouget reconsidered his own position, strongly resenting revolutionary excesses. But his resentment had deeper roots.

He belonged to a family whose numerous branches had for centuries provided crown servants; among them military governors, judges, and magistrates. Rouget himself was born into a well-established family, his father being a crown advocate at Lons-le Saunier, on May 10, 1760. The small town lay in the Jura region of the *Franche-Comté,* known for its piedmont scenery and hardy population.

At the time of his birth, his parents had already decided on a military career for their firstborn. To open the way toward it, he was christened Claude-Joseph, Sieur de l'Isle. The aristocratic patronymic, given him by his common-born parents, made it possible to become an officer, since commoners were excluded from receiving the king's commission.

Probably under his mother's influence, Rouget developed an early interest in poetry and music. His adolescent verses and musical sketches were sentimental pieces, much in keeping with the conventional lightness of the rococo. Not by chance did he compose a short romance for the daughter of Pierre Beaumarchais, of *Le Figaro* fame, whose house he frequently visited while at a military school in Paris.

When the revolution erupted in the early summer of 1789, he returned as soon as possible from his post as an engineer officer to his home town, where he supported the fundamental reform measures, participated in public activities, and joined the newly created national guard. Yet, when he came to the capital in February 1790, his primary interest focused on the theater stage rather than the political one.

Literary success, however, still eluded him. He was not unhappy to leave Paris for Strasbourg, where he had been posted as of May 1, 1791. After all, the Alsatian capital was second only to the national capital among French cities as a center of the arts. He greatly enjoyed his stay there, benefitting from its cultural ambiance and not least so at the mayor's mansion.

Shortly after the outbreak of war, Rouget was detailed to supervise work on the fortifications at Huningue, a few miles from the Swiss border at Basel. It was at this outpost that news of two successive mob intrusions of the *Tuileries*, the royal residence in Paris, had reached and shocked him. The first of these intrusions had been a rather harmless affair that ended when the flustered king donned a Phrygian red cap, symbol of the revolutionaries. The second invasion, in August 1792, proved far more serious; it ended in the slaying of nearly one thousand Swiss guards, who were defending the palace, and in the transfer of the royal family to the uncertain protection of the legislature. Some twenty years later Rouget still was to refer to "the catastrophe of 10 August."[10]

There can be no doubt as to the intensity of his feelings at the time of the event. Toward the end of August 1792, a delegation from the legislature arrived at Huningue. Its members were making the rounds to ensure that all officers on active service accepted the new situation with the royal family in protective custody of a legislature increasingly under pressure from a radical minority. Rouget was the only officer at the garrison to refuse a sworn commitment to the new order, and the commissioners felt compelled "to suspend the author of the *Chant des Marseillais*."[11]

By fall, however, his patriotism outweighed all other considerations. The newly proclaimed republic struggled precariously for survival against numerous domestic and external enemies. Rouget was hardly more favorably disposed toward the republic than to those who had stormed the *Tuileries* and all but ended the constitutional monarchy. But now "la patrie est en danger."

He asked General Jean Baptiste Valence, an old acquaintance, for reemployment, and the general replied: "I very well could use the author of a tune which has become the general expression of the Republic."[12] With such encouragement the suspended officer decided to take the requested loyalty oath to the constitution of the republic, provided the former "would be neither modified nor replaced."[13]

He then joined General Valence's staff and served creditably in the siege of Namur, a key Belgian fortress. But early in 1793 he returned to Paris. For unknown reasons he refused to draw his army pay any longer. Perhaps he was so deeply shaken by the execution of the king in January that he preferred not to be in the pay of regicides; very likely he also may have wished to give more time to his literary activities. Never quite decided on which of two careers to follow, he had himself transferred to the inactive list.

The new Robespierrist Republic of Virtue saw little virtue and less use in a career officer who, in the hour of greatest patriotic needs, preferred the pen to the sword. Moreover, several of his close friends were under investigation for counterrevolutionary contacts or activities. In mid-September 1793, a law was passed to detain all those suspected of disloyalty or opposition to the republic. The ever watchful *Comité de Salut Public*, center of governmental power, soon thereafter ordered Rouget's arrest and before the end of the month he found himself in prison.

It was not, however, one from which an ever-longer train of tumbrels carried prisoners to the guillotine. In fact "citoyen Rouget" was treated quite leniently. After all, even the most ruthless prosecutor or suspicious jailer must have realized quickly that this prisoner was the author of the national anthem.

It indeed had become popular not only among the soldiers but also among the civilian population. As André Grétry, among the foremost French composers of the era and one-time collaborator with Rouget on a musical comedy, wrote to him: "Your stanzas . . . are sung at all shows and at all the corners of Paris."[14] About the only negative comment came from Rouget's mother who was quoted as writing to her firstborn: "What is all this I hear regarding that revolutionary hymn which is sung by a horde of brigands and which is mixed up with our name?"[15]

Whatever the popularity of his composition, he remained imprisoned. There were suspicions. His friend Mayor Dietrich, the very sponsor of the *Marseillaise*, was charged with counterrevolutionary activities and ended up under the guillotine in the Christmas week of 1793. The first elected mayor of Paris, a distant relative of Rouget, met the same fate. The author's renown as the creator of the Republic's national anthem still might accord some protection against such an eventuality. Yet in the frenzied months of the Robespierre dictatorship in the first half of 1794, when even the most stalwart revolutionaries and republicans were guillotined, nothing could be taken for granted—least of all life.

So as not to miss any opportunity of securing his own life, Rouget addressed a statement to the French people and such governing authorities as the Committee of Public Safety and the Revolutionary Tribunal. Declaring himself the author of the *Hymne des Marseillais,* he hastened to assert that he no longer considered it to be his personal achievement! Instead, the hymn, whose "motives of inspiration could be no more denied than its national importance or the services rendered," belonged to the nation.[16]

Such self-serving assertions proved unnecessary, both for his own survival and that of his foremost creation. The Robespierrist firestorm did not consume him. It burned itself out on the 9th of Thermidor, the middle month of the new republican calendar. Robespierre's rule and life came to an abrupt end at the hands of those who feared for their own.

The prison gates sprang open for many of the "antiregime" suspects. Rouget gained provisional release within a week. In a reflex reaction to the traumatic experiences of the past year, he joined the most reactionary group of counter-revolutionaries. During the post-Thermidorean period, Rouget identified readily with the "Incroyables" who, in their extravagant dress and conduct, represented the antithesis to the preceding years of revolutionary rigor. And he became a welcome visitor to the fashionable new salons to which his legitimist politics, recent imprisonment, and not least his artistic inclinations gave him ready access. Nor was he forgotten in the reconstituted Convention, the latest national assembly, now dominated by a moderate republican majority.

On July 14, 1795—sixth anniversary of the storming of the Bastille—the deputy Jean Debry rose in the Convention. "I demand that the author of the *Hymn of the Marseillais* be mentioned honorably in the proceedings of today. This excellent patriot was incarcerated . . . during the Robespierre tyranny while the song which he had composed . . . led our brothers to victory."[17] And on Debry's subsequent motion *La Marseillaise* was declared that day—for a second time—the official anthem of the first French republic.

But such sanctioning did not guarantee general acceptance. The anthem that was to exemplify as well as symbolize national unity soon presaged deep divisions. The Thermidorians had no use for it. Instead, they rallied to the tune of *Le Reveil du peuple*, with its vitriolic disclaimer of the "assassins and brigands" who had caused the revolutionary excesses. And they hooted down the hymn of the revolutionaries whose collective expression of faith remained the *Marseillaise*.

Rouget himself must have soon become aware of this dualist interpretation. In the words of Mayor Dietrich's grandson, the author had written his piece exclusively for the national defense effort. "When he saw that piece changed to a rallying cry of hate towards royalty he complained bitterly that it had been distorted."[18] Yet his own loyalties did not divide. On two occasions in 1795, he demonstrated against the radicals in and around the Convention where he was once shot at in a melee with a mob. He did, nevertheless, still take pride in his most widely known creation, which was given place of honor in the first collection of his printed work, the *Essais en vers et en prose*, in 1796. As long as the *Marseillaise* led French troops to victory—or even out of defiant defeat—there was no reason for him to lessen that pride of authorship.

Once more he accepted reinstatement to active service as of March 1795, only to leave for good within a year. In his most argumentative vein he complained about lack of promotion and alleged prejudice as its cause. Underlying the growing tension between him and his superiors was Rouget's inborn uncertainty whether to follow the drums or the muses, and he resigned his commission one last time.

His literary production, now resumed, did not yield a very encouraging response. He wrote several librettos for second-rate composers, enhancing neither their nor his reputation. But there was always the *Marseillaise* to draw on for success! A young general by the name of Buonaparte conducted a victorious campaign in northern Italy. Better still, he had ordered all bands in his command to play the *Marseillaise*. And it was "sung with enthusiasm by the soldiers."[19]

Rouget applauded both Napoleon's successes and his own song's share in them. It was one thing, however, to put together—with the support of *La Marseillaise*—a string of brilliant victories; it was quite another if the dynamic general were to expand and exploit them for his own ends. Yet that happened precisely on the 18th of Brumaire, 1799, when he posed as France's savior from ignominy and inefficiency.

Napoleon's coup caused Rouget, like many other Frenchmen, misgivings. These increased when the newly proclaimed First Consul took a sudden dislike to Rouget's masterpiece because the opposition had used it to protest his coup. Not for the first time and certainly not for the last, the new national anthem had been turned into a double-edged sword of partisanship. But the First Consul still respected Rouget and commissioned him to write another "warlike song." The flattered author obliged. His *Chant des Combats*, however, met with a lukewarm response. There was apparently no substitute for the *Marseillaise*.

Nor was he any luckier in his further dealings with Napoleon. Appointed as an agent to the Netherlands, he took the occasion to criticize the Consul's principal councillors. In 1803, he requested Napoleon's authorization to travel to England because "he felt frustrated at home in every respect."[20] There was no answer to that request, either because of the impending renewal of war between Britain and France or because Rouget was under suspicion of wanting to contact anti-Bonapartist groups in London.

His prolonged frustration soon vented itself in a letter to Napoleon on February 9, 1804. In it Rouget displayed an astonishing boldness, considerable prescience, and a complete disregard for his professional future. He admonished the Consul—soon to be emperor of the French—"to open [his] eyes to the corruption, the infamy, the crimes which usurp insolently the place and privileges of talents, patriots, and virtue." And he warned him in an extraordinary statement of frankness as well as recklessness: "Bonaparte, you are going to lose and what is worse you will lose France too."[21]

For the time being it was Rouget who lost. Predictably, he remained unemployed as long as Napoleon held power. He made a scanty living from copying music while his literary production all but dried up. The only significant piece, the *Hymn to Peace*, by its title alone antithetical to the *Marseillaise*, was written during Napoleon's ill-fated Russian campaign of 1812.

Quite naturally, Rouget hailed the return of the Bourbons in 1814, in an effusive if short poem that began and ended with the same telling line, "Vive le Roi.''[22] From a committed royalist like Rouget such an exclamation might be expected. Far more surprising, however, was the call in the same poem upon Tsar Alexander I—a major partner in the anti-Napoleonic coalition—to "punish the execrable oppressor of the West" and to restore the Bourbons to their throne. Less than a quarter of a century had gone by since the same author had sounded his clarion call for all true Frenchmen to resist foreign invaders!

A still more striking reversal occurred during the brief return of the erstwhile emperor in March 1815. Just before Napoleon's reentry into Paris, the author of the *Marseillaise,* in a spectacular ironic twist, all but denigrated his most famous creation. Belatedly arriving at a dinner party because of demonstrations against the hurriedly exiting Bourbon king, Rouget exclaimed, "It's going badly. They are singing the *Marseillaise!*''[23]

For him it was no longer the triumphant battle hymn of the defenders of the national soil and of liberty, but a disagreeable partisan outburst against royalty and legitimacy. The Bourbons, however, showed no gratitude for such faithful devotion. Their second return after Waterloo in June 1815, where the imperial guard in its last desperate attack had once more rallied to the cadencies of the *Marseillaise,* did not benefit its author. For the restored Bourbons it remained the theme song of the detested revolution, with neither creator nor creation deserving any kind of recognition.

Rouget fared no better now than in the latter stages of the revolution or under Napoleon. He had worked on a couple of Shakespearean plays—Macbeth and Othello—to make them into operas. When one of them was ready for rehearsal at the royal opera in 1817 he learned to his consternation that "the author of the infamous *Marseillaise*" could have no access to that stage.[24]

His disappointment at Bourbon rule grew apace with professional and financial difficulties. The Bourbons were unwilling to pay any pension to an officer who had opted out of service over a quarter of a century ago and whose best verses had stemmed from the despised revolution. A new edition of mainly old poetry, the *Cinquants chants français,* did not produce much revenue. Significantly, his pièce de résistance, the *Marseillaise,* was only given place 23 in that collection of fifty poems.

In 1826 one of several creditors pressed action against the luckless and listless Rouget, and after more than thirty years he was again imprisoned—not as a political suspect but as a debtor. But there were those who remembered him and his masterpiece and now came to his assistance. Foremost among them was the best-known French poet of the post-Napoleonic era, Pierre Béranger. In a letter of encouragement he counselled Rouget not to be embarrassed. Rather, he wrote, "it is the entire nation which should blush over the misfortunes which have not ceased to befall the author of *La Marseillaise.*''[25]

Released from prison after seventeen days, Rouget still lacked in financial means. He did not lack, however, devoted friends. General François Blein had offered him shelter in his house. Located in the village of Choisy-le-Roi, one could not think of a more suitable name for the refuge of a staunch royalist like

Rouget. But he now questioned whether it might not have been better "if I were not the author of that *Infamous Marseillaise*."[26] That sarcastic reference to the very words used by the Bourbon authorities to deny him access to the royal opera stage nevertheless indicated that he had second thoughts about the impact of the *Marseillaise* on his life.

Official recognition and a measure of compensation were finally accorded the hapless author in his closing years. In July 1830, the rule of the Bourbons, who had "learned nothing and forgotten nothing," came to an end. They were replaced by the rivalling Orléans dynasty, and their head, Louis Philippe, remembered Rouget. Within one month of his ascent to the throne the "citizen king" informed him that he recalled with pleasure the *Marseillaise* as contributing to victory at Jemappes, first French battle success on foreign soil in November 1792, where Louis Philippe had led a charge. Now the time had come to offer overdue appreciation and compensation.

He failed to mention, however, that two days earlier a crowd at the opera had spontaneously sung the *Marseillaise* and then collected money for its composer. Not to be outdone, the new government offered a small pension to the ex-officer. It was quickly doubled by contribution from the king's private purse. But what pleased the recipient of these donations most was the *légion d'honneur* award.

Like its creator, the *Marseillaise,* too, had benefitted from the dynastic and political changes. It was proclaimed the anthem of the July monarchy. Alas, as Rouget's life ebbed in the mid–1830s so did the prominence of his foremost creation. That fateful partisan interpretation and utilization, previously noted and not least by the author, reasserted itself. Demonstrating and often unemployed workers sang it as a rallying tune of defiance against an uncaring government, In retaliation, the *Marseillaise* was heard less and less at official ceremonies.

Fortunately, Rouget was spared another round of disappointment and disillusion. He faded away almost unnoticed. Never married—a fate of several anthem authors—he had no family of his own. No records exist regarding his relations or lack thereof with women: a situation that gave rise to a variety of insinuations from homosexuality through impotence to profligacy. But, after living in solitude for much of his adult life, Rouget's death caused an upsurge of awareness and appreciation.

At his funeral in Choisy-le-Roi on June 28, 1836, friends and villagers spontaneously broke into the *Marseillaise*. General Blein saw to it that a memorial stone was erected over his grave and provided the inscription:

Here rests Claude-Joseph
Rouget de Lisle
When the French Revolution
in 1792
Had to fight the kings
He gave to it for victory
The Song of the Marseillaise

Yet that song had a far greater role to play than indicated on his tombstone. Destined to international fame, it crossed frontiers and then continents. In the first decade of its existence it was translated into several languages.[27] Hungarian patriots possessed copies in 1795; it served as a model for the first Greek national hymn a year later and inspired the equally short-lived Spanish anthem of 1812. It was struck up by the Belgians in their fight for independence in 1830 and influenced the Italians fighting for the same goal in 1848–49.[28] And the radical leader Felix Pyat could state without much exaggeration in 1841: "The *Marseillaise* is the hymn of deliverance . . . sung in Polish, Italian, German, even in Turkish . . . in all languages by those who want to be free."[29]

Deliverance, however, meant more to Pyat and his associates than national independence. It meant social progress and workers' rights, and soon the use of the *Marseillaise* manifested that change in emphasis. Its primary function changed from one of national defiance and defense to one of social challenge and change. The *Marseillaise* moved from ready acceptance in palaces, theaters, and city halls to one in working quarters and thence to prisons and transports. The dual character of the anthem, now unifying the French people, now dividing them, was its indelible mark. It clearly showed in such perceptive comments as that of one of Rouget's best biographers. "While he fought in the ranks of the enemies of the Revolution, the *Marseillaise* remained the song . . . of the Jacobins and Montagnards."[30]

His most famous creation was fated to keep bobbing along with the turbulent course of modern French history. Governments and their opposition alike made the one enduring piece of Rouget's pen and violin into a political tool to serve respective needs. And various regimes used it accordingly, at times by insertion into and at other times by its withdrawal from public life. This had been the case in the era of Napoleon I. It happened again under Louis Philippe. When his reign abruptly ended in 1848, the *Marseillaise* sprang back into prominence during the short-lived Second Republic. Within three years its life was ended by another Napoleon. Like his illustrious uncle, he had little use for an anthem associated with revolution and later on with republicanism. Those ardent republicans who broke into the *Marseillaise* as they boarded the transports for Cayenne in 1852 endeared themselves as little to the newly proclaimed emperor as did the tune they sang so defiantly.

Only after the outbreak of the Franco-Prussian war in 1870 did a jittery Napoleon III allow the anthem official status, much as his forbear had reinstated it during the months preceding Waterloo. In the one case as in the other, it could not turn the tide on the battlefields. Worse still, it again was made to serve conflicting interests and groupings at home. The Communards in Paris sang the *Marseillaise* in defiance of both the besieging Prussians and of the capitulants and "reactionaries" who bartered from Bordeaux for terms with the German conquerors in March 1871. It was in that southern French city where the provisional national assembly struck up the same tune in a demonstration of bitter antagonism toward the Parisian radicals.

For several years after the proclamation of the Third Republic in 1871 the *Marseillaise* remained in limbo. Half a decade later it made a semiofficial reappearance; appropriately so at the funeral of Adolphe Thiers, the wily statesman who had forecast that a republic would divide France the least. And in 1879, Rouget's song became by order of the minister of war once again the *Chant National Officiel.*

Nor did its author go unacclaimed any longer. Perhaps because of the previous neglect, two statues were erected in the same year (1882), one in his birthplace, the other in the village where he died. At that ceremony Premier Charles de Freycinet stated with more conviction than foresight: "*The Marseillaise* is the hymn of the country . . . .Foreign people know . . . that it is more than a hymn of war . . . .The banner which France carries forward today is that of progress, civilization, and liberty."[31]

Indeed, the premier's triumphant words were echoed beyond France's borders, albeit in a setting quite different from that envisaged by him. As early as 1868, a publication of the International Workers Association contained this passage: "Our *Marseillaise* no longer sounds for the soldiers . . . .Our *Marseillaise* is the hymn of work, [social] freedom, and justice."[32] And before the end of the century an observer commented: "The *Marseillaise* remained the password of the international revolution."[33]

Not until August 1914 did the French national anthem resume its original function of uniting the nation in the face of war. Almost a year later Rouget was accorded ultimate honors, less for his attainments than for political and propagandist reasons. There was an urgent need for a viable symbolism that could rally the nation to still greater sacrifices and lasting endurance. His remains were transferred from Choisy-le-Roi to the national shrine of France's great, the Panthéon. At a solemn ceremony on July 14, 1915 President Raymond Poincaré declared, "The *Marseillaise* evokes the idea of a sovereign nation . . . whose songs prefer death to servitude . . . .Gentlemen, it needs an anthem like this in a war like this to express the noble thoughts of France."[34] As such it was heard as the ultimate expression of the national will to resist on battlefields like Verdun.

In the Second World War, official acclaim soon was denied to the *Marseillaise.* The Vichy government, satellite of Nazi Germany, suppressed or at least curtailed the rendering of the anthem in public. Instead it became, appropriately, the battle song of the *résistants.* On yet another July 14, this one in 1942, some 20,000 Marseillois sang it defiantly in spite of a local ban by Vichy authorities, and it could be heard in concentration camps such as Ravensbrück.[35] Not until August 1944, however, did the *Marseillaise* regain official status. General Charles de Gaulle, upon entering liberated Paris on August 25, was among the first to sing it publicly with much emotion at the *Place de la Concorde.*

Since that time the anthem has been untrammelled by the governments of both the IVth and the Vth French Republic. That does not mean, however, that its survival in status is guaranteed. Among young French people of today, remarks can be heard that the *Marseillaise* is too much of a war song. And there are efforts under way to replace the text, once branded by no less a literary authority than Victor Hugo as inferior.

In June 1990, the recently founded association *Pour une Marseillaise de la Fraternité*, led by the social reformer Abbé Pierre, published an appeal for a new *Marseillaise*. That appeal, in its first sentence, declared, "The national anthem is the soul of a people." It went on to point out that "because we love France we do aspire to a message in harmony with its ideal of liberty, equality, fraternity,"[36] the very triad engendered, like the *Marseillaise*, by the first French revolution.

The appeal specifically excluded the musical score from any revision since it has resonated "throughout the great moments of our history." But could one, the signers of the appeal asked, expect people—especially young ones—who aspired to live in friendship and solidarity with other nations to sing of hate and vengeance? The hour had come, in the opinion of these signers, to search for verses that would acknowledge only the war against hunger, illiteracy, unemployment, and want. Among those who underwrote that appeal, coupled with a request for contributions to a fund for a new *Marseillaise* text, were Madame Danielle Mitterand, wife of the president of the republic, the singer Charles Aznavour, government ministers, generals, industrialists, and scientists.

Yet for all the well-known names and groundswell of support for a textual replacement, there was no effective follow-up on the demand for change. Not unexpectedly, however, that issue came to the fore again in the early spring of 1992. At the opening of the Olympic winter games at Albertville in the French Alps, athletes, spectators, and television audiences throughout the world were treated to the first stanza of the *Marseillaise*. Rendered ever so touchingly by the solo voice of a young schoolgirl, reaction from mostly French people was anything but enthusiastic: not on account of the uniformly acclaimed presentation, but because the verses and the occasion were so incongruously juxtaposed.

Within days, objections that inveighed against the ferocity and xenophobia of such lines as "their impure blood will drench our furrows" reached the media. That negative reaction, on the other hand, proved a godsend for the movement in favor of the anthem's revision. A retired commander of the French firefighters corps led the charge against the unwelcome lines. He argued rather convincingly that at a moment of international togetherness of young people from all over the world, phrases of hate and violence were especially inopportune. And he lost no time in bringing to public attention a possible new text far more consonant with the times and France's current standing in world opinion. It so happened that the author was a retired firefighter and that his stanzas thus made them still more commendable to the erstwhile chief of the corps.

Armand Thuair's revision[37] certainly does not lack either in patriotism or pacifism. He even saved quite generously and, no doubt sincerely, a couple of lines from Rouget's original lyrics. But the thrust and theme of Thuair's version was peace and cooperation, not war and confrontation. Moreover, his verses would fit snugly into the existing score. The new lyrics paired successfully with the old melody would almost certainly prove acceptable, not only to the new France within the new international setting, but to the world at large.

Yet he and his sponsor probably had not quite expected the counterswing of the pendulum. No sooner had the reformers of the *Marseillaise* made their pitch when the traditionalists weighed in with arguments hardly less fervent if perhaps more defensive. The most committed and eloquent defenders of the original version are also those who admit outright that some of the stanzas are totally inapplicable and even unacceptable today.

The top editorialist of conservative *Le Figaro* flatly stated that the *Marseillaise* "is not a poem but an uproar" and that its stanzas "indeed are incredible."[38] Yet in the same categorical vein he had declared in the opening sentence of his editorial: "One must not touch *La Marseillaise*. She is part of our history." And he concluded by asserting that it is "not an ordinary national anthem" but had become "the universal hymn of liberty."[39]

The defenders of the anthem have by no means been limited to conservative groups and their spokesmen. A left-socialist former minister has spoken of the anthem as "a symbol of the nation and the republic" and gone in the same statement so far as to call the *Marseillaise* "indispensable in the forming of the citizen."[40] Still further to the left, the chairman of a much weakened communist party is on record as defending the stanzas with the plausible argument that they have an international appeal to revolutionaries the world over.

None of the proponents of the original version have denied its martial character. The author of the potential replacement lyrics has pronounced it the most belligerent among the 175 anthems that he claims to have examined. Even such staunch advocates as the then minister of defense admit that the *Marseillaise*, throughout, is warlike. Yet he added at once that the words did denote a defensive rather than an aggressive war. Making his final pitch, Pierre Joxe declared, "Why should we renounce [our] past? For me, the *Marseillaise* is and must remain the song of liberty and the rights of man."[41] Nor is this view solely that of an individual. A public opinion poll revealed that even though forty percent of the respondents found the anthem too sanguinary, a large majority (75%) did not wish to see the lyrics changed.[42]

Just to make sure that any intended or actual move by those in favor of revision would be effectively countered, a committee for the defense of the Marseillaise has been organized. It is likely to clash with the Committee for a Marseillaise of Fraternity organized by Abbé Pierre. The future of the French anthem thus hangs in a precarious balance. Even American media have become involved in the controversy and made their preferences known.[43]

There seems to be no dearth of proposed alternates. Yet even if there should be agreement on a desirable replacement, a lengthy acceptance procedure would have to be followed from parliamentary approval to a possible plebiscite. As in other countries where replacement efforts have been made—as will be seen in some of the subsequent chapters—such efforts are not likely to yield quick results. National tradition is not easily broken nor a consensus on a new national anthem readily obtained. In the case of the *Marseillaise* its élan in word and tune reflects that of the French nation; discarding the text would mean denying the image.

Equally important in carrying the anthem from generation to generation is the fact that it carried with it the pride in an inspiring tradition: the victorious fight against reactionary invaders in the opening stages of a great revolution which made France the premier European power to lead that continent into the modern age. In the final analysis the *Marseillaise* may prove inextricably interwoven with the immortal triad of liberty-equality-fraternity, all stemming alike from an epochal decade in western history. In that case the noble efforts of Abbé Pierre or like-minded revisionists would have a tough row to hoe for the obvious reason that France can no more be separated from its 1789 revolution than the United States of America from their revolution a decade and a half earlier.

NOTES

1. Julien Tiersot, *Rouget de Lisle–son oeuvre–sa vie* (Rouget de Lisle–his work–his life) (Paris: Librairie Ch-Delagrave, 1892), quoting mémoire of Desiré Monnier, a friend of Rouget's in Lons-le Saunier.

2. Louis Fiaux, *La Marseillaise; son histoire dans l'histoire des français depuis 1792 (La Marseillaise;* its history in the history of the French since 1792) (Paris: E. Fasquelle, 1918), 28.

3. Tiersot, 387.

4. Philippe Parès, *Qui est l'auteur de La Marseillaise?* (Who is the composer of the *Marseillaise?*) (Paris: Editions Musicales Minerva, 1977), 70, fn. 24.

5. Tiersot, quoting Monnier mémoire, 388. As in the case of several other anthems, the origins and originality of the musical score were subject to as much debate as doubt. The *Marseillaise* had its complement of those who either doubted or denied that Rouget had composed its melody. This issue has been thoroughly examined by Parès, 58–115. He concluded that as far as it can be determined the *Marseillaise*'s melody originated with Rouget but did not rule out the possibility that the score was influenced in part by that of the *Oratorio Esther*, composed by Jean-Baptiste Grisons, a little-known contemporary of Rouget.

6. Parès, 32.

7. This translation of the two most often sung stanzas of the *Marseillaise* is that of the present author.

8. See, for example, the chapters on the Belgian and Portuguese anthems.

9. The three verbal accolades are cited by Alfred Leconte, *Rouget de Lisle: sa vie, ses oeuvres, La Marseillaise* (Rouget de Lisle: His life, his works, *La Marseillaise*) (Paris: Librairies–Imprimeries Réunies, 1892), 20–21.

10. Ibid., 19.

11. Rouget stated within a few days of his suspension that he could "never capitulate

to his conscience." Letter to officials in the Jura *département* as quoted by Marguerite Henry-Rozier, *Rouget de Lisle* (Paris: Gallimard, 1937), 83.

12. Tiersot, 171.

13. Henry-Rozier, 83.

14. Georges de Froidcourt, *Grétry, Rouget de Lisle et La Marseillaise* (Liège-Paris: Gothier-Clavreuil, 1945), 34.

15. Parès, 25, fn. 13.

16. Tiersot, 385–86, quoting from Rouget's "Au Peuple et aux réprésentants du Peuple, an II de la République."

17. Parès, 43.

18. Ibid., 67, fn. 18 quoting August Dietrich, one of the mayor's grandsons.

19. Fiaux, 133.

20. Ibid., 180.

21. Ibid., 181–86, where this extraordinary letter has been printed in full.

22. Rouget titled this polemic poem *Le Chant du Jura*, perhaps because of the conservative disposition of many of the Jurassiens, including his own. He praised the returning Bourbons as "the hope of the country." The poem has been reprinted in Parès, 48.

23. Fiaux, 193. The returned emperor reluctantly allowed the *Marseillaise* to be sung in public for the sake of winning support.

24. Ibid., 200.

25. Leconte, 35.

26. Ibid., 195.

27. Before 1800 the *Marseillaise* was translated into Danish, German, Greek, Hungarian, and Swedish. On its rapid spreading see especially Daniel Fryklund's two monographs: *La Marseillaise dans les pays scandinaves* and *La Marseillaise en Allemagne* (Hälsingborg: Schmidts Boktryckeri A-B, 1936 for both titles).

28. See the chapters on the Belgian and Italian anthems.

29. Felix Pyat, in a literary notice appended to *La Marseillaise: Chant patriotique* (Paris: Jules Laisué, 1841). A great-grandson of Mayor Dietrich reported that he had heard the *Marseillaise* in Brazil in 1888. Albert de Dietrich, *La création de la Marseillaise* (Paris: Bibliothèque d'Alsace Lorraine, 1917), 25. And it was sung by revolutionaries in the Antilles, according to Fiaux, 140.

30. Tiersot, 183. Fiaux, 6, succinctly observed that the *Marseillaise* was living "two lives; one military and warlike; the other civilian and political."

31. Quoted in Fiaux, 266.

32. Statement by François V. Raspail in #1 of the short-lived journal *La Marseillaise*, and quoted by Frantisek Gel, *Internationale und Marseillaise* (Prague: Artia, 1954), 244.

33. Ernest Chapuis, *Rouget de Lisle et l'hymne national* (Besançon: Imprimerie et Litographie de Paul Jacquin, 1892), 16.

34. Fiaux, 408.

35. Marie Mauron, *La Marseillaise* (Paris: Librarie Académique Perrin, 1968), 225.

36. *Le Monde*, June 29, 1990.

37. *The New York Times*'s translation of the proposed new anthem is given in the issue of March 5, 1992.

38. George Suffert editorial in *Le Figaro*, March 3, 1992.

39. Ibid.

40. *The New York Times*, March 5, 1992, quoting Pierre Chévènement.

41. *The Washington Post*, July 14, 1992, quoting Pierre Joxe.

42. *L'Actualité*, March 3, 1992.

43. See, for instance, the comments in the op. ed. piece "A Milder 'Marseillaise'," in *The Washington Post*, March 13, 1992, and "Meddling with the Marseillaise," in *Time*, March 16, 1992.

5

Poland

Dąbrowski Mazurka
(Jozef Wybicki)

For many a Polish exile in the late 1790s, the home country lay a thousand or more miles away but the craving to return there persisted. Yet the Poland they longed for had disappeared from the map altogether, swallowed up by its rapacious neighbors: Austria, Prussia, and Russia. Many of the patriots who had fought so recently for Poland's survival had not only lost their properties and home; the homeland had lost them for an indeterminate time after they fled abroad in the wake of the country's final partition in 1795.

But was that *finis Poloniae*? Was Poland never to rise again? Hopes had ever more diminished after each of the three partitions since 1772.[1] Now in the summer of 1797, however, those hopes were on the rise again, at least among the expatriates on French and Italian soil. Here a nucleus of Polish resistance took shape. A military force was in the process of forming, far away from the native land but all the more dedicated to it. And one day it might serve as a vanguard in the retrieval of Polish sovereignty.

That hope was buoyed by the support of one major country: France. The new French government, the Directory, continued the traditional policies of friendly and at times close relations with the Poles. Better still, the Directory's most important military commander and guarantor of its uncertain authority had just scored a string of brilliant victories in northern Italy. General Bonaparte not only had defeated large Austrian forces but, on the Directory's urgings, had consented to the formation of a Polish legion in Italy.

In the early spring of 1797 its first battalions were formed, following a convention signed by the provisional government of Lombardy and the Polish General Henryk Dąbrowski. Under its terms the future Polish legion would be taken into the employ of the Lombardian government, since the French constitution of 1795 forbade the employment of foreigners in the armed forces of the republic. So as to satisfy all parties concerned, the volunteers were to be clad in Polish uniforms, wear a French tricolor cockade on their hats, and have sleeve patches with the embroidered legend in Italian: "All free men are brothers."[2] There were dreams and even plans among the eager legionnaires of marching all the way from Italy to Poland to resurrect it by the sword.

In early July 1797, a tired traveller in civilian clothes approached Polish outposts near Reggio d'Emilia, southeast of Parma. He spoke Polish like a native, but the sentries who had stopped him were suspicious since he insisted on seeing their commander, General Dąbrowski, at once. An officer who happened on the scene just then recognized the visitor as General Jozef Wybicki and undertook to lead the unexpected guest to Dąbrowski's headquarters.

The two men had last met in Paris some six months earlier, and their embrace betokened a close relationship. Yet they differed much in upbringing, temperament, and career as well as in their very looks. Wybicki, now fifty, had the countenance of a somewhat aloof and disdainful aristocrat. The hooded eyes were skeptical, the nose prominent, the lips sardonic. Dąbrowski, by contrast, had a florid and jovial face. He had made his name and career in battle while Wybicki owed his military rank mainly to administrative skills, relying more on the pen than on the sword to serve the needs of his compatriots and the destiny of his country.

Yet both men had come closer to one another in their quest for a resurrected Poland. In October 1796, they had set to work in Paris on organizing a Polish legion. Support by the Directory was obtained quickly and Wybicki recorded: "I never was happier than when Dąbrowski informed me about the answer of the Directory."[3] Within a couple of months that legion came into being. Polish soldiers, commanded by their own officers, were once again under arms and ready to march.

On the way to the headquarters of the legion—gradually expanded to number three legions—Wybicki had passed through several encampments of French troops in northern Italy. Almost everywhere he had heard the vibrant *Marseillaise,* whose words and tune were still in his mind when he finally arrived at Reggio in his search for Dąbrowski.

In conversation over a bottle of wine, Wybicki had brought up the question of what the legionnaires were singing. The general replied that the officers still liked traditional hymns such as the *Bogurodzica* (Mother of God), with its martial undertones and religious fervor. The soldiers, however, preferred folk songs of the Krakoviak and Mazurka variety.[4]

As for himself, Dąbrowski said, he thought the time had come for a new song, one more attuned to the spirit that now existed among the troops under his command. He added that some two months ago he had received a fine march melody from Prince Michael Oginski, a fellow exile in Paris and well known to Wybicki. The general then suggested to his guest that as a man of literary talent he might provide some verses to the melody, thus giving the legionnaires a song of their own.

A few days later Wybicki attended a parade of Polish troops. He was much impressed by the reassuring sight of the marching volunteers and even more so by their buoyancy. And he listened in the evening with fascination to the singing of familiar but half-forgotten songs that brought back childhood memories.

With those songs still ringing in his ears, the serried ranks of the marching soldiers still before his eyes, Wybicki's rational mind was flooded by a rare exuberance. The vision of a Poland reclaimed and restored took form in the shape of six stanzas written in the third week of July 1797.

> Poland has not perished yet,
> Whilst we are still alive;
> What foreign powers have taken away
> We at sword point shall retrieve.
>
> March, March Dąbrowski,
> From Italy to Poland!
> Under your leadership
> We shall join up with the nation.[5]

The rousing first line was not so much a call of defiance as of hope. This line arose spontaneously, almost jubilantly, like a songbird after a thunderstorm. Shaped by the stimulating experiences of the last few days, the author could not possibly have anticipated the significance these words were to acquire. Except for the substitution of a single word—perished for dead—this opening line would literally reverberate through the centuries. It reassured successive generations of Poles that whatever misfortunes had befallen their country, its resurrection would be assured.

Such assurance could also be drawn from the second line of the poem. As long as Poles survived Poland would! National life depended on the life of its nationals. If they could no longer live in their country because it had ceased to exist, the country would continue to live through them. It was the nation rather than the state that would guarantee survival.

Nor were the next two lines any less unequivocal. The recovery of the lost homeland could only come by the sword. Here, among the only Polish fighting force in existence, the steel lay close to hand. The second stanza invoked examples of victorious leadership: the Polish hetman Stefan Czarniecki turning back Swedish invaders in the mid-seventeenth century. And the third stanza reverberated to a triumphant if unsubstantiated optimism including a bow to General Bonaparte.

We will cross the Vistula,
We will cross the Warta,
We shall be Poles,
Bonaparte set the example
How to win.

As if to reaffirm the hope of victory, the following stanza asserted that "German and Muscovite will not settle down when we take up the sword." And to add a homey touch to such grand predictions, the fifth stanza had a Polish father tell his daughter with tears in his eyes that he could hear the kettledrums of the approaching liberators. Projecting this folksy and local image onto the national scene, the last stanza has every Pole cry out "enough of bondage." To lend weight to this outcry, Wybicki reminded his fellow Poles of "the scythes of Raclavice," where peasants and townsmen under Tadeusz Kosciuszko's command had scored the one salient victory in the uprising of 1794.

It was, however, the refrain, with its electrifying call to action—echoing the refrain of the *Marseillaise*[6]—that ultimately provided the title of the Dąbrowski March. Wybicki had titled his creation *Song of the Polish Legions in Italy,* but such were the intensity and popularity of the refrain that within weeks it was known as the *Dąbrowski Mazurka.* Its first presentation took place at the Café Luterani on Reggio's main square. Polish officers who frequented the Café responded enthusiastically when hearing it on July 20, 1797, and the rousing refrain was taken up by the soldiers gathered around the square.[7]

But Wybicki's vision of the restored homeland was more sophisticated than that of much of his present audience. Many of the legionnaires were a generation younger, republican in their political leanings, and radical in their social demands. His concepts had been shaped by the Enlightenment, his views were rational rather than radical, and he remained at heart an eighteenth-century seigneur, even though there was now an overlay of dramatic experiences drawn from the French Revolution.

Born in September 1747 on a country estate of moderate size in Bedomin, some dozen miles southwest of Gdansk, he had received his education at a Jesuit school. Politics and public administration, however, soon appealed to him more than theology. He secured his first appointment with the help of two *wojewods*— the title of provincial governors—at the Poznan law court when all but seventeen years old. And one of his benefactors took him to the capital in September 1764.

Coming to Warsaw was an exciting experience, one enhanced by the pending coronation of a king. After nearly a century of foreign-born monarchs, a Pole had been elected by the Polish gentry, the *Szlachta.* Except perhaps for the wirepullers of this election, the Prussian king and the Russian empress, nobody anticipated that Stanislaw Augustus Poniatowski was to be Poland's last king.

In 1767 Wybicki returned to the capital; this time in his own right. He had been elected by the gentry of the Koscierzyna district to the *Sejm,* the national assembly, where he joined a group dubbed the Patriots. His patriotism flowed from two sources: the perceived need for institutional and social reforms along with resistance to foreign dominance, primarily Russian.

Count Nicholas Repnin, the Russian envoy in Warsaw, exerted his powers ruthlessly, as though there was no Polish sovereign or a sovereign Poland. When Repnin ordered the deportation of both spiritual and secular leaders, Wybicki was among the most outspoken protesters in the *Sejm*. Early in 1768, he poured his red-hot resentment against "Russian outrages" into a pamphlet, the first of many to emanate from his skillful pen. And such was the tenor of his daring that he wisely went into hiding rather than await certain imprisonment.

He emerged soon afterward in the southwestern part of the country where a confederation, the traditional Polish instrumentality of regional gentry association and assertion, had been formed at the township of Bar. In spite of his youth, Wybicki was chosen to act as the Confederation's spokesman. Before long, however, he became disenchanted with the Confederation because of its lack of national appeal and its inherent conservatism, and returned to Warsaw.

Always eager to travel, he briefly went to study at Leyden University in the Netherlands in 1770. It was there that he became imbued with the spirit of Dutch tolerance and was drawn closer to the credos of Protestant rationalism and masonic beliefs. He was equally impressed by the self-government of the Dutch provinces; it contrasted so sharply with the lack of unity, the fossilized infrastructure, and the chaotic socioeconomic conditions in his own country. Worse still, these conditions lured the rulers of the neighboring powers to annex long-coveted border areas. When the first partition occurred, only a few voices of protest were heard, none perhaps as telling as the fable of the three black eagles which had gathered to tear the Polish white eagle apart.[8]

Wybicki voiced strong disapproval when hearing about the joint action by Austria, Prussia, and Russia, recording in his diary at an unspecified date in the fall of 1772, "Vienna . . . and Moscow aim at our destruction."[9] He might have included Berlin as well, since Frederick the Great had been a prime mover in bringing about the first partition. Moreover, Wybicki's birthplace and property had just come under Prussian jurisdiction as the borders had shifted.

But if Poland suffered considerable loss both in status and lands, it unexpectedly gained on another level. A reform movement got under way in the rump country. There was hardly a sector of public life that did not require urgent reform. Wybicki was offered several opportunities to serve the cause of reform in judicial and educational commissions. Always ready to put his thoughts to paper, he also published several essays as well as a series of letters.[10] They soon established his credentials as a moderate reformer, a true son of the Enlightenment, and a dedicated patriot.

However eloquent and diligent in advocating reforms directed at the very structure of public life in the truncated country, such efforts and hopes soon came to naught. The opposition within the *Szlachta* and the Roman Catholic Church, to say nothing of the surrounding foreign powers, stymied the reform movement by 1780. Wybicki thereupon stepped aside and, befitting a nobleman with literary inclinations, went into semiretirement on one of his estates. It was there that his second wife—the first had died childless—bore three children, and there he turned his always active pen to both literary and musical composition.

In one of his pieces he included a mazurka which anticipated the melody of the later national anthem. In *Polka* he called on his countrymen "to mount horse, draw the sword [if] faith and freedom still have meaning."[11] Patriotic exhortations ran through much of his work and culminated in a poem titled "Still I am a Pole."

At the end of the 1780s, new opportunities and hopes offered for the aborted reform movement. A new *sejm*, not undeservedly called the *Great Sejm*, passed legislation that embodied many of the proposals that Wybicki had made earlier. Although not a member of the *Great Sejm* for much of its four-year duration, he did get elected as one of the new urban delegates after passage of the reform constitution of May 3, 1791. At least he could bask in its afterglow.

Alas, that was to fade soon. The reform constitution remained but a blueprint because the Russian Empress Catherine II willed it so. Worse still, she found collaborators among the reactionary Polish nobles. Organized as the Confederation of Targowica, they acted as her Fifth Column when Russian troops crossed into rump Poland. Prussia, not to be deprived of the spoils, soon did likewise and the country was amputated anew in January 1793.

But this time around such patriots as Kosciuszko and Wybicki organized armed resistance. Unexpectedly successful, the insurgents gained control of Warsaw and Vilnius. A provisional government was set up in which Wybicki, promoted to general, served as deputy chief in the military department in charge of supplies. He also drafted several appeals to the Polish people enjoining them to achieve reforms by legal means. Yet the rank and file of the population had more pressing and less lofty interests. Radicalization followed liberation. Agitation accelerated against real or assumed collaborators with the partitioning powers, and lynch justice was practiced. Wybicki, who had helped to save General Dąbrowski from that fate,[12] went briefly into hiding in July 1794 to escape mob violence. His aversion to lawlessness or any kind of radicalism caused him to resign from all official functions.

There was no opportunity this time around, however, to return to the tranquillity of one of his estates, now all under Prussian jurisdiction. Its authorities had marked him down as one of the principal instigators of the uprising. Moreover, he continued to support the remaining Polish forces. In September 1794, he assured soldiers at a camp in western Poland that the enemies of "the freedom and name of Poland" would be defeated, and he ended his peroration with an emphatic "You are free; you are Poles."[13]

Only after Kosciuszko's final defeat in October did military resistance end. Wybicki, like so many of his compatriots, could be free and Polish only in exile. Yet the umbilical cord with the motherland was never cut. Fearing imprisonment similar to that which Kosciuszko suffered at the hands of the Russians, Wybicki fled the country in disguise. Travelling a circuitous route through Prague, Vienna, and Basel, he arrived in Paris by March 1795. The French capital offered refuge to leading Polish emigrants, as it was to do for later generations of exiled Poles.

Half a year after Wybicki had reached Paris, the "three black eagles" had fastened and feasted once more on the remains of Poland. By the fall of 1795 it had disappeared altogether from the map; even its name was officially obliterated. The effete king, shattered symbol of national sovereignty, had obsequiously thrown himself at the mercy of his former paramour, only to find himself out of the Tsarina's grace, though not out of either pocket or comfort in imperial St. Petersburg.

Wybicki and his fellow exiles showed themselves to be better patriots. He kept showering the Directory in Paris with appeals and memoranda. The Directory, preoccupied with ensuring its own survival, was not unmindful of such entreaties and neither was its strongman, General Bonaparte. On him now centered the hopes not only of the Directory but also of the Polish exiles.

Wybicki, as their foremost publicist, indulged a rather fanciful comparison between Generals Washington and Bonaparte. "As our Kosciuszko has learned . . . from the immortal Washington how to defend the native country so we shall learn under Bonaparte's banner how to defeat our enemies."[14] This rhapsodic assumption was soon to flow into the third stanza of the *Dąbrowski Mazurka*. Its instant popularity was not least due to the popularity and prestige of Bonaparte as the seemingly predestined victor. As early as August 1797, Dąbrowski wrote from his headquarters at Bologna to his friend Wybicki: "Soldiers here and in other places like your song more and more and we sing it frequently with the respect due its author."[15]

The legionnaires sang the verses with as much conviction as gusto upon entering Rome in May 1798. But when the fortunes of war turned in mid–1799, the first of the many parodies could be heard. The refrain now no longer assured Dąbrowski that the legionnaires would march under his command to Poland; instead they would "die of hunger" here in Italy.

Parody or not, the *Song of the Polish Legions in Italy* remained theirs wherever they marched and fought. Decimated in various battles alongside their French allies during the disastrous campaigning in Italy through much of 1799, their numbers dwindled as did their hopes. Most of the remaining formations disappeared in the ill-fated Haitian expedition of 1802-1803. Their song, however, survived.

Its creator followed the fortunes—and misfortunes—of the legionnaires with concern. But his interest centered on political rather than military action. He attempted to bring together a provisional *sejm* in exile while at the same time mitigating the sharp differences among the Polish exiles, not least the most important generals. However, unsuccessful in his attempt to organize a *sejm* and disappointed at the unending personal rivalries, he once again withdrew from public life in 1800.

His request to return to the ancestral estate at Bedomin was denied by Prussian authorities. During the next half dozen years, he travelled restlessly from country to country, the worst scenario for an exile. Having no known means of supporting his family, with which he was reunited in 1802, he again took to writing, now mainly scientific and educational as befitted his eclectic tastes.

Unsettled as his situation was, that of Europe at large was hardly less so as long as Napoleon was the epicenter of cataclysmic changes. In October 1806, Wybicki received an unexpected summons from Dąbrowski, then in Berlin. French imperial headquarters had just been established there after the seemingly ever-victorious Napoleon had crushed the vaunted Prussian army. In the decade since 1797, when the Polish emissary had passed through the encampments of French troops under General Bonaparte's command in northern Italy, much had changed. The upstart young general, now emperor of the French and master of much of Europe, continued his amazing series of victories that changed the European map almost at will. He might also be the one who would put Poland back on that map, not least because he remembered the Polish legionnaires, some of whom now served him as an elite lancer formation.

Here at Berlin, talk among the Poles centered on new hopes for marching behind the emperor eastward and toward the restoration of Poland. Perhaps the thrilling refrain of the *Dąbrowski Mazurka* might, after all, soon become an even more thrilling reality! Wybicki himself was so carried away by the prospects of Poland's resurrection that he viewed the emperor as a redeemer rather than a schemer moving people and borders to fit his imperial designs. In an effusive proclamation of November 3, 1806, which had been drafted by Wybicki and was signed by him and Dąbrowski, all Poles were called upon to support "Napoleon the Great . . . who will enter Poland with an army. . . . Prove to him that you are willing to shed your blood for the recovery of your homeland."[16]

In December the author of the *Dąbrowski Mazurka* presented to the emperor recommendations on the borders of a resurrected Poland and soon referred to him as "our father and master."[17] If Wybicki could be charged on more than one occasion with opportunism, that trait stemmed at least in part from his passionate quest for opportunities that might help Poland. Now such an opportunity occurred. Napoleon did live up to the Wybicki-Dąbrowski proclamation by entering Poland with a strong army. In early November 1806, Poznan was liberated, and it was there that Polish insurrectionists enthusiastically struck up the *Dąbrowski Mazurka*. It never sounded more moving to the author and his friend than when they heard it for the first time on Polish soil.[18]

Wybicki exuded high hopes. "One single moment is sufficient . . . for Napoleon to restore Poland."[19] The flattered emperor reciprocated: "Without Wybicki I would have nothing to eat."[20] Indeed, the effective provisioning of French and Polish forces was Wybicki's major contribution to the ongoing liberation of Poland. In recognition of these services he was awarded the *légion d'honneur*. Better still, his sequestered properties were restored. Best of all, however, was the restitution—by Napoleon's grace—of a semblance of Polish sovereignty. The Grand-Duchy of Warsaw, established in 1807, was little more than one of several satellites created by imperial policies. But at least it put Poland back on the map, made Warsaw again the capital, provided a national army, and revived the *sejm*.

Yet within less than a decade the emperor, the reforms, and the Grand-Duchy itself had disappeared. Once more Poland, as much as the creator of its national song, faced a very uncertain future. And once more Wybicki changed his service connection, accepting the presidency of the superior court in Warsaw. That high position was offered to him by Tsar Alexander I, newly crowned head of the kingdom of Poland, an autonomous part of the Russian empire.

Becoming a tsarist officeholder seemed incompatible with the anti-Russian stance that Wybicki had taken for almost half a century. His readiness to serve one more foreign master and a Russian at that was not, however, as opportunistic as may appear. He did hold office in the Polish capital of a kingdom of Poland with its own constitution and a national legislature. The *Dąbrowski Mazurka* could be heard on official occasions and was sung freely among the people. There was no censorship until a couple of years before Wybicki's death in March 1822.

It was just as well that he died prior to the onset of heavy-handed Russian policies under a new and rigid tsar. The oppressive regime of Nicholas I would have left Wybicki a Hobson's choice: either renewed exile or debilitating compromises. As it was, his most famous composition no longer enjoyed official acceptance.

Yet *Jeszcze Polska* was to resonate anew within a decade. Like a tocsin it again called the Poles to arms and freedom. The uprising of November 1830 lacked in everything—planning, leadership, weapons, manpower—but patriotic spirit and lore. A new anthem was composed, but its first stanza retained the familiar lines. Grafitti on Warsaw buildings read "Poland is not lost as yet." Polish troops converging on the capital enthusiastically sang the original stanzas, though the refrain now called on all Poles to march, substituting Dąbrowski's name with an appeal to God who would grant victory.

Alas, ultimate victory belonged to the Russians. Not only did they crush Polish resistance within a year; the *Dąbrowski Mazurka* was expressly forbidden in a vain effort to extinguish all hope of a future rebirth of a free Poland. But a new wave of exiles kept both anthem and hope alive.

Nor were the verses forgotten nearer home. The Springtime of Nations in 1848 left much of Poland dormant except for its westernmost parts, governed by Prussia. For a fleeting moment the traditional animosity of Germans and Poles had been put aside. At Poznan town hall the assembled burghers and students who were forming a new Polish legion joined in singing the familiar Wybicki verses. And the same tune was heard in Berlin where Polish patriots, just released from Moabit prison, eagerly joined their Prussian fellow revolutionaries in March 1848.

At the end of that fateful year, with progressivism and republicanism on the wane, reaction and repression came to the fore. Western Poland was repossessed in full by Prussian authorities and denied any form of self-government, not least so by Prussian liberal nationalists. In turn, resistance flared, however briefly, in Galicia. Even though the Austrian administration was the least oppressive among the partitioning powers once it had reestablished control, the *Dąbrowski Mazurka* was banned in Austrian Poland as it was in the Prussian and Russian parts of the chopped-up country.

Once again the fiery song could be heard only where Polish exiles gathered or fought for foreign governments on foreign soil. In the early 1860s, however, Wybicki's driving stanzas echoed anew on home soil. The third aborted effort to regain independence fared no better than its predecessors. The 1863 uprising soon fizzled into guerilla activities and came to an end altogether within less than a year. This time around the *Dąbrowski Mazurka* was mostly heard from among the long lines of deportees wending their way on forced marches to Siberia.

The defiant song also had other use and users. Translated into several European languages, it gained wide popularity in the German states and Slavic countries. It became, like the *Marseillaise*, especially popular among radicals challenging the existing social order. More surprisingly, the verses were also heard on such far-away battlefields as Bull Run and Gettysburg.[21] But however far-flung and diverse its use, ultimately the Legionnaires Song needed, as all other anthems, a homeground to flourish. So long as there was not an inch of territory the Poles could claim as their own, the national anthem remained an exile, or a prisoner, or an underground phenomenon. And so long as the three partitioning powers held sway, all hopes for a restored Poland remained illusory.

World War I at last destabilized that oppressive situation. The Austro-Hungarian and German empires engaged their Russian counterpart in war. Soon the hard-pushed Austrians resorted to arming Poles as an auxiliary force. In December 1914, a new Polish legion was formed on Austrian soil by Jozef Pilsudski, renegade socialist turned nationalist. The first two battalions mustered to the strains of the familiar *Jeszcze Polska nie zginęła* but the reviewing Austrian general cut short as inappropriate the band's rendition of the Polish anthem. Notwithstanding such disturbed beginnings, Polish troops were quickly given frontline duty. The First Rifle Brigade fought along imperial Austrian forces against the Russians in the Carpathian mountains.

What more suitable song for this new generation of Polish legionnaires than that of their forefathers in Bonaparte's Italian campaign! To be sure, the refrain had to be fitted to a new leadership. Now it became "March, march, Pilsudski."

In November 1918, Poland at long last regained independence upon the collapse of the empires of the "three black eagles." Attempts in the early 1920s to replace Wybicki's piece with one more contemporary and selected in open competition failed when the telling point was made that the nation had decided long ago! In February 1927, the *Sejm* affirmed by legislative action that the

Dąbrowski Mazurka was the anthem of the republic. But, if Poland at last had an official national anthem, its national existence was by no means assured.

By 1939, the latest, if unofficial, version of the anthem defied the latest challenger of Polish sovereignty and territory.

> Hitler will hang head down;
> March, march against Hitler
> And may the cholera take him.[22]

That dare was to prove as illusory as an earlier one directed at the eastern bully power, anticipating wishfully that "the Russian will clean the boots of the Pole."[23] The pipedreams of sweet retribution turned into the nightmare of September 1939. Within three weeks Poland once more had been swallowed up by its powerful neighbors to the east and west. Once more Poland existed solely "in the hearts of the Poles," as Jean-Jacques Rousseau had observed more than a century and a half before.[24] And again its anthem had to take refuge in exile unless it was sung in open defiance.

On numerous occasions resistance fighters broke into "Poland has not perished yet," as they faced execution squads. The same spirit and song animated the Poles who had managed to escape to the free world. They assembled at camps in the highlands of Scotland, the sands of the Middle East, the swamplands of Polesia bordering the Ukraine, and the vintage verses of Wybicki had the same ring and meaning as in 1797. They again reverberated on battlefields, this time from Tobruk to Monte Cassino.

After the failed insurrection in the tragic Warsaw uprising from August to October 1944, national resurrection followed anew. Only now it assumed a different pattern of frontiers and government. A communist regime was superimposed, running counter to the traditional institutions and the very faith of the Polish people. Yet that regime was not so far out of touch—and tune—as to break the century-old bond between people and anthem.

On the contrary! The Communists promoted a veritable renaissance of its author. A surprisingly large number of monographs and biographies, always favorable to Wybicki, have been published since the 1960s. Memorial tablets and at least one impressive monument were unveiled. In 1972 a symposium was arranged at Gdansk to honor the eighteenth-century nobleman on the 150th anniversary of his death.

Obviously, the Communist regime wanted to preserve a semblance of national independence and patriotic pride. By the same token, it hoped to add some lustre to its dubious legitimacy. Article 103 of the revised constitution of the People's Republic of Poland in 1976 stipulated that the *Mazurka Dąbrowskiego* would be the national anthem.

As a treasured symbol it lived through successive communist governments and easily made the transition into the post-Communist era. After all, it had been in existence long before the word *communism* ever existed. Not surprisingly perhaps, Lech Wałęsa himself reportedly said that he would like to take the top position in Poland—as he finally did—so that "everywhere I went, they would play the National Anthem."[25]

If there has been one constant in the often tragic and always uncertain history of modern Poland it is Wybicki's poem. Its numerous variations attest to the vicissitudes of that history. But they also have tested the viability of the *Dąbrowski Mazurka* and not found it wanting, even if its literary value, like that of other anthems, has been questioned.

As an indicator, however, of Polish history and proclivities, Wybicki's creation has undisputed validity. That companionship has been succinctly summarized by Poland's greatest nineteenth-century writer. Adam Mickiewicz, following Wybicki's road to Paris and exile in 1831, stated soon thereafter: "All the history of Poland up to the rising of 1830 was contained in the few stanzas of the Legionnaires Song."[26] Without undue stress on either credence or pertinence, this summation could well be extended to the present day if allowance is made for the numerous variations of *Jeszcze Polska* since that time.

NOTES

1. The second and third partitions occurred in 1793 and 1795, respectively.

2. The Convention of January 9, 1797, which provided for the formation of the Polish legion in Italy, has been reprinted in Leonard Chodźko, *Histoire des légions polonaises en Italie*, 2 vols. (Paris: J. Barbezat, 1829), 1:203–4.

3. Stanisław Hadyna, *Droga do Hymnu* (The road to the hymn) (Instytut Wydawniczy, Warszawa, 1976), 65.

4. Karol Koźmiński, *Józef Wybicki* (Warsaw: Nasza Ksiegarnia, 1963), 97.

5. This and the translation of the following stanza have been kindly provided by Dr. Stanisław Skrzypek.

6. Among the numerous references to the impact of the *Marseillaise* on Wybicki's composition, see especially Koźmiński, p. 97 et seq., and Jan Pachoński, *Jeszcze Polska nie zginęła* (Poland has not perished yet) (Gdańsk: Gdańskie Towarzystwo Naukowe, 1972), 14–16, hereafter cited as Pachoński, *Jeszcze Polska*.

7. Ibid., 55.

8. This allegory was the creation of F. D. Kniaźnin, a late-eighteenth-century poet. The black eagles were the heraldic symbols of the three countries partitioning Poland; the white eagle symbolized Poland itself.

9. Extract from Wybicki's *Journal*, as reprinted in *Archiwum Wybickiego*, ed. A. M. Skałkowski, 3 vols. (Gdańsk: Nakl. Tow. Przyjaciół, N. S. 1948–71), 1:38.

10. The letters published under the title *Lettres patriotique au ex-chancellier Zamoyski*, and *Idées politiques sur la liberté civile*, published in 1775 and 1776 respectively, made Wybicki's reputation as an essayist of progressive leanings and spokesman of the Enlightenment.

11. Edmund Rabowicz and Tadeusz Swat, eds., *Józef Wybicki: Wiersze i Arietki* (Verses and songs) (Gdańsk: Wydawnictwo Morskie, 1973), 405.

12. Pachoński, *Jeszcze Polska*, 40. As a temporary member of a "people's court,"

Wybicki pleaded successfully for Dąbrowski's life, stating that "if you want to defeat the enemy you must respect the military leaders."

13. Ibid., 65.

14. Jadwiga Lechicka, *Józef Wybicki: Życie i Twórczość* (Jozef Wybicki: Life and works) (Toruń: Praca wydana z zasiłku Polskiej Akademii Nauk, 1962), 74.

15. Dioniza Wawrzykowska-Wierciochowa, *Mazurek Dąbrowskiego* (Warsaw: Wydawnictwo Ministerstwa Obrony Narodowej, 1974), 99.

16. *Archivum Wybickiego* II, 32–33.

17. Ibid.

18. In 1808, Dąbrowski recorded his recollections of entering Poznań together with Wybicki on November 6, 1806. "In all streets . . . one could hear the well-known . . . Dąbrowski March . . . composed by Wybicki . . . when he saw Polish troops in Reggio." Jan Pachoński, *Legiony Polskie, 1794–1807*, 3 vols. (Warszawa: Ministerstwo Obrony Narodowej, 1969–1971), 1:132, fn. 50.

19. *Archiwum Wybickiego*, II:85.

20. Ibid.

21. Some 5,000 Polish nationals fought in the ranks of the Union army and about 1,000 with that of the Confederacy. Reports that the *Dąbrowski Mazurka* was sung at Gettysburg caused a protest by the Russian ambassador in Washington. Wawrzykowska-Wierciochowa, 368.

22. Rabowicz, 463.

23. Ibid., 462.

24. Norman Davies, *God's Playground: A History of Poland*, 2 vols. (New York: Columbia University Press, 1984), 2:274.

25. Lech Wałęsa statement as quoted by Daniel Broder in the *Washington Post*, November 17, 1989.

26. Pachoński, *Jeszcze Polska*, 104.

6

Portugal

A *Portuguesa*
(Henrique Lopes de Mendonça)

Portugal, Britain's oldest ally on the European continent, owes its current an-them—in a manner of speaking—to that ally. Ironically, however, the Portu-guese anthem sprang from a rare moment of sharp tension in the almost six hundred-year-old alliance.[1] And, perhaps even more ironically, the cause for conflict lay in a remote region of Africa.

The two countries, which had cooperated for so long, not least in the Napo-leonic era, confronted one another in the 1880s as colonial powers. Portugal had been the first European state to establish a foothold on the "Dark Continent" in the early fifteenth century, thanks to Prince Henry the Navigator and his band of determined explorers. Yet it was Great Britain which had gained control over large parts of Africa in the course of the nineteenth century.

The race among European powers, large and small, for the remaining pieces of the territorial pie, however, was far from over. Collisions of interest were bound to occur. One such collision occurred in the late 1880s, when the British felt increasingly challenged by what looked to them like a deliberate effort of the Portuguese to expand their sphere of influence in southeastern Africa.

An intrepid Portuguese explorer and expansionist, one of several among other European nationals, had penetrated with a contingent of troops into Mashonaland on his way to the southern end of Lake Nyasa. If Major Serpa Pinto, who had already traversed southern Africa on an earlier expedition, dreamt of forging a link between Mozambique and Angola, the two principal Portuguese colonies in Africa, he and his Lisbon backers had a rude awakening. British empire builders also had dreams—and plans. Their minds focused on establishing an African north-south axis that one day might link Alexandria and Capetown, and they would not brook any attempt at creating a Portuguese east-west axis across southern Africa.

Using a chieftain of the Matabele tribe as their point man, British agents supplied Chief Lobengula with rifles and urged him to resist Portuguese infiltration. But Serpa Pinto was not easily deterred from advancing into the Shiré highlands[2] in his quest for a possible connector between Mozambique and Angola. Beset by alarming reports from British officials and agents and by the rising clamor of a jingoistic press, Her Majesty's Government warned the Lisbon government to desist from a further incursion into the disputed region and any infringement of the rights of natives under British protection.

Alas, the Portuguese government had already committed itself to the vision of a compact Portuguese Africa, several times the size of the homeland and a great deal richer in raw materials. In 1887, the Portuguese foreign minister had displayed "the pink map" in the lower house of parliament, where it met with strong approval. That map's rose coloration, no less alluring than its configuration, showed the two major Portuguese colonies as an entity.

But it was one thing to indulge a chimera and quite another to face realities. The Portuguese government, fully aware of the limited resources of the country and its fiscal weakness, showed a willingness to compromise on territorial claims. Not so the British. Their prodding in November 1889 yielded little, and the latest reports indicated a further advance by Major Pinto's small force.

Shortly after the new year, the British prime minister and avowed imperialist, Lord Salisbury, despatched an ultimatum to Lisbon requesting the withdrawal of Portuguese troops from the contested region. Initial reaction came in a grandiloquent statement by Portugal's foreign minister: "Portugal, who [sic] conquered India and created Brazil, has a past exceeded by no other nation. That past gives her . . . hopes of a brilliant future. Africa alone can guarantee it for her. When she defends her right on that continent, she defends her future."[3]

Such scintillating words were soon to prove as hollow as soap bubbles. The British government ordered a naval squadron to the Tagus and threatened an imminent break of diplomatic relations. The Portuguese government, under a new and inexperienced king, understood the critical situation well enough to draw in its tentacles. What they did not anticipate, however, was the eruption of public furor, first in Lisbon and thereafter in Oporto, second largest city in the kingdom.

As the American ambassador soon came to observe, "Portugal mourns and rages alternately."[4] Protesting crowds rampaged through the streets of the capital, tearing down the escutcheon of the British consulate, breaking the windows in the house of the Portuguese foreign minister, and setting fire to places of entertainment. More refined expressions of national defiance and pride came from outraged artists in musical and poetic creations.[5] None, however, enjoyed lasting renown except for a march by Alfredo Keil, a prominent composer, written late in 1889.

This composition was a curious mixture of fanfare-like measures and the more subdued notes of a specific Portuguese musical style. Without words, however, his *marcando* melody lacked maximum appeal. Fortunately, the versatile composer, who also painted, knew just the right author to provide the needed lyrics. Henrique Lopes de Mendonça had previously contributed the libretto for Keil's score of a comic opera, their first of several common productions.[6] Better still, he was even more patriotic than the composer, a first generation Portuguese of German ancestry. The author's patriotism stemmed in large part from his fascination with Portugal's maritime tradition and from his long service as an officer in that country's navy. In the service, he had developed a love for the sea, the pride in Portugal's overseas empire, and his skills as a romantic writer of adventure, biography, and history.

Lopes de Mendonça was quickly caught up in the strong current of anti-British sentiment which swept the country as a result of the ultimatum. But in his case that sentiment had deeper roots and more literacy than that of the numerous demonstrators. As a naval officer he had felt early a resentment of the global dominance of the British navy. Not by chance had his first poem, written well before the ultimatum crisis, carried the title *Delenda Albioni* (Albion must be destroyed). In later years he was to change his views on Great Britain, but in January 1890 he avidly set to work on Keil's request for some rousing verses to enhance the appeal of the tune.

That undertaking proved rather more difficult than the author had anticipated in his initial surge of enthusiasm. When Keil had first played the melody to him, he had struck the piano keys most emphatically to the rhythm of the *Marseillaise* as well as to the beat of the Portuguese *Fado*, the country's plaintive national music.[7]

Lopes de Mendonça recalled some twenty years later "the difficulties of fitting the verses into the already existing melody."[8] Nor was his task made any easier by Keil's insistence that the lyrics be completed quickly, while public agitation was still at its peak. He visited the composer's house almost daily, and within a week he heard Keil clap approval as they blended lyrics and score.

Not surprisingly, the most evocative lines were those recalling Portugal's maritime tradition and overseas exploration. The sea served as a point of reference from the first to the last but one line of the three stanzas. They were titled *A Portuguesa* (The Portuguese woman). In choosing that caption the author followed the lead of *La Marseillaise* and the vogue of romantic artists depicting liberty, victory, and the nation itself in female form.

Having fashioned a symbolic cynosure that would guarantee popular acclaim, he proceeded to invoke Portugal's past greatness and glory in the hope of reactivating national passion and pride. How better to do that than by a sweeping salutation to his countrymen, coupled with a reminder to show themselves as worthy patriots.

Heroes of the sea, noble people.
Brave and immortal nation.
Raise today once more
The splendor of Portugal!
From out of the mists of memory,
Oh motherland, thy voice is heard
Of your illustrious forbears
And shall guide you to victory.

To arms! To arms! Upon the land, upon the sea,
To arms! To arms! Do fight for the native land!
March, march against the hostile guns.

Unfurl the invincible flag
Against the luminous light of your skies!
Call out to Europe and the entire world:
Portugal did not perish!
Kiss your jocund soil,
The ocean roaring its love:
It's your conquering arm
That gave new worlds to the world!

[Refrain][9]

Apart from such a felicitous turn of phrase as the opening line of stanza one and the last line in stanza two, the verses followed a rather conventional pattern. There were the customary pleas to defend the homeland, to remember the deeds of the forefathers, to stand together, and to love the country. In fact, Lopes de Mendonça borrowed here and there from existing European anthems as well as from classical Portuguese poetry. To mention the *Marseillaise* is to point to the obvious, since *A Portuguesa*'s refrain bears a striking similarity to that of the French anthem. The somewhat gratuitous reminder that Portugal has not perished does recall the opening line of the Polish anthem ("Poland has not perished yet"). And the powerful locution of "the new worlds given to the world" by Portuguese daring was culled verbatim from Portugal's greatest epic, Luiz Vaz de Camões' *Lusiad*.

But if the verses were not altogether original, they had a sufficient national texture to reveal both current Portuguese sentiments and psychological undercurrents, particularly the intermittent hope for a revival of grandeur. A people reduced through the centuries from world rank to one of minor position would almost of necessity have recourse to millennial illusions, expressed in the form of *Sebastianismo*, the messianic expectation of the return of a young king lost on a crusade.[10]

Sebastianismo may have seeped, perhaps unconsciously, into some of the lines of *A Portuguesa*, but their author put it squarely to his compatriots that resurrection of the country now could only come by facing up to the British challenge. "Let the echo of an insult be the signal for our revival"—as the third stanza had put it—reflected for all to see the circumstances of the song's creation. And for that reason above any other, the new march quickly gained not only prominence but preference as the collective expression of national agitation.

In immediate reaction to the British ultimatum, demonstrating crowds had intoned the *Marseillaise*.[11] Three weeks later the Portuguese had acquired their own national voice in *A Portuguesa*. It was first heard in the Lisbon Coliseum on February 1, 1890, during a benefit concert for national defense. Such was the impact that the audience stood for a second rendering. For several weeks thereafter nightly performances at Lisbon's principal theater closed with *A Portuguesa*.

Yet the vibrant piece was far more than the finishing flourish to an evening's entertainment. The song rapidly became public property. "Children would sing it at the playgrounds, urchins whistle it in the streets."[12] Before long the new tune seemed likely to displace the existing anthem.

The *Hino da Carta* (Hymn of the Charter) dated to 1822 and had the unique distinction of having been created by a monarch. When Pedro I, erstwhile emperor of Brazil, assumed the throne of Portugal (in absentia) as Pedro IV upon the death of his father in 1826, his hymn (which initially had celebrated Brazil's newly proclaimed independence) found a second home in Portugal. There it survived as the official anthem of the kingdom until challenged by *A Portuguesa*, which was propelled forward not only by anti-British resentment, but also by a burgeoning antimonarchical attitude.

Three successive governments were toppled in 1890. Upon the urgings of King Carlos I, each had attempted to come to terms with the British but failed to win approval of the *Cortes*. These failures had endangered the monarchy itself as a republican movement gathered momentum. Just one year after the ultimatum to which a new government had finally acceded, a military rebellion —one of many to pockmark the country's history—broke out in Oporto.

On January 31, 1891, a few hundred troops staged an uprising that lasted but a few hours. Before it was crushed by royalist forces, however, a republic was proclaimed, its red-and-green flag raised, and *A Portuguesa* struck up. A band accompanying a mass of demonstrators, partly civilian and partly military, played the rousing march and its combative words soon resounded from a host of defiant voices, shortly being stilled.[13]

The quick defeat of the republican rebels had far-reaching effects, not least on their fight song. Understandably, the royal government banished it forthwith. After all, *A Portuguesa* had served as the collective expression of those who had taken up arms against the crown or had supported them. By banning it, the government transformed the unofficial anthem of monarchical Portugal into the quasi-official hymn of the republican opposition.

That opposition was to reassert itself in ever more formidable strength. The growing unpopularity of King Carlos stemmed as much from his yielding to British demands as from the prolonged economic and fiscal malaise of the country. Conditions were not improved by the manipulations of the two major parties, more concerned with playing a game of political musical chairs in the formation of alternate governments than with the future of Portugal. By contrast, that future was frequently conjured up in the ceaseless propaganda activities of republican militants.

In a desperate effort to govern effectively, the king endorsed a de facto dictatorship by his chosen premier. That move soon was to prove fatal to both the monarch and the Bragança dynasty. Early in 1908, republican extremists assassinated both King Carlos and the crown prince. The hapless younger son, Manuel II, did not fare much better. Within little more than two years the monarchy was flooded out of existence on a tidal wave of republicanism.

The state visit of the Brazilian president-elect in the first days of October 1910 may have rekindled memories of the ousting of the last Bragança on Brazil's throne two decades earlier. In any event, support for the Braganças in Portugal had worn quite thin, if the feeble rendition of the *Hino da Carta* during the Brazilian state visit is any measure.[14]

Lisbon was astir with not just rumors of revolution but with preparations for it. Several plots had been uncovered during the preceding months. Agitation and unrest in the capital and other urban centers soon exploded in labor strikes and student demonstrations. The assassination of a prominent republican leader by a deranged former army officer provided the spark that detonated the explosive force of revolutionary action.

During the night of October 3, fighting between republican and royalist forces erupted in Lisbon. Within days the republicans had gained the ascendancy not only in the capital but throughout the country. The rise to power by the republican mass movement was almost invariably accompanied by the singing of *A Portuguesa*, sometimes in conjunction with that of the *Marseillaise*.[15]

Even before young King Manuel II and other members of the Bragança family decided to leave the country to seek refuge in Great Britain, a republic had been proclaimed. And with its proclamation came the opportunity to proclaim—twenty years after its creation—*A Portuguesa* as the national anthem. Its composer could not enjoy that moment of gratification since he had died three years earlier, but its author fully savored the honor.

In November 1910, Lopes de Mendonça recalled with as much pride as pleasure the circumstances leading to the creation of the anthem. His remarks were occasioned by an order of the new minister of war requiring all military personnel to stand to attention and all officers to salute when *A Portuguesa* was played. The same order stated that "the people fondly regard this hymn as that of liberty and emancipation."[16]

A leading Lisbon newspaper, which published the minister's injunction, carried on its front page the same day Lopes de Mendonça's recollections of the anthem's origins. He remembered "the admirable spectacle of the reinvigoration of the old Portuguese race and their exuberance" and how he himself was swept up in the recitation of "inflammatory verses amidst delirious acclamations."[17]

A Portuguesa's stanzas, as their author took pains to explain, did not arise solely from the challenge of the British ultimatum. Admittedly, the country was in need of a song which could assuage "the wounded spirit of the nation."[18] In larger measure, however, the verses were a protest against "the laxity, weakness, and corruption of our monarchical politics."[19]

Quite possibly, such latter-day asseveration may have overstated the original motivations of the anthem's creators. There is no indication that Alfredo Keil composed his allegro march with any other purpose in mind than to give vent to patriotic ire. As for Lopes de Mendonça, he may have sympathized with the republican movement early on, as did some of the naval officers, but his account leaves the impression that either the wisdom of hindsight or the urge to give to the anthem a more timely aura may have colored his recollections. Yet even if the stanzas did not have specific antimonarchical origins, they soon acquired their republican association with the revolt of January 1891.

If on that occasion *A Portuguesa* had become a republican tune, it stood to reason that it would now become the tune of the republic. On June 5, 1911, the protest march of 1890 was incorporated into the constitution of the republic and promulgated as the national anthem. As such, it was widely intoned in the immediate aftermath of the revolution and perhaps overused.[20] But that use waned in later periods of the first republic. Its unsteady course was punctuated by coup after coup. Pulled alternately left and right, the buffeted young republic presented few opportunities for manifestations of national solidarity.

One of these came in March 1916, when Germany declared war on Portugal. Crowds surged through Lisbon's streets as did the powerful words and throbbing melody of *A Portuguesa*. It was heard in other massive demonstrations in support of the war effort[21] which, however, left the nation deeply divided over the despatch of an expeditionary corps to the western front.

A decade later the anthem served as a salutation to the nearly completed metamorphosis of the republic from a highly volatile state to one of rigid solidification. The pronunciamento of May 28, 1926 sounded the death knell to the ineffective parliamentary system of the republic. Its government was now taken over by the military. Formal installation of the new regime climaxed in a great parade to the tune of *A Portuguesa*, struck up on Lisbon's main square.

In the same year, the septuagenarian author commented rather whimsically, "I was awarded the commandery of Sant 'Iago by King Carlos who during the ceremony closed his ears to the sounds of *A Portuguesa* whose lyrics, written by me, were shaking the throne."[22] When Lopes de Mendonça died in 1931, one of his close friends eulogized him as "one of the greats in our literature."[23] Notwithstanding the author's biographical work on Portugal's great explorers, from Bartolomeu Dias to Fernão de Magalhães, and the large variety of plays, novels, poetry, and essays, that accolade has not been bestowed by experts on Portuguese literature, who rarely include references to these works. The eulogist was closer to the mark when he spoke of Lopes de Mendonça's "civic pride and impassioned patriotism . . . which is reflected for us in the eternal verses of our national anthem.''[24]

These verses have certainly lasted to the end of this century, in spite of the cataclysmic changes affecting Portugal both at home and overseas. In 1930, the military regime gave way to a civilian government. That transformation, however, did not mean an easing of heavy-handed controls. On the contrary! The *Estado Novo*, now coming into its own, resembled that of fascist Italy and soon francoist Spain.

The autocratic and corporate "new state," fashioned by Dr. Antonio Salazar, saw changes in almost every facet of public life. But he did not interfere, as some other European dictators did, with the national anthem. There was indeed a plenitude of opportunities for its use. After all, *A Portuguesa* conjured up the glories of a once-powerful Portugal, global in magnitude, and the resurgence of a proud nation. Not surprisingly, therefore, the anthem was frequently intoned at parades, pro-government demonstrations, and public ceremonies. *A Portuguesa* was a fixed item in the elementary school curriculum. The anthem opened and closed the daily broadcasting program of the *Emisora Nacional*, and it was anchored in its official function by government decree of September 5, 1957.[25]

Although the song was routinely used by the Salazar regime, the growing opposition had not forgotten *A Portuguesa*'s republican and revolutionary past. Much like the *Marseillaise*, the Portuguese anthem served dual needs: official representation and spontaneous manifestation, often in protest.[26] On VE-Day (May 8, 1945), jubilant antifascist groups, mainly drawn from university students, gathered on Lisbon's main square to acclaim the victory of the Allies. They struck up the anthem while unfurling a big national flag.[27]

Patriotic demonstrations of this kind, however, could hardly be expected to bring down the Salazar state. The ultimate danger to its survival lay, ironically, in the very overseas possessions that had proven to be the small country's greatest assets and motivated the most striking lines in its national anthem. It had found ready acceptance in *ultramar* Portugal, not only with the Portuguese settlers but also among the natives, all of whom had been legally Portuguese citizens since the early nineteenth century. Thus everybody, regardless of color, joined in singing *A Portuguesa* when a new governor arrived, a troop detachment was reassigned, a new public structure dedicated, or a national holiday celebrated.

But this apparent amity did not last. Three decades after the death of Lopes de Mendonça, the Portuguese Kipling, the empire's breakup began. The tidal wave of a new African nationalism, which already had engulfed most of the continent, swept Angola and soon thereafter Mozambique and Guinea-Bissau. The ensuing anticolonial wars, which lasted for thirteen years, put an ever-heavier burden on the metropole while yielding ever-diminishing returns. To fight in three separate areas required large-scale mobilization. The new conscripts were inducted to the strains of *A Portuguesa*, which likewise was played regularly at military ceremonies on African bases. But the anthem was also struck up at outlying posts as an antidote to isolation and a reaffirmation of national commitment.

As guerilla warfare dragged on, however, the combative spirit lessened, as did the anthem's use. The number of draft evaders ultimately equalled almost two-thirds of the men under arms. Many escaped to France and Spain rather than serve. They would indeed have little reason for singing *A Portuguesa*. There was not much more evidence of its use by the troops in Africa. Some draftees could not remember singing it while serving in the early 1970s. Many of their officers had realized by then that the guerilla wars could not be won and—worse still—that they had lost all faith in the Lisbon government.

The most active officers planned on putting a quick end to both the wars and to the regime. Their newly formed Armed Forces Movement (MFA) staged a *golpe* in the early morning hours of April 25, 1974. Two popular songs rather than the anthem provided the broadcasting signal for the coup. But jubilant crowds, hailing their new freedom, soon struck up *A Portuguesa*.[28] It could be heard repeatedly during the next twelve months, which saw conflicting moderate and radical groups struggling to gain ultimate control of the country.

With the triumph of a pluralist democracy and stable institutions, the anthem was anchored once more in a constitution. Article 11 of the constitution of April 2, 1976, proclaimed that "the National Anthem shall be *A Portuguesa*." Its survival through strikingly different republics is even more astounding because of the complete disappearance of overseas Portugal, except for Macao. Yet it was *that* Portugal which had inspired the verses of Lopes de Mendonça.

How then can the persistence of the anthem be explained? There is, after all, at least one major rival in *Maria da Fonte*, a popular and patriotic song which antedates *A Portuguesa* and is openly concerned with the struggle for domestic liberty.[29] Yet while the older song is sometimes played in lieu of the anthem, the latter was never displaced by it.

As in the case of some other anthems, tradition and symbolism helped the anthem to survive. But in the final analysis it must be remembered that the melody has an endearing and enduring Portuguese character.[30] The stanzas, in turn, are equally acceptable to conservatives and progressives. To the former because of the invocation of past grandeur; to the latter because of the anthem's republican function. And thus, *A Portuguesa* can be sung by all with equal fervor on such different national days as the 10th of June, which celebrates both the Portuguese Community and Camões Day, honoring the national bard of Portuguese exploration and expansion; the 5th of October, which commemorates the republican revolution of 1910; and the 1st of December, which has long marked Portugal's breakaway from Spain and renewed independence in 1640.

NOTES

1. The first British-Portuguese treaty dates to 1373.
2. The area at the southern end of Lake Nyasa is now in Malawi.

3. George Bailey Loring, *A Year in Portugal, 1889–1890* (New York: G. P. Putnam's Sons, 1891), 292.

4. Ibid., 197.

5. Among those creations were a symphony, *A Patria*, and even a "March of Hate."

6. Their most famous joint work was the first Portuguese national opera, *Serrana*.

7. In addition to the *Marseillaise* and the *Fado*, a recent monograph on the origins of *A Portuguesa* lists a third seminal influence: *Maria da Fonte*, a traditional Portuguese song of freedom. See Teixeira Leite, *Como nasceu "A Portuguesa"* (How *A Portuguesa* originated) (Lisboa: Terre Livre, 1978), 28.

8. Henrique Lopes de Mendonça, "Como nasceu 'Portuguesa'," in *Diario de Noticias*, November 18, 1910.

9. This translation has been kindly provided by one of my students, Ms. Ruth Ferszt.

10. Sebastian I, together with the flower of Portuguese nobility, died in battle with the Moors in 1578. Two years later, Spain assumed suzerainty in a single Iberian state.

11. Brazilio Telles, *Do ultimatum ao 31 de Janeiro* (From the ultimatum to the 31st of January) (Porto: Livraria Chardron, 1905), 130 and 381–82.

12. Joao Pinheiro Chagas, *Historia da revolta de Porto de 31 de Janeiro 1891* (History of Porto revolt of January 31, 1891) (Lisboa: Empreza Democratica de Portugal, 1891), 13–14. So popular were the verses that they appeared on porcelain and even decorated ashtrays.

13. Telles, 381–82.

14. Russell E. Benton, *The Downfall of a King: Dom Manuel II of Portugal* (Washington: University Press of America, 1977), 95.

15. Douglas L. Wheeler, *Republican Portugal* (Madison: University of Wisconsin Press, 1977), 55 and 57.

16. *Diario de Noticias*, November 18, 1910.

17. Ibid.

18. Ibid.

19. Ibid.

20. Humberto da Silva Delgado, *The Memoirs of General Delgado* (London: Cassell, 1964), 17.

21. A leading republican politician recalled attending a major demonstration in support of the war effort in May 1917. "A band played the national anthem, enhanced by enthusiastic vivas for the country." Sebastiao Magalhaes Lima, *Episodios da minha vida* (Episodes from my life), 2d ed., 2 vols. (Lisboa: Livraria Universal, 1928), 169–71.

22. Henrique Lopes de Mendonça, "Auto biografia," in the introductory section to a reissue of his *Estudos sobre navios portugueses nos seculos XV e XVI* (Studies of Portuguese navy vessels in the 15th and 16th centuries) (Lisboa: Ministerio da Marinha, [1971]), n.p. That decoration was awarded to him for the play *Afonso de Albuquerque*, one of Portugal's empire builders.

23. Ibid., xii.

24. Ibid.

25. This enactment was sponsored by Dr. Salazar's deputy and ultimate successor, Dr. Marcelo Caetano.

26. That point has been made repeatedly by Professor Jorge Borges de Macedo, Director of the National Archives of Portugal, in communications to this author.

27. The incident has been referred to by Portugal's current president, Mario Soares,

in his book *Portugal's Struggle for Liberty*, trans. Mary Gawsworth (London: George Allen and Unwin, Ltd., 1957), 36.

28. *Diario de Noticias*. April 27, 1974, reporting the singing or playing of the *Hino nacional* in such cities as Santarem and Setubal.

29. That song, referred to previously, takes its title from a rural uprising, initiated by women and reportedly led by one Maria da Fonte, in 1846.

30. See, for instance, the comment that Keil's composition reflects such traits of the Portuguese people as sentimentality and melancholy in the article by Frederico de Freitas, "Hino Nacional," in *Enciclopedia Luso-Brasileira*, 18 vols. (Lisboa: editorial Verbo, n.d.), 10:191–93.

7

Ireland

Amhran na/bh Fiann
(Peadar Kearney)

The perennially troubled and troublesome Anglo-Irish relationship showed signs of amelioration in 1907. The Liberal government formed in London the previous year was expected to prove slightly more amenable to Irish demands for autonomy than its Conservative predecessor. In the words of the new prime minister, a "modest, shy, humble effort"[1] was made to give to the Irish a measure of local self-government. There might even be brought, in the foreseeable future, yet another Home Rule bill in Parliament at Westminster, where two previous bills had failed.

Such tranquilizing prospects calmed agitation among the Irish political elite for stronger pressures upon British authorities in both Dublin and London. Most of that elite belonged to the Irish Nationalist Party, a party that had lost some of its sharpness in "treading on England's toes," as its first leader, Charles Stewart Parnell, had once put it. Instead, the party aimed at deals with the two major parties in Britain. But century-old tensions between two conflicting cultures—one Celtic and the other Anglo-Saxon—locked into a contest of national wills could at best be eased only temporarily.

The existence of a substantial Protestant and Anglo-Saxon population in the northern and smaller part of the island, in contrast to the largely Catholic and Celtic south, triangulated an otherwise bipolar confrontation and made a solution so much more complicated. Regardless of the absence of large-scale violence during all-too-brief periods, or a lull in controversial legislation, or a consensus on reforms—contemplated or carried through—tensions persisted.

If most of the Irish early in this century abstained from radical action, and the Nationalist Party leaders endorsed cooperation at Westminster, it did not follow that British dominance in Irish affairs went unchallenged. That challenge was mounted by various organizations with a variety of objectives and procedures, but all of which had an anti-English bias and a commitment to Irish independence, though not necessarily to be obtained by force. Whatever form these organizations took, whatever means they chose were part of a self-perpetuating tradition of animosity toward a British presence, be it cultural, economic, social, or political.

After all, the continued British presence, if not dominance, served as a constant challenge to Gaelic Irish sensitivities; nor had the latter abated during the more than seven hundred years since the English had first penetrated the emerald island. Each successive generation of the native population added its often all-too-bitter experiences to the expanding national trauma and devised ever more ingenious or violent means of striking back.

These means ranged from local raids to national insurrections, from acts of heroism to those of terrorism, from mayhem to murder, and from public demonstrations or passive resistance to secret organizations. The Irish Republican Brotherhood, the IRB, carried the credo of an independent Ireland through three generations into the twentieth century, and that credo carried with it the myth and wrath of the older Fenian movement,[2] which had exhausted itself in the abortive uprising of 1867. If there was to be another—and few of the IRB members had given up on that goal—their clandestine brotherhood would constitute its main force.

The Gaelic League had an entirely different structure and program, save the "de-Anglicization of Ireland." Nonpolitical and nonsecret from its creation in 1893, it aimed at reviving the almost lost Gael language. Its founders, like the cultural nationalists in Greece, Hungary, and Norway,[3] believed that a linguistic revival was the prerequisite for any meaningful awareness and assertion of nationhood. And unlike the predominantly Catholic IRB with its republican tendencies, the Gaelic League strove to encompass all of the Irish in a Celtic union, with scant regard for religious affiliation or future political structure.

Another association set out to bring together young Irishmen for the purpose of activating both their minds and bodies in behalf of a new Ireland. The Gaelic Athletic Association was to shape citizens fit to form the backbone of this new polity. And before long the ancient game of hurling had its rebirth along with Gaelic football, route marches, and other manly exercises—provided they were native in origin.[4]

The most active promoter of nativism in the political field was the *Sinn Féin* movement, which had gotten underway in 1905. As its name *"Ourselves Alone"* suggested, the Irish would solely rely on themselves to struggle free from their bonds with Britain. Noncooperation with that country thus provided the key to independence.

Quite a few nationalist militants were associated with several of these organizations. But membership was not the sole criterion for testing the strength of commitment to the noble cause of an independent and united Ireland. What counted most was the intensity of dedication to it.

Peadar Kearney possessed that in full measure—so much so that he preferred to spell his surname O'Cearneigh. But even without that Gaelicization, nobody could doubt his Irishness. He marched in the ranks of the young men of the Gaelic Athletic Association who, in shouldering their hurley sticks, conjured up visions of Irish soldiers marching proudly into battle. But in Kearney's opinion the music hall tunes that they sang or whistled were inappropriate for such a destiny.[5] He wanted them to sing something more purposeful and inciting, something that would focus their minds on the ultimate task: Erin's liberation.

Resolved to create such a song, he set to work in 1907 and completed it within a week. Suitably, he titled his poem *The Soldier's Song*. Just to make sure that this martial aspect would remain the dominant theme, Kearney repeated the words in the opening line and for good measure in the refrain. The first stanza set the scene: a campfire around which eager fighters gathered, awaiting the morning light "impatient for the coming fight."

But it was the second stanza, nowadays most often sung as part of Ireland's anthem, that breathed fiery defiance.

> Soldiers are we, whose lives are pledged to Ireland.
> Some have come from a land beyond the wave.
> Sworn to be free; no more our ancient sireland
> Shall shelter the despot or the slave;
> Tonight we man the bearna baoghail
> In Erin's cause, come woe or weal;
> 'Mid cannon's roar and rifle's peal
> We'll chant a soldier's song.[6]

Curiously, the *bearna baoghail*—the "danger gap"—were the only two Gaelic words that Kearney used in his original version, perhaps because they conveyed a special meaning in Gaelic and added a specific flavor. The third stanza, in common with other anthems, proudly recalled the forefathers' deeds. Rather grandly, it asserted: "We're children of a fighting race that never yet has known disgrace." As if to affirm that assertion, the final stanza burst into a rhapsodic appeal.

> Sons of the Gael! Men of the Pale!
> The long watched day is breaking;
> The serried ranks of Innisfail
> Shall set the tyrant quaking.
> Our camp fires are burning low
> See in the east a silvr'y glow
> Out yonder waits the Saxon foe,
> So chant a soldier's song.[7]

But it was one thing to visualize the day of glory and triumph and quite another to realize it. Nor did the rousing verses by an unknown rhymer necessarily translate into an immediate, collective patriotic response. To convert a poem distinguished as much by passion as by its uneven meter into a fetching song proved a formidable difficulty. It was certainly not made any easier by the fact that the likely composer could not read music! Patrick Heeney was an amateur musician to an even greater degree than Peadar Kearney was an amateur poet. Fortunately, they were linked in a close personal relationship and had worked in tandem for some years. Moreover, they shared not only their passion for Irish independence but also an underprivileged background.

Yet, upon completion as a song, it was not vouchsafed the immediate enthusiastic reception which had greeted the other resistance anthems. Even members of the hurley clubs failed to respond with spontaneous acclaim, if only because *The Soldier's Song* was not that easy to sing.[8] The absence of sheet music and of a printed version of the text did not facilitate public awareness. Kearney's one attempt to have his poem published in the widely read *United Irishman* came to naught.

For five long years the poem remained largely unknown as did, no doubt, both the author and the composer.[9] Heeney died at the age of thirty in June 1911, leaving no professional record and hardly a reputation. But in the following year Kearney had the satisfaction to see his poem printed at last. In September 1912, *Irish Freedom* carried the four stanzas to public attention.

Publication, however, benefitted the poem rather than the poet because it appeared anonymously. That anonymity lent to *The Soldier's Song* a folk-song character which increased its popularity. Since Kearney wrote his most effective verses in the homey terms of a political balladeer, alternately plucking humorous and patriotic strings, author's pride meant less to him than the message.

There were additional reasons for the lack of initial name recognition, probably none more fundamental than Kearney's blending with the masses. In appearance, habits, outlook, and upbringing he was a typical working-class Irishman. He drew his personal, political, and not least his poetical strength from that background. His rather haggard face had a wistful expression with a touch of an impish smile. Dressed in his Sunday's best, he looked for all the world more like a laborer than a poet.

And laborer he had been since adolescence.[10] Descending, as so many Irishmen did, from farmstock, his paternal grandfather had moved the numerous family to Dublin. His son John, Peadar's father, trying hard in the grocery business, left upon his death as little as he had started with. But he bequeathed to Peadar, the oldest of half a dozen children, something far more lasting: scorn for everything English.[11]

The same year his father died, Peadar, at fourteen, got his first job, alas one of many. His real interest lay elsewhere: in the world of books and the theater. Never caring to amass property, to acquire status or reputation, he drifted in and out of jobs until he hired out as an apprentice painter. Coincidentally, he had his first poem published at that time.[12]

Between jobs he went on writing patriotic poetry and a play based on the life of Wolfe Tone, unforgotten martyr of the 1798 uprising. All of his literary outpourings had Irish themes: legends, countryside, history. Kearney's poetry was homespun, and some of it became widely known, if only for the entertaining primitivism and droll humor.[13] His artistic qualifications were as semiprofessional as his tradesman's status, and with equal readiness one could think of Peadar Kearney as a house painter who wrote poetry on the side or as part-time author whose livelihood depended on house painting.

But there was one field of action to which he was and remained wholeheartedly committed: the righting of great wrongs inflicted intentionally or unintentionally by British rule. His Gaelic awareness flared up like sudden lightning. In 1901, he joined the Gaelic League and two years later the Irish Republican Brotherhood. Henceforth he would be a soldier serving the cause of a free and united Ireland. But the military part of that role had to await its time. First and foremost were the moral, spiritual, and physical preparedness. The spoken and written word alike were the primary instrumentalities in the regeneration of an Irish national will.

Early in the twentieth century, Kearney, like so many other Irishmen of his generation, came under the spell of a resurgent Irish literature. Probably no one piece had greater impact than William Butler Yeats's one-act play *Cathleen ni Houlihan,* which climaxed in an apotheosis of a restored and rejuvenated Ireland. Several other plays, if not as poetic then at least as patriotic, subsequently appeared as dramatic incarnations of Irish history, in itself incarnate drama for most of the time. And Kearney occasionally acted in supporting roles, greatly enjoying himself. On the stage he could audibly and visibly identify with the great moments in the history of his country. Moreover, the stage served as a convenient and little-challenged outlet to denounce British rule.

Since acting was at most an avocation for him, he merely added this occasional activity to his other part-time occupations. In 1908, while employed as a house painter in County Wicklow, he taught Gaelic to the local people.[14] Three years later he was drawn back to the stage now centered on the soon famous Abbey Theatre, established half a decade earlier. His employment there, however, was as a property man. As such, he went with the company on tour to England.

Not surprisingly, Kearney viewed the English as "an alien people with whom contact best be avoided."[15] He felt comfortable only among his own countrymen. Nightly, after showtime, they gathered for their Guinness stout at an Irish pub. There they happily sang familiar tunes, some sentimental and others militant, and it was there that Kearney first heard, to his deepest regret, of Heeney's untimely death and raised at once a collection for the widowed mother of his friend and collaborator.

After the troupe's return to Dublin in mid-summer 1911, tension throughout the island began to build anew. A third Home Rule bill, far from heralding an era of good feelings, threatened to divide the country irrevocably.[16] In the northern nine counties, Protestants, though barely more numerous than Catholics, formed themselves into the Ulster Volunteer Force (UVF). Their ostensible aim was to fight off any possible aggression from their southern neighbors; in reality they wanted to impress His Majesty's Government in London with their resolve to resist the pending Home Rule enactment in Ulster, if necessary by force.

Not long after the founding of the UVF in January 1913, in something resembling a knee-jerk reflex, the southern Nationalists determined to assert their interests through a counterorganization, suitably named Irish National Volunteers (INV). Among the earliest and most enthusiastic members was Peadar Kearney, and before long he and his fellow Volunteers just as enthusiastically drilled with the few rifles in their possession while dressed in sport suits of semimilitary cut.

Better still, the Volunteers adopted his *Soldier's Song* as their marching tune, giving it for the first time wide prominence. More urgently needed, however, were rifles, probably the most sought-after goods in Ireland, north and south, as the Home Rule bill neared promulgation. In the race for arms, Ulster, with its Unionist leadership and their close ties to British authorities, was far better positioned than the southern separatists. Gun running for the UVF was more of a lucrative game than a dangerous undertaking.

By contrast, the Irish National Volunteers had to scrape for funds as well as for rifles. In the land where the harp is the national symbol, one sure means of raising money was to stage benefit concerts. What could arouse an audience more than a rendering of *The Soldier's Song*? According to one eyewitness it was heard "at all concerts."[17] The money, however, came in faster than the rifles.

But on July 26, 1914, the INV had its hour of elation. Ostensibly on a route march, some eight hundred Volunteers—Kearney among them—suddenly converged on the small port of Howth, just north of Dublin. There a yacht had docked with nine hundred rifles to be unloaded forthwith. As Kearney recorded, he "could not attempt to describe the scenes of wild enthusiasm."[18] While the unloading proceeded smoothly enough, a subsequent fracas between agitated civilians and a company of Scottish troops ended with substantial casualties for the demonstrators. Even that bright day in the Volunteer annals had a dark ending.

Confrontation on a far larger scale, however, soon overshadowed local or regional tensions. On the very day when another arms shipment was successfully landed, World War I began. The "Irish Question" quickly became a sideshow for the imperial government in London. Home Rule was passed quickly by Parliament only to be put on hold for the duration of the war. The last thing that the London government wanted to see was renewed confrontation over Ireland's future now that deep divisions had been papered over as Nationalists and Unionists committed themselves to support the British war effort.

The great majority of Irish National Volunteers followed the call of such prominent politicians as John Redmond to rally alongside Britain—not so much to help as to win first gratitude and then concessions. A minority, however, decided to have no part in the war and to take the fullest advantage of Wolfe Tone's 1798 dictum that "Britain's difficulty is Ireland's opportunity."

That diehard minority soon banded together as the Irish Volunteers, and Peadar Kearney readily made the transition from the mother organization to its errant offspring. It was not he who had broken faith but those who compromised themselves by compromising with Britain. He marched proudly in demonstrations and parades, rifle shouldered, in behalf of a republican and united Ireland. But he had to shoulder other responsibilities as well. In February 1914, he had married a dark-eyed, shy, and serious girl. Eva Flanagan not only inspired him to write some turgid love poems but also to look for work. He returned to the Abbey Theatre as property man and, early in 1916, again toured England with the company.

While preparing for performances in Liverpool, Kearney requested immediate leave and departed over the objection of the manager, who threatened never to employ him again. But for Kearney there were more important activities to be considered than making money or keeping a job. Word had reached him of a momentous undertaking by his organization, the Irish Volunteers.

Its leaders, grouped in a Military Council, had long planned a direct challenge to British authority. They hoped to enlist German support for an outright attack and had been given some indication of such a support.[19] Liberation Day was set for the Easter weekend of 1916. Kearney was one of many who had received advanced notice to prepare for action; nor were the Irish Volunteers and the Irish Republican Brotherhood the only ones to have received warnings. Those in the know of a possible uprising included the German, U.S., and British governments.[20]

The last ones to become aware of a possible rising were the authorities in Dublin Castle, center of British administration in Ireland, although there were almost as many informers as rumors that indicated forthcoming action. But whatever information was about, it soon became outdated and contradictory. Developments during Holy Week ran counter to the plans of the Military Council and—before long—to the hoped-for success. German support never materialized to the degree anticipated. The one ship that carried a large load of rifles, ammunition, and some machine guns was intercepted and scuttled itself.[21]

The few Irish prisoners of war in German camps who had been talked into offering their services to the insurrection never arrived. The most important go-between for the Irish revolutionaries and German authorities was almost accidentally seized on Good Friday by the Royal Irish Constabulary.[22] Worst of all, mobilization orders for the Volunteers were cancelled on Easter Sunday, only to be countermanded in some of the Dublin districts, while they did not reach some of the backcountry districts at all.

The disappointment of many of those who were unexpectedly told to either go or stay home was as intense as the elation of those who mustered on April 24, Easter Monday, in small numbers and much confusion. Peadar Kearney, not quite sure whether his mobilization order was valid, decided, upon Eva's urgings, to don his semimilitary outfit, grabbed his rifle together with 200 rounds and a haversack of supplies, and eagerly rushed to the assembly point. There he found but a couple of men from his company. Undaunted, they joined the next small group of insurgents. Told at high noon of the proclamation of an Irish Republic, "a cheer of pent-up relief greeted the news and instinctively we went down on one knee to say a short prayer."[23]

Later that day his makeshift unit took up positions at Jacob's biscuit factory, and there the eager men stayed for a whole week in expectation of a heroic struggle with British troops in hand-to-hand fighting. It never materialized. Instead, a pall of first isolation and then dejection began to hang heavy, much like the ever-increasing fires and smoke over the inner city, whose strategic buildings were bombarded by British artillery. Kearney welcomed the opportunity to carry food supplies at night to the besieged insurrectionists at the College of Surgeons, though it meant crossing streets under fire from encircling British forces.

Safely back at base, he could have cheered his comrades with a verse or two of his *Soldier's Song*, now more appropriate than ever. But Kearney's account of that hectic week merely mentioned that the men "cheered one another with quip and jest and, very often, a snatch of a song."[24] Maybe modesty kept him from striking up his own stanzas. Certainly, *The Soldier's Song* was heard elsewhere among the would-be liberators who only too soon were the beleaguered. One Volunteer, a female, recalled that her detachment in the College of Surgeons had broken spontaneously into the chorus of Kearney's song.

When news came to the insurgents holed up in Jacob's factory that their central command had ordered surrender, many broke into tears or voiced despair. Most of them surrendered and their leaders were summarily executed. Rather than face the execution squads or, at the very least, long-term imprisonment, Kearney and a few other Volunteers disappeared quickly and quietly. They left behind not only their illusions but worse still their weapons, not used once in earnest. Instead of soldiering for an Irish republic they now were hunted men, "on the run" from British soldiers. Kearney for one moved furtively and sometimes desperately from shelter to shelter, changing into ill-fitting and nonsuspect clothing when opportunity and helpful hands offered that choice.

If arms had failed, words did not. If rifles had to be put aside for the time being, the pen remained handy. The execution of sixteen leaders who individually had acted as heroes and collectively like fools, and the imprisonment of hundreds of other patriots churned up a flood of poetry and songs in a country never short of either. The quality ranged from the exquisite phrasing of William Butler Yeats who, in *Easter 1916*, coined the striking phrase of "terrible beauty" to the treacly verses of an unidentified nun.[25]

Kearney lost no time in making his own literary contributions to the lore which embroidered the Easter Rising. True to his most natural poetic expression he composed several ballads. *A Row In A Town* was his salute to the dead heroes of the rising, and each of the stanzas ended in the familiar St. Patrick's Day greeting "Erin Go Bragh." *The Devil's Crew* commemorated for their tenacity, not without a touch of humor, those "very low down" in the ranks like himself, who would fire the last shots in the ruins of Dublin.

How much of this homespun poetry with its easy rhymes and folksy narrative reached the public, even in Kearney's later years, remains uncertain.[26] But *The Soldier's Song* gained ever-wider publicity, mainly because of its fighting stance. And a growing number among the southern Irish, in the aftermath of the Easter rebellion, hardened their views on British dominance. What the hapless makers of the rising failed to achieve in life, they brought about in death as some of them had foreseen. For Kearney and his comrades it was impossible to think of the insurrection as ill-conceived, ill-timed, and ill-fated.[27] Whatever its outcome, the rebellion would set an example for future generations to emulate. The sacrificial death of its leaders would add new luster and a new chapter to the voluminous record book of Irish martyrology. Moreover, the objectionable misrule of Britain in Ireland would be brought anew to world attention.

What the author of *The Soldier's Song* could not have anticipated was his poem's significance as a rallying symbol in the unfinished struggle for Irish self-determination. The comment, by the Irish-American leader John Devoy, that Kearney's piece had replaced the Fenian hymn *God Save Ireland* toward the end of 1916 as the national anthem of the Irish may have been premature. After all, in 1916 there was no sovereign Irish state, and its possible creation seemed further away than at any other time in the preceding fifty years.

Yet if the song's prominence be judged on how widely it was used, then such comments as Devoy's did not lack altogether in credibility. The first boatload of Easter Rising prisoners released from British jails arrived in Kingston on June 17, 1917. The prisoners had been freed for political rather than humanitarian reasons; partly as a gesture of goodwill toward the United States as the newest and most essential wartime ally, and partly to give the planned all-Irish Convention a flying start to overcome the rift between Nationalists and Unionists. As Eamon de Valera, the only surviving senior commandant in the rising, led his fellow returnees ashore, they struck up *The Soldier's Song*.[28] It was a familiar tune in the internment camps, an incantation of faith and a declaration of resolve. Before long some of the lines served as political slogans or demonstrations. In a fall meeting in 1917, organized by *Sinn Féin* and addressed by an unbending de Valera, the front of the rostrum was covered by an enormous bunting with the inscription "Soldiers are we, whose lives are pledged to Ireland."

A group of political prisoners in Cork jail rolled their chargesheets into make-believe trumpets from which, "in a fair imitation of a bad brass band," emerged the defiant sounds of *The Soldier's Song*. But the most unexpected if also, perhaps, the most telling attestation to its inherent power came from the opposite side. In the same Cork jail a gruff sergeant of the military escort was heard to remark, "If a kid sings *'The Soldier's Song'* coming down O'Connell Street the 'ole bloomin' garrison is turned out."[29]

Kearney's poem was not only heard in jails or in the streets. A first printing was undertaken by a Dublin firm in December 1916. Significantly, the cover showed a rifle placed between "Soldier's" and "Song." An American edition was sponsored by a New York Irish priest. Not only did he get one of the best-known music publishers in the city to print the sheet music; better still, Victor Herbert rearranged the musical score. Apparently, it sold quite well, since the priest was able to hand Kearney royalties estimated to total slightly more than £100.[30]

But whatever the rewards and recognition, the most troubled years for Kearney and many of his compatriots still lay ahead. At the end of World War I, *Sinn Féin* was the dominant political force in all of the island except the Ulster counties in the northeast. And in January 1919, with much of continental Europe in revolutionary turmoil, Irish Nationalists convened their first legislative assembly, the *Dáil Eireann*. However, within eight months it was outlawed along with *Sinn Féin*, the Volunteers, and even the Gaelic League by the challenged and edgy authorities in Dublin Castle, as Irish militants increased their hit-and-run activities.

It was mainly the Irish Republican Army, soon known as the IRA, which, as the newly formed clandestine combat organization, resumed the struggle against the British in the spirit of 1916, albeit by other means. The war now was to be waged by guerilla action, and that entailed a spiraling bitterness, nastiness, and ruthlessness. The ill-reputed *Black-and-Tans* and the still more hated *Auxiliaries*[31] indelibly stamped the postwar years in Irish history and minds, as no less frightful and unforgettable than the Great Hunger of the 1840s. Yet IRA raids and assassinations also made their contribution to such dark shadows.

In late 1920, the vicious circle of attack and reprisal churned anew at high speed. During the night of November 20, a dozen British intelligence officers were slain in their quarters. In retaliation the *Black-and-Tans* and the *Auxiliaries* attacked spectators at a Sunday Gaelic football game and exacted an equal loss of life. More assassinations occurred during the following week, and police and troops began to round up hundreds of suspect Nationalist sympathizers.

If Kearney had been suspect to British authorities in 1916 he was even more so in 1920. His reported election to the Supreme Council of the Irish Republican Brotherhood, now nearly defunct, may have sharpened suspicion. In the small hours of November 25, *Auxiliaries* backed by a squad of British soldiers rushed the Kearney home. Despite the protestations of Eva and their two small sons, he was taken away. The following morning he and other suspects found themselves in a holding camp near Dublin.

They stood uneasily around in the cold morning air when one of the detainees, later to become the publisher of Kearney's poetry, recognized "the small, spare man,"[32] and he broke encouragingly into *The Soldier's Song*. Those detainees standing nearby joined in while the British sentries looked askance. For the first time the tune had rung out defiantly within earshot of British troops and in the presence of its author.

Most of those assembled at that holding camp were later transferred to a detention camp near Belfast, Kearney among them. Ballykinlar was to house some 2,000 internees in spartan surroundings for many a long and weary month. Kearney tried to overcome homesickness and a growing lethargy by occasionally writing poetry. Out of this urge came the verses to be titled *Arise*, set to music by Martin Walton, fellow internee and close friend. Subtitled the *Ballykinlar March*, the new poem did not lack in patriotic verve—or bathos.

> List ye, nations of the world,
> To the message of the free;
> Ireland stands with flag unfurled
> Sword in hand for liberty![33]

Other poems written in his year of detention reflected the longing to return home. In late November 1921, Kearney finally received permission to leave on parole—and then only for two weeks—because of his wife's reported illness. As it turned out, he was spared renewed internment.

On December 6, representatives of both the British government and *Sinn Féin* signed an agreement soon known as the Anglo-Irish Treaty. It was the result of prolonged and labyrinthine negotiations after both sides to the "Damnable Question" had realized that they were at a dead end. The treaty provided a workable compromise. At long last it gave to the great majority of Irish people a "Free State" of their own. But the *Saorstat na hEireann* was to remain a member of the British empire; its government had to take an oath to the British Crown, and—most objectionable—the northeastern counties could opt out of it, as they did almost at once.

Still, the treaty offered for the first time in over seven hundred years a measure of independence for the largest part of Ireland and a hope for conciliation on both sides of the Irish Sea. But if it eased Anglo-Irish relations, it acerbated those among Irishmen; not just Nationalists and Unionists but, far worse, among the citizens of the new state. The most tragic phase in the long drama of Irish history was about to open at the very moment when that drama at last seemed to have taken a turn for the better. It was to pit the irreconcilables of the de Valera persuasion against the conciliators led by Arthur Griffith, president of the Free State, and Michael Collins, the almost legendary young hero who combined derring-do with a strong sense of realism.

Collins epitomized the Irish fighting spirit along with its buoyancy, generosity, and volubility. Kearney had known the "Big Fellow" since 1911 and fallen under his spell. He backed Collins' painful decision to vote for the Anglo-Irish treaty and even supported him when, after much hesitation, Collins ordered an attack on antitreaty combatants.[34] Not long into the resulting civil war, Collins was killed in an ambush, and Kearney commented in sorrow as much as in praise that he "will remain the one great figure . . . , head and shoulders above all others."[35]

However bitterly divided, not only during the ten months of civil war but also for quite some time afterwards, the warring sides had two things in common: devotion to the future of the country and *The Soldier's Song*. It could be heard from both Free-staters and Republicans. Yet its author all but withdrew from public life, much like the author of the *Marseillaise*. He disliked work as a censor at a Dublin prison where many Republican insurgents were held. After resigning from that uncomfortable position in late 1922, not least because of his own strong republican views, Kearney eked out a meagre living in his old trade as a painter.

The Soldier's Song, however, flourished. In July 1926, the Free State's minister of defense acknowledged, in reply to pressing questions from a deputy in the *Dáil*, the lower house of the legislature, that the army considered *The Soldier's Song* to be the national anthem.[36] That declaration had the backing of the council of ministers which, on July 12, 1926, had informally agreed that the song should be used as the anthem of the Free State "for all purposes at home and abroad."[37]

If the government considered the matter settled, not everybody concurred. In 1934, a noteworthy debate ensued in the *Dáil*, not just over the merits of the Irish anthem but over the character and significance of the national anthem per se. That debate grew out of a proposal by the minister of finance to remunerate both the living author and the dead composer for their creation of the anthem, which came in for some sharp criticism. One deputy put that criticism quite bluntly when he remarked, "from both a literary and a musical point of view I would regard the 'Soldier's Song' a jaunty little piece of vulgarity and I think we could have done a lot better."[38]

Defenders of *The Soldier's Song* made their strongest pitch by pointing out that it was not the artistic quality but the popularity of a song that made it into an anthem. That point was made most strikingly in the statement that "national anthems come about not because of the suitability of the particular words or notes but because they are adopted generally by the nation."[39] That line of argument may well provide an answer as to why so many of the anthems dealt with here have survived to the present day, regardless of their literary or musical shortcomings.

Bringing the lively debate back to the specifics of the Irish anthem, one deputy observed that "it happened to be the Anthem on the lips of the people when they came into their own and when the outsiders evacuated the country. . . . It was adopted by the people here before it ever was adopted by the Executive Council."[40] Such incontrovertible arguments led to a favorable vote on remuneration to Kearney and Heeney,[41] and by implication on the continuance of *The Soldier's Song* as the country's anthem.

As for Kearney himself, he never doubted that he spoke for Ireland and his compatriots at one and the same time. In true Irish fighting spirit he had challenged, in the late twenties, a proposal made by a Dublin newspaper to base the selection of the Free State's anthem on the consent of the paper's readers. The author of *The Soldier's Song*, his dander up, asserted in a stinging reader's letter that the song was written for just one purpose: "the destruction of everything that stood for British supremacy in Ireland." He added for good measure and not without hyperbole that his poem's "spirit of militant Irish nationalism has carried it around the world and with that spirit it will live and die."[42]

This very spirit manifested itself anew in 1937, when Kearney felt compelled to add a stanza to the anthem—without adding anything to its concinnity. Tentative British plans for a possible new partition triggered a pathetic stanza.[43] Its unfiltered fieriness stood in stark contrast to the deteriorating frailness of the author and to his ever more reclusive attitude. In November 1942, with death near, he remarked to one of his nephews, "I would live the same life over if I had to live it again."[44] Obviously, he had no regrets either in regard to his militancy, literary output, or way of living.

Kearney's death, like his life, caused little public attention; not so much because he had become a homebody or published nothing in his last years. but because for all of his life he had remained undistinguishable from the mass of the Irish people. No official ceremonies embellished his funeral services, although President de Valera, the defense minister, and the lord mayor of Dublin honored the late author of the Irish republic's anthem with their presence.

Brief obituaries in the newspapers recalled Kearney's authorship of the anthem but made few references to his other poetic work. Instead, they referred to him as a professional housepainter, leaving the impression that he was a literary amateur. They did, however, also leave no doubt as to his record of soldiering for Ireland and dedication to its cause.[45]

As in the case of many an anthem, Kearney's piece had to compete with poems of far better-known and qualified authors. At least three of the executed leaders in the Easter Rising had more substantial claim to literary accomplishment and standing, quite apart from such highly regarded writers as William Butler Yeats and Thomas Davis, who had produced great national poetry. Why, then, were the laurels of national anthem author bestowed on someone who was first and foremost a street balladeer and that on a part-time basis? The contention that his *Soldier's Song* was already in a place of honor for a decade or more before it received official sanction begs the question. An answer must be looked for elsewhere. *The Soldier's Song*, with its down-to-earth lines, descriptive imagery, fighting stance, and patriotic passion, had become vox populi much the same way its author had remained a part of the common people throughout his life. Indeed, it might be said without dubious exaggeration that it was not so much Kearney who gave this poem to his countrymen as the latter who gave it to him in a spiritual osmosis, a point made in the *Dáil* debate of 1934.

His author's pride presumably would be fully satisfied if he could hear his verses boom out annually from among the 80,000 spectators assembled at Croke Park, Dublin for the hurling and Gaelic football finals in September. No less striking testimony to the continued appeal of *The Soldier's Song* comes from the other side of the partitioning line still dividing the island. The Catholic Irish in Ulster know the stanzas from childhood and can hum the tune, yet often don't know the names of either author or composer.

As long as the emerald island remains partitioned, it seems unlikely that *The Soldier's Song* will lose its raison d'être as the national anthem of the Republic of Ireland. The words spoken some sixty years ago during the 1934 *Dáil* debate retain an incontestable relevance today. The anthem, a deputy said, "reflects the aims and aspirations of our people and until such time as these aims and aspirations are fully satisfied there is . . . no need to change the words of the song."[46] That point of time, much like a fata morgana, may seem closer in some years than in others; the most recent example being the joint declaration of December 15, 1993, by the British and Irish prime ministers who called for a major conciliation effort by all parties to the conflict. Yet in the six months following grim realities, historical animosities, and encrusted traditions kept reasserting themselves, thus granting the fiery anthem a renewed, if temporary, lease on life.

NOTES

1. George Dangerfield, *The Damnable Question* (Boston: Little, Brown & Co., 1976), 55. This is the title of probably the most thoughtful and objective book ever written on the highly complex issue of Anglo-Irish relations in modern times. The author has drawn that title in part from a comment by the British prime minister, H. H. Asquith, who had visited Dublin shortly after the Easter Rising. Dangerfield, 217, fn.

2. *Fenianism* is one of several Irish terms that directly date back to Celtic mythology. The *Fianna* were the warriors of prehistoric and legendary Ireland. Fenianism as a derivative dates to the formation of Irish militants in the United States into a political pressure group by 1856.

3. See Chapters 8, 9, and 11.

4. Founded in 1884, GAA rules called for a ban on any "foreign" viz. British sports such as cricket, rugby, and soccer.

5. Seamus de Burca, *The Soldier's Song* (Dublin: P. J. Bourke, 1957), 1. This is the only biography of Peadar Kearney.

6. The four stanzas of the original version of *The Soldier's Song* have been reprinted in several collections of Kearney's poetry. The one quoted here is contained in J. W. Hammond, ed., *The Soldier's Song and Other Poems by Peadar Kearney* (Dublin and Cork: The Talbot Press Limited, 1928), 11–12.

7. Ibid. *Innisfail* is the poetic synechdoche for all of Ireland.

8. The melody's pentatonic scale may be the root cause for the difficulties encountered at first.

9. Kearney recorded that in the early summer of 1911 neither his nor Heeney's name was widely known among Irishmen gathering at a London pub. Burca, 67.

10. Kearney is the only blue-collar worker among all the authors presented in this book.

11. John Kearney once tore a page out of a school library book that Peadar had brought home because it praised Great Britain. Burca, 18.

12. It appeared over his name in *St. Patrick's Weekly* in 1900.

13. One of the best known of his ditties is the jocular if anti-British *Whack Fol The Diddle*.

14. Among those who took instruction from Kearney was the playwright Sean O'Casey.

15. Burca, 61.

16. Under the provisions of this third Home Rule bill, as amended in 1920, six of the nine Ulster counties were allowed the choice of exclusion from Home Rule, leaving them in a close union with Britain.

17. Margaret Skinnider, *Doing My Bit for Ireland* (New York: The Century Co., 1917), 237.

18. Quoted in Burca, 98.

19. Sir Roger Casement, a former British diplomat of Irish descent, had been in contact with German officials in New York and Berlin since the fall of 1914.

20. The German ambassador in Washington had repeatedly informed his Berlin superiors of ongoing preparations by Irish nationalists, both in the U.S. and in Ireland. New York police had raided a German suspect's office in New York early in April 1916 and confiscated documents subsequently made available to London authorities.

21. The tramp steamer, renamed *Aud,* reached Tralee Bay but shore contacts failed before she was compelled to follow a British warship into Queenstown harbor. She was blown up on the way, on orders of her captain.

22. Sir Roger Casement had been landed at the coast of Kerry but was detected before he could move inland. He was transferred to England, where he had to stand trial for high treason and subsequently was hanged.

23. Burca, 115.

24. Ibid., 121.

25. In addition to *Easter 1916* Yeats wrote *Sixteen Dead Men*, which commemorated the executed leaders of the rising.

26. The first published collection of his poems, put out by Martin Walton, dates to 1928.

27. Years later Kearney remarked that if the rising had not taken place "it would have been fatal. Indeed, it would have been the end for a generation at least—another 1865, perhaps." Burca, 217. Kearney's reference was to the Fenian attempt at rebellion, originally set for 1865 but delayed by two years.

28. Mary Bromage, *De Valera and the March of a Nation* (New York: The Noonday Press, 1956), 64.

29. Robert Brennan, *Allegiance* (Dublin: Browne & Nolan Ltd., 1950), 158.

30. Burca, 56.

31. The *Black-and-Tans*, mainly composed of demobilized British soldiers, wore makeshift uniforms of khaki and dark colors. The *Auxiliaries* were mainly ex-officers with higher pay than the *Black-and-Tans* and a still worse reputation among southern Irish.

32. Quoted in Seamus de Burca, ed., *My Dear Eva: Letters written from Ballykinlar Internment Camp by Peadar Kearney* (Dublin: P. J. Bourke, 1976), 3. The future publisher and patron of Kearney was Martin Walton.

33. Burca, 245.

34. The Irish civil war opened on June 28, 1922, when Collins ordered Free State troops to clear the Four Courts building which the Republicans had occupied since April.

35. Burca, 220.

36. *Dáil Eireann, Parliamentary Debates* (Dublin: Cahill & Co., Ltd., 1926), 16:2198.

37. Ibid., 50:408 (1934).

38. Ibid., 412.

39. Ibid., 414.

40. Ibid.

41. The amount of £1,200 was equally divided between Kearney and the legal representative of the deceased composer. The award stemmed from a threatened suit by Kearney against the Free State for having made unauthorized use of *The Soldier's Song*. By this action the anthem became property of the state.

42. *Evening Herald*, September 14, 1928.

43. The supplemental stanza began as follows. "And here where Eire's glories bide/ Clann London fain would flourish./But Ulsterwide what e'er betide/No pirate blood shall nourish." Burca, 246.

44. Ibid., 222. One of Kearney's nephews was the remarkable if controversial Brendan Behan.

45. Obituary notices in *The Irish Times*, November 25, 1942, and in the strongly nationalist *Irish Press* of the same date. The latter paper did feature a sketch of the deceased author's face on its front page. It also stated that *The Soldier's Song* had become "the national anthem of the Republican movement by instinct."

46. *Dáil Eireann, Parliamentary Debates*, 50:417.

Liberation Anthems

8

Hungary

Himnusz
(Ferenc Kölcsey)

An anthem marked as much by melancholy and lament as by the absence of an
assertive or at least emphatic nationalism is an oddity among the anthems presented here. It may seem even more odd that a poem of elegy and passivity
should become the anthem of a strongly nationalist and ethnocentric people,
known for their vivacity and dash. Thus, it looks like a strange match of anthem
and nation at first glance. Yet when taking a closer look, it will become apparent
why, in the fullness of time, Ferenc Kölcsey's *Himnusz* was accepted as the
unchallenged and unchanging anthem of the Hungarians.

Its origins were as inconspicuous as the milieu in which the poem was written.
No explosive event or situation touched off its creation; no impending or ongoing war engendered a stirring call to arms; no defiant challenge to oppressors
was voiced, and no glorious vision of national union and power filled its verses.
But then the Hungary of 1823 was a stagnant political backwater, its public life
dormant, and its social structure fossilized.

Outwardly becalmed, Hungary did not, however, lack in causes for unrest or
in potential centers of agitation. The imperial authorities in Vienna continued
their traditionally heavy-handed policies of utilization if not outright exploitation
of the country. The decade-old Metternich government merely used more pro-
ficient but no less insidious methods, such as an elaborate spy system and a
tightened censorship, while the perennial demands for taxes and recruits continued.

There existed, to be sure, Hungarian institutions and instrumentalities to ventilate grievances. First and foremost, the constitution whose origins could be traced back to within seven years after the *Magna Carta* of 1215. A Hungarian national assembly or Diet had given the country a means of collective expression and legislative action since. In the Diet the lower house had far more members than the upper house, composed of the great nobles. But these were far more influential and often in tune with Vienna. The Diet's role was further weakened because the Habsburg rulers called and disbanded it at will.

Ultimate remedial power rested with the monarch himself. Kingship had deep roots in Hungarian civic culture. The crown of St. Stephen had been the sacred symbol of Magyar nationhood since 1000 A.D. The Habsburg dynasty, first by election and since 1687 by heredity, held claim to that crown. Unfortunately, the same dynasty had anterior interests and obligations elsewhere, not least in its Austrian crownlands and in the emperorship of the Holy Roman Empire.

Still, king-diet-constitution—whatever their restrictions as guarantors of Hungarian interests—formed a workable polity in Kölcsey's time. A graver concern of the Magyar intelligentsia to which he belonged was that of national survival. Its fragility had been brought into sharp focus when most of the country had been overrun by the Turks after the disastrous battle of Mohacs in 1526, an event that left an indelible imprint on the collective memory of the nation and its literature.

Early in the eighteenth century, when the last vestiges of Ottoman control had disappeared, the process of Hungary's amalgamation within the Habsburg empire continued at an accelerated pace. Such resistance as was offered to "Austrianization," commonly interpreted as Germanization, came mainly from the gentry. Their primary concern was the preservation of feudal privileges, including exemption from taxation, and the exploitation of the servile peasantry. Many of the gentry believed that survival of the national entity would guarantee these privileges.

Yet that survival seemed in renewed doubt at the very time when Ferenc Kölcsey was born in 1790. The removal of the sacred crown of St. Stephen to Vienna and the planned use of German in public institutions throughout Hungary during the reign of Emperor Joseph II were indicators of the likely disappearance of a national identity. To add weight to such ominous signs, the Magyars, once in a clear majority in their own country, constituted no more than a narrow plurality at the time of the French Revolution.[1] The nightmare of *nemzethalál*—the death of the nation—darkened the thought of quite a few of Kölcsey's compères.[2]

The past rather than the future had to safeguard national survival. Not surprisingly, the politically most active population, the gentry, remained in their majority also the most conservative in matters social and economic. Local or county affairs preoccupied them to a degree that proved simultaneously a bane and a blessing, since their benighted provincialism also provided strength to the Magyar identity and autonomy. Unified in clinging to their privileged status, the roughly half million *dzsentri*—as distinguished from the aristocracy—divided into almost a half-dozen categories. These ranged from the prominent landowners with substantial holdings to the "sandalled" nobility, too poor to buy boots and living much like the serf family that worked their minuscule property. Much of the gentry differed but little from one another in their rustic character and limited education. Perhaps nothing typified the encrusted traditionalism better than their use of Latin in all official proceedings.

There were, however, noteworthy exceptions to this collective immobility and intellectual inertia. Most literary luminaries belonged to the gentry. Some had moved to the few urban centers, including Pesth, in quest of more congenial company; others stayed in the bucolic environment of their estates. Yet none withdrew so far and so much into himself as Ferenc Kölcsey.

His isolation mirrored in a curious way that of the nation. For a millenium the Magyars who had settled in the Carpathian basin along and across the middle Danube in the tenth century had felt surrounded by German, Slavic, Rumanian, and assorted other population groups. Ethnic and linguistic separateness engendered a psychological backlash. Numerical inferiority triggered a superiority complex within some of the Magyar elite not unlike that of the Spartans.

An assertive national pride which had become a natural component of the perceived isolation was to flare up, perhaps subconsciously, even in the humanistic and introverted Kölcsey. He had been cast into an involuntary solitude at the remote Cseke estate in northeast Hungary. A family property of moderate size, it offered few amenities except for the books that he had brought with him when settling down in 1815. The solitude to which the young poet had become accustomed since childhood at times felt oppressive.

It was never more so than in January 1823, when the gloomy atmosphere of the wintry countryside seemed to correspond to the spirit of the master of the house. His inborn pessimism, deepening at times into despondency, was unrelieved. Contact with the outside world had all but stopped. Newssheets arrived rarely, and they contained almost no stimulating information since they were heavily censored by Austrian fiat. Correspondence with literary friends proved more satisfactory, yet thoughtful exchanges were often delayed if not by censorship then by a haphazard mail service.

Remote as he was in both location and attitude, the life of the nation remained close. Hemmed in physically, his mind was free to roam through all of Hungary's history. Now, in the short days and long nights of a harsh winter month, desolate surroundings, and unbroken solitude he reflected on the evolution and the meaning of that history, contemplating it with more sorrow than satisfaction. National survival, he felt, could only be secured by the grace of God.

To Him he turned in the very first word of his new poem, and to Him he returned in the first line of the last of eight stanzas. While some other anthems opened or closed with the same appeal or invoked deity more often, none is referred to as "prayer-song."[3] The theme of divine involvement both as a retributive and as a redeeming power runs like a leitmotif through all but two of the stanzas. God's grace alternately is acknowledged and implored:

God! The Magyar bless
With Thy plenty and good cheer!
With Thine aid his just cause press,
Where his foes to fight appear.
Fate, who for so long did'st frown
Bring him happy times and ways;
Atoning sorrow hath weighed down
Sins of past and future days.[4]

But the God of bounty and support is also one of Calvinist rigidity. His wrath
at the "misdeeds" of the Hungarians is discharged like lightning and in the
form of invasions by "murderous Mongols" and "Osman hordes." Interspersed
with this gloom are brighter verses of praise for the beauty of parts of the
country. But all too soon darker hues reappear:

'Neath the castle, a ruin now,
Joy and pleasure once were found,
Only groans and sighs . . .
In its limits now abound.
But no freedom's flowers sprout
From the spilt blood of the dead,
And the tears of slavery burn,
Which the eyes of orphans shed.[5]

And the final stanza repeats, for emphasis, the plea to God for forgiveness and
redress from "a sea of grief that engulfs the Magyar." If that theme constituted
the leitmotif of the *Himnusz*, setting it apart from other anthems, it also differed
from them in the absence of a challenge to existing political conditions.

The *Himnusz* did not contain a single word chastising, let alone challenging,
Austrian dominance. Perhaps Kölcsey feared censorship,[6] but such concerns had
not stifled the impulses or bold defiance of other authors. Perhaps the age-old
practices of successive Habsburg governments applying indirect pressures rather
than outright coercion offered few opportunities for direct response. Most likely,
the introvert poet did not possess a revolutionary temperament; nor did he have
a sufficient political involvement at remote Cseke to cast seditious lines, like so
many banderillas, to arouse both the combativeness of his compatriots and the
ire of their prospective target.

Kölcsey's thoughts and emotions focused on quite different issues. He eschewed returning to the glories of the past in the belief that they would do little
for Hungary's future. National revival and even survival was not a matter of
heroics but of purification. The true enemy was not external but internal, not
foreign aggression but domestic retrogression.

The poet's real aim was the arousal of Hungarians to a national awareness of
shortcomings through the centuries of a stormy history, the subtitle of his *Himnusz*. Hence the absence in it of moments of national glory or reference to

leaders of uprisings on behalf of national reassertion; an omission all the more surprising because many of these leaders had come from the eastern border area where the author, too, had been born: Transylvania.

If that was the principal cause of omission of Transylvania in the *Himnusz*, there may have been additional reasons for not drawing on the rich lode of the region's pride and tradition. The Kölcsey family had moved away from the Transylvanian border area soon after Ferenc was born there in August 1790. His father, a learned lawyer, settled his expanding family on one of the estates that he owned in Szatmár county in northeast Hungary.

He died before Ferenc was six, one of several losses that were to afflict him in early life. The loss of one eye, resulting from scarlet fever, was to have a profound effect on the development of his personality, probably causing the withdrawal syndrome at Cseke. And on the eve of adolescence he became an orphan upon the death of his mother, to whom he was strongly attached.

These calamities impacted on his psyche, leading him into a pessimism that was to affect his writings. The education that he received at Debrecen, bulwark of strict Calvinism, hardly brightened his outlook or tempered his loneliness. He came to dislike the mental coldness of the Calvinist milieu and retreated further into himself. His principal companions were books. With one eye he probably read more in one month than many of his fellow students did in a year.

He viewed most of the gentry as intellectually backward and preoccupied with their rural concerns.[7] Nor did his first stay in Pesth, the largest Hungarian town, make him more sanguine. He had gone there in 1810 to finish his law studies but found it more of an outsized village than a cultural center. His idealized vision of Greek and Roman cities of antiquity clashed with the less-than-inspiring reality.

He envied poets who lived "in a beautiful country where genius could flourish and win appreciation."[8] At times he actually wished himself away from the country of his birth. In 1813 the author of the future Hungarian anthem wrote to his closest friend. "If my soul had a choice, coming up from Hades, I am sure that I would not have chosen the country in which I was born."[9] Hardly a position common to authors of national anthems!

Growing isolation and frustration ventilated themselves in the writing of sentimental juvenile poetry. What distinguished it was the heavy pessimism that hangs over most of Kölcsey's creations like a dark and stationary cloud. Foreshadowing the lament and gloom of much of his work, notably the *Himnusz*, one of the early poems contrasted the elysian lands of his visions with Hungary as it existed. Here in his homeland "the wine is mixed with tears and no gay tune could be heard from a poet's lute."[10]

Yet such deep-seated pessimism was not only a trait of the author of Hungary's anthem but one of national dimension. A contemporary of Kölcsey's trenchantly observed: "Melancholy is the national veneer."[11] Nor was that pessimistic trend confined to the period. Present-day native commentators have confirmed its existence and coined such descriptive terms as "creative pessimism"[12] for a nationwide attitude of rising defiantly from the depth of despair. In June 1991, the then Hungarian premier Joszef Antall declared, "A Hungarian will always see the worst. . . . Every renewal in our history was always born in pessimism." And he clinched that point by continuing, "Even our anthem is pessimistic."[13]

Quite possibly, the ever present melancholia has been conditioned by the cultural and geopolitical isolation which like a plasma had enveloped Hungarians for centuries. Wedged between central and eastern Europe and subject to influences from both directions, Mihaly Vörösmarty, one of Hungary's great authors and creator of a second national anthem, could observe in 1828, "The Hungarian looks West, and then looks East with dismal eyes; he is an isolated, brotherless branch of his race."[14] And if Kölcsey's pessimism was not atypical of his fellow citizens, that sense of isolation was an even more common feature of both author and nation.

Like other authors and composers of anthems, Kölcsey realized the importance of folk songs and legends as a vital element in national rebirth. As early as 1818, he had commented, "If my gloomy mood permits I experiment with the tone of peasant songs."[15] By his own admission their conversion into more refined lyrics proved a difficult task. Yet he did work some of the simple themes and sentiments into several poems, often in ballad form. Before long his initial reservations gave way to a full understanding that "the driving force of the poetry of the nation is to be sought in the songs of the common people," a view shared by several anthem authors.[16]

Kölcsey's thinking on this subject evolved gradually as it did on other issues, causing him to change from cosmopolitanism to nationalism, classicism to romanticism, or political passivity to outspoken activism. One characteristic, however, remained constant: his pessimism. In the year when he penned the *Himnusz*, he also wrote one of the most despondent pieces in Hungarian or any other literature. *Vanitatum Vanitas* recalls by its very title a doomsday mood.

But however heavy the pressure of his pessimism, it would not suffocate the flame of his patriotism. That flame shone most brightly in his essay *National Traditions*, dating to 1826, which contained this revealing passage: "National character can be preserved only by bestowing care on the monuments of the past, [and if lacking them] it is the poet's duty to erect poetic monuments to the past deeds of the nation."[17]

Yet his cerebral patriotism also found outlets other than a revival of the past. The *Ode to Liberty* (1825), with its passionate and even erotic appeal to an imaginary goddess of freedom, typified a whole generation of romantic poets including several of the anthem authors. Like some of them, Kölcsey's compassion for liberty, both of the individual and of the nation, drove him into the political arena. That breakthrough from his psychological shell was due mainly to his urge to improve the lot of the subjected peasantry in his county. Offering himself as a candidate for public office, he was elected an assistant registrar and notary for Szatmár county in July 1829.

Compassion for his underprivileged countrymen as much as his concern for the future of Hungary now made Ferenc Kölcsey express himself in behalf of either by means other than the written word. That means was at hand. The Diet was called into session in December 1832 and became known as the Reform Diet. Proposed reforms of whatever nature had few if any spokesmen more eloquent or applauded than the author of the *Himnusz*.[18] He owed his election as one of the two deputies from Szatmár county probably more to his participation in public affairs than to his reputation as a poet. For some three years now the erstwhile recluse had taken a prominent part in drawing up resolutions and petitions for the people of the county. And it was *the people* he wanted to represent at the national Diet in Pozsony (now Bratislava) rather than just the gentry, even though they alone had voted him the county's representative.

Arriving in the city shortly before Christmas 1832, he felt out of place at first. He was neither a calculating politician nor an experienced team player. His motivation and goals derived from moralism, humanism, and patriotism. Beholden to no interest group, sectionalism, family, or even a mistress, he could freely speak his mind. The purity of his endeavor was recognized by contemporaries and posterity alike.

Kölcsey's appearance alone set him apart from the other deputies. He stood out among them in his black frock coat, sharply contrasting with the colorful, Hussar-like garments that so many Hungarian gentry sported; resembling a missionary among a tribal flock yet to be converted. A contemporary observed that "it was an interesting phenomenon to see this tall, frail, bald and . . . modest man . . . among the red-cheeked, potbellied officials and judges who were influenced by his gentle and noble humanism."[19]

No issue was more salient and divisive than that of rural reform, and that issue made Kölcsey the central figure of the reform group in the Diet. The shy author unexpectedly turned public speaker with telling effect. He waxed most eloquent on the controversial subject of serf manumission.

His impassioned call for it had been made first in the Szatmár county assembly. "A nation of ten million freemen" should replace the one "consisting of seven hundred thousand demoralized souls."[20] In his speech *The state of the taxpaying people of Szatmár*, Kölcsey had drawn a dismal picture of the conditions of the dependent peasantry. Now he eagerly took up their case on the national stage which the Diet furnished.

As soon as opportunity offered in January 1833, he demanded that the ancient constitution, sheet anchor of Hungarian autonomy, be revamped for the benefit of the whole nation. Such radical proposals could hardly be expected to find ready acceptance in the Diet, let alone by the government. A rather diluted bill on rural reform passed the Diet in November 1833. Sent on to the King of Hungary, that is, the Habsburg emperor, a decision was held up for months. Not surprisingly, Kölcsey's pessimism reasserted itself. "Our prospects darken, our hopes are waning and all the worries . . . about the future of the country are again stirred up.''[21]

Almost one year after its submission to Vienna the bill was indeed returned as unacceptable. Its rejection triggered a flood of protesting speeches, none more moving—or lengthy—than that of Ferenc Kölcsey. Lajos Kossuth, leader of the Hungarian independence war of 1848–49, recorded the effect of Kölcsey's peroration. ''The poet Kölcsey . . . drew so touchingly a picture of the . . . oppressed peasant that after the sound of weeping . . . deafening cheers followed, evincing how deeply . . . sympathies accorded with the orator.''[22] On February 9, 1835, that poet delivered his swan song at the Diet. One last time he thrilled a large audience as much by his sincerity as by his oratory. ''We were motivated by two strong desires: to raise up the level of the taxpaying people from servitude and to expand the ownership of land . . . Fatherland and Progress were our motto.'' And in words recalling the last stanza of the *Himnusz,* he once more invoked the help of ''God to guard this nation against evil; may God let dawn the beautiful day of the nation's full bloom.''[23]

Kölcsey's brief appearance on the political centerstage had ended. The reformers felt that loss so deeply that Kossuth's famed lithographed reports of the Diet's proceedings bore black borders on the day of the poet's retirement. Young patriots wore black armbands in token of their grief. Yet, paradoxically, on that day of mourning the author of the *Himnusz* had entered the life of the nation for generations to come. In short order he had become a much respected public figure. His purity of purpose, probity of conduct, and intensity of effort on behalf of the nation had secured for him a standing in national awareness that his literary work alone could hardly attain. And the elevation of one of his poems to national anthem status over several others of like merit was ultimate proof of this respectful awareness.

The owner of Cseke, however, knew little of the widening esteem around and ahead of him. Once more he fell into the depression that had shadowed so much of his life. Once more he took up pen to give expression to his ever-deepening pessimism and his constant patriotism, still linked to one another. The sequel to his *Song of Zrinyi*, a plaintive poem dating to 1830, was *Zrinyi's Second Song.* Both titles referred to Count Miklos Zrinyi, a seventeenth-century soldier and poet who had become a role model for the patriotic reformers of the early nineteenth century, and both poems were cast in the dark shadows of Kölcsey's reflections. In *Zrinyi's Second Song* he gloomily predicted that a people other than the Magyars would prevail in the Carpathian basin.

It seemed fitting that Kölcsey's life should come to an end in the year in which he struck up the darkest notes of pessimism. A neglected cold undermined his always frail health. Medical help was called for too late. He died as lonely as he had lived on August 24, 1838.

Had he been alive for another half-dozen years the poet, modest introvert that he was, would almost certainly have been pleased at the news that his *Himnusz* had been set to music. In 1844, the director of the National Theater initiated a prize competition for a musical score of the *Himnusz*. The winner, Ferenc Erkel, had already made a name for himself as a composer of romantic operas with national themes. In later years he remembered that it took less than an hour to create the score.

Erkel also recalled that he heard the church bells of Pozsony while perusing the poem and that they made him doubly aware of its solemn character. Within two months after winning the competition, the *Himnusz* was heard publicly for the first time. A magazine commented with remarkable foresight that "the outstanding quality of the composition assures the widest popular recognition and, thus, it will become *the* hymn of the Hungarian people."[24]

The composer indeed had fashioned a melody whose gripping solemnity and choral quality would carry the poem like powerful wings to the most remote villages and through successive generations. Quite possibly, it was the music which greatly assisted Kölcsey's verses in gaining anthem status. Certainly there were, as in other countries, both actual and potential competitors, among them the lively *Rakoczi March*, best known through the compositions of George Bizet and Franz Liszt; the *National Song* by Sandor Petöfi, Hungary's most famous poet, and *Szózat* (Summons). The latter was written a couple of years before Kölcsey's death by Mihaly Vörösmarty, generally regarded as the greatest Hungarian author of the pre-1848 era.

Szózat has rivalled the *Himnusz*, its predecessor by a dozen years, ever since its creation. It has been informally used as a second national anthem. Certainly, its affirmative and even assertive stanzas, emphasizing the fight for liberty, fatherland, and the ultimate triumph of the nation by its own efforts, are more in keeping with the nineteenth-century anthems than the prayerful *Himnusz*.

Both the *Himnusz* and *Szózat* made their national appearance by the same means and at about the same time. *Szózat* was set to music a year before the *Himnusz* when the same director of the National Theater sponsored a competition for the most suitable melody. That the awards committee chose the *Szózat* ahead of the *Himnusz* indicates a preference for the more contemporary and forceful stanzas. Throughout 1843, the prize-winning composition attained both public presentations and acclaim.[25]

Yet, in the following summer, *Szózat* lost ground to its powerful rival. On July 2, 1844, "the joint harps of Kölcsey and Erkel launched the hymn of the people."[26] The *Himnusz* rapidly gained prominence. What better occasions than the launching of the steamship *Széchenyi*, banner name of national reform and strength, on August 10; followed a few days later by the flag consecration of the militia on Rákos field, the historic meeting place of ancient Hungarian assemblies. During both events the assemblage broke fervently into the *Himnusz*.

To widen its circulation, sheet music and text were distributed by an enterprising publisher in September 1844, and before year's end the *Himnusz* was sung for the first time on the stage. It was to be heard again on a different stage and in different circumstances less than four years later.

On March 15, 1848—destined to become the national holiday of Hungary—

the political quake that was to shake much of Europe erupted in Budapest. At the Café Pilvax the turbulent crowd first listened to and then joined in a new revolutionary song composed by a young and radical patriot glowing with enthusiasm and ready to take up arms. Sandor Petöfi had just given life to the *National Song* and soon was to give his own for Hungary's independence.

Yet the remembrance of Kölcsey's stand and stanzas would not let the *Himnusz* fade away. Soon it rang out during a torchlight parade. In mid-August it attained quasi-anthem status when sung for the first time at an official ceremony in the Matyas Cathedral of the capital. Within a year, however, it was officially banned. Joint intervention of Austrian and Russian forces had ended the last efforts and hopes of the Hungarian revolutionary army with the capitulation at Vilagos. That tragic ending, symbolized by the execution of no fewer than thirteen generals, seemed to add another verse to Kölcsey's mournful recital of Hungarian woes.

The *Himnusz* and its creator came together again when a memorial stone was consecrated at Cseke on May 18, 1856. Words and melody blended into a final tribute to Kölcsey by the small group gathered in his honor. A far larger crowd joined their voices and esteem on a similar occasion a few years later. As many as 80,000 people had congregated to honor the national reformer István Széchenyi—dead by suicide in April 1860. Appropriately, they broke into the *Himnusz*, that dirge of tragedy, during a requiem mass.

But Kölcsey's poem fitted less well into the rough-and-tumble of political activities. In the electoral campaign of 1861, the *Szózat* rather than the *Himnusz* provided the setting for patriotic speeches and gatherings. Kölcsey's passionate lament all but disappeared from official ceremonies in the decades to come. The historic *Ausgleich*, the equalization compromise of 1867, at last gave to Hungary constitutional as well as institutional equality with Austria. It allowed for a distinctive national flag and coat of arms. Still, that hard-fought-for limited sovereignty did not include an official anthem other than the imperial one. In fact, Emperor Franz Joseph, whose reign of nearly seven decades included the *Ausgleich* era, expressly forbade the use of any rivalling anthem.

Nor did Hungarians push hard for a formal recognition of their own anthem. In 1903 a Hungarian deputy introduced a bill to formalize usage of a national anthem. Not surprisingly, the bill failed to reach even the debate stage. On the other hand, the imperial hymn *God Sustain Our Emperor*, dating back to Haydn's day, was last heard in mid-October 1918. That its final official airing should be in Debrecen, the city where Kölcsey had received his advanced schooling, must appear as rather ironic.

But within fourteen days quite a different tune was heard, and one more attuned to national sentiment. In the evening of October 27, 1918, restless crowds roamed the streets of Budapest in quest of peace, bread, and—not least—independence. Count Mihaly Karolyi, about to assume governmental authority, heard the *Himnusz* rise up from a demonstrative gathering at Vörösmarty

Square.[27] It seemed altogether fitting that the authors of the two pre-1848 national poems should thus be linked.

An independent republic was proclaimed on November 16th, but patriotic hopes were all too soon dimmed by Czech, Rumanian, and Serbian intervention backed by the major western allies. A mere four months after its proclamation the tottering republic gave way to a Soviet-type and Soviet-sponsored dictatorship. Its leaders despised the symbols of bourgeois nationalism. The green-white-red flag disappeared from sight in favor of the red flag, and the *Himnusz* was displaced by the *Internationale*.

Neither of the two substitutes were to outlast the brief Béla Kun dictatorship. A counterrevolutionary drive, led by Admiral Nicholas Horthy, quickly gained ascendancy. On November 16, 1919, to the day one year after the proclamation of Hungary's second and equally ill-fated republic, a high mass celebrated the restoration of a conservative order and the liberation of the capital from Rumanian occupation.[28] Rain doused that Sunday's outdoor ceremony but not the spirit of those gathered. They broke into the first stanza of the *Himnusz,* yet it was the last stanza with its plea for a better future that had a special meaning at this watershed moment.

The Horthy regency, established in 1920 with the possibility of monarchical restoration left open, accepted the national anthem in the spirit of national self-assertion and in anticipation of better times. Yet such times still proved elusive. Even though the *Himnusz* was not formally designated as the Hungarian anthem, its very nature—not to mention that of its deeply pessimistic author—corresponded to the mood of melancholic resilience and chiliastic resurrection so typically Hungarian.

Not until 1938, however, did the opportunity occur to recover some of the regions lost under the Trianon Treaty.[29] Additional territorial recoveries were made in the following years. But the price was too high since Hungary, to the remorse of some of her most patriotic leaders,[30] sold herself to the Axis powers. Since opposition came mainly from conservative groups, the *Himnusz* did not immediately become the rallying song of an underground resistance. When the latter formed in late 1944, it was as much directed against the advancing Red Army as against the gradually retreating Germans.

Soviet pressures were increasingly felt in the postwar years. Yet the Hungarian communists who gained control of the government by 1947 had learned from the fundamental mistake of their predecessors in 1919. They did not this time around discard the treasured national symbols. Anthem and flag—the latter modified by a red star, sheaves of wheat, and a hammer—remained in place except for one abortive effort to replace the *Himnusz*.[31]

Although officially sanctioned, the anthem was used in anti-communist demonstrations, which reached their climax in the October rising of 1956. Then the anthem was heard as a call to both resolution and revolution. On the afternoon of October 23rd, excited students sang it at Budapest Technical University. From there anthem and revolution spread simultaneously, first through the capital and then throughout the country.[32]

In the oppressive atmosphere of the years after the aborted independence struggle, recalling that of 1849, the *Himnusz* retained its official status but was bereft of any real meaning when intoned under government auspices. It did not regain that meaning until the late 1970s. In January 1978, the crown of St. Stephen, ultimate symbol of Hungarian history and pride, was returned to Budapest from U.S. guardianship. An elaborate ceremony at the majestic parliament building marked the festive occasion. It was suitably enhanced by the singing of the *Himnusz* and then the *Szózat*; the latter being heard publicly for the first time in some thirty years.

In the final decade of the communist regime, the *Himnusz* was occasionally struck up in defiance of police trying to dissolve minor demonstrations. More often, however, the anthem acted as a bracket rather than as a wedge for the nation, not least because of the reforming efforts of the communist government. There was no apparent need, therefore, to intone the *Himnusz* in defiance of authority, since the transformation from a monolithic to a pluralist system of government evolved both smoothly and gradually in the late 1980s.

The transition when completed in early 1990 did not require either restyling or reintroduction of the national anthem; nor did it have to serve in mass demonstrations calling for the overthrow of tottering communist regimes in the winter of 1989 as anthems did in Czechoslovakia and East Germany. But while the *Himnusz* had no specific role to play, its author was the subject of special attention and soon of honors. Some of these laudations focused on his reform efforts in the Pozsony parliament; others on his literary work.[33] A commemorative session was held by the Academy of Sciences on the occasion of the bicentenary of his birth, in August 1990.

But the ultimate honor was bestowed on Ferenc Kölcsey on January 22, 1991, when the Hungarian government decreed that henceforth this would be National Culture Day. It was on that day in 1823 that he had completed the *Himnusz*. No other anthem author has acquired such a distinction.

NOTES

1. In 1787, the ratio of ethnic Hungarians to the total population of the kingdom of Hungary lay somewhere between 29 and 39 percent. Andrew C. Janos, *The Politics of Backwardness in Hungary, 1825–1945* (Princeton: University Press, 1982), 10. Half a century later it was 37.4 percent. Ibid., 11.

2. Count István Széchenyi, Hungary's foremost nineteenth-century reformer, observed in the 1820s, "Every day I am more convinced that . . . the Hungarian nation will soon cease to exist." Quoted in George Barany, *Stephen Széchenyi and the Awakening of Hungarian Nationalism, 1791–1841* (Princeton: University Press, 1968), 19 and 179.

3. Jancso Benedek, editor of a selection of Kölcsey's works in *Kölcsey Ferencz: Valogatott Munkai* (Budapest: Lampel Róbert, 1903), xiv.

4. English translations of the *Himnusz* vary considerably because of the difficulties in translating poetry, compounded in the Hungarian case by the special character of that language. The translation of this stanza is by William N. Loew, *Selections from Hungarian Poets*, rev. ed. (n.p.: 1899), 196.

5. Ibid., 197.

6. In a letter of July 28, 1823, Kölcsey remarked caustically, "My notes on Greek philosophy might not be forbidden if I were to keep them in a strictly historical perspective." Ferenc Kölcsey, *Minden Munkái* (Collected Works), 3d ed., 10 vols. (Budapest: Franklin-Tarsulat, 1886–87), 9:298.

7. Kölcsey commented rather acidly, "The Hungarian nobleman . . . when tired from laboring in meetings rushes back to his village to keep his shepherds and farmhands in line. His only source of livelihood is the management of the estate. And how does he manage it? Answer: just like his serf." Julius von Farkas, *Die ungarische Romantik*, 1st ser. of *Ungarische Bibliothek*, vol. 15 (Berlin: Walter de Gruyter, 1931), 59.

8. This line occurs in *Andalgasok* (Meanderings), one of his first poems, written in 1811.

9. Janos Papp, ed., *Kölcsey-Brevárium* (Budapest: Tarköny Kiadó, 1975), 6.

10. *Andalgasok*, in a collection of Kölcsey poetry in *Minden Órám*, ed. Ferenczi Laszlo (Budapest: Kozmoszkönyvek, 1984), 26.

11. Karoly Kisfaludy, an early romantic poet, as quoted by Farkas, 143.

12. The term has been coined by Dr. István Csicsery-Ronay, one of the readers of this chapter.

13. From an interview reported in *The New York Times*, June 24, 1991.

14. Lorant Czigany, *The Oxford History of Hungarian Literature* (Oxford: Clarendon Press, 1984), 128.

15. Ibid., 111.

16. See, for instance, the chapters on the Greek and Norwegian anthems.

17. Czigany, 113.

18. The *Himnusz* appeared in a volume of Kölcsey's poetry for the first time in 1832. The poem had been originally published in the literary magazine *Aurora*, in December 1828, but the magazine's circulation was very limited.

19. *A Magyar Irodalom Története* (A history of Hungarian literature), ed. Pal Pandi, 6 vols. (Budapest: Akadémia Kiado, 1964–1966), 3:428.

20. Janos, 63. This figure includes all of the nobility.

21. Mihaly Horvath, *Fünfundzwanzig Jahre aus der Geschichte Ungarns* (Twenty-five years of Hungarian history), trans. Joseph Novelli from the original Hungarian, 2 vols. (Leipzig: Brockhaus, 1867), 1:313–14.

22. E.O.S. [*sic*], *Hungary and Its Revolutions . . . With a Memoir of Louis Kossuth* (London: Henry G. Bohn, 1854), 195.

23. Horvath, 1:273.

24. *Honderü*, July 6, 1844.

25. The composer of *Szózat* was Beni Egressy (1814–1851), who as a semi-professional musician also doubled as a librettist and actor. Egressy did not attain Erkel's musical level and reputation, although he wrote librettos for some of the operas of his more famous colleague.

26. *Honderü*, July 6, 1844.

27. *Memoirs of Michael Karolyi: Faith without Illusion*, trans. Catherine Karolyi (New York: E. P. Dutton, 1957), 112.

28. Rumanian troops had entered Budapest on August 4, 1919, and withdrew on November 14 in the same year.

29. Hungary lost nearly two-thirds of its prewar territory under the provisions of Trianon which became operative in June 1920.

30. Count Pal Teleki, then premier, committed suicide on April 3, 1941, in protest of Hungary's joining Nazi Germany for the invasion of Yugoslavia.

31. In 1951, the communist dictator Matyas Rakosi asked the widely respected poet Gyula Illyes to write a new anthem, but that request was effectively sidestepped by the author.

32. In the evening of October 23, 1956, Radio Budapest reported that 50,000 people were singing the national anthem near the statue of General Jozef Bem, a Pole, who fought as a senior commander of Hungarian forces in the independence war of 1848–49.

33. See, for instance, the articles on Kölcsey's role in the Pozsony Diet and on his contributions to Hungarian and European culture in *Magyar Nemzet* of September 10, 1990, and January 22, 1991, respectively.

9

Greece

Hymnos eis ten Eleutherian
(Dionysios Solomos)

Less than six months after Kölcsey's creation of his *Himnusz*, another poem with a very similar title and destined to the same role as a national anthem was created in Greek. The respective authors probably never heard of one another, certainly did not know the title of each other's poem, and were unaware of both similarities and dissimilarities in their two poems as well as in their lives. Yet Ferenc Kölcsey and Dionysios Solomos had more in common than just their patriotism.

They had grown to manhood without parental care and each remained a loner. Both men were deeply committed purists and moralists who wished not only to see their country independent but reformed in its political and social structure, along with a cultural revival. And both wove into their future anthems, sometimes in a striking similarity, the theme of ruthless invasion by "Osman hordes"; small wonder, since Hungary and Greece alike had at one time or another come wholly or partly under Ottoman control.

But there the similarities ended. Kölcsey entered public life, however belatedly, while Solomos would not deign to descend into the political arena. The skepticism of the Greek author did not match the pessimism of his Hungarian counterpart. Their differences showed most clearly in their future anthems. Kölcsey's religious emphasis centered on Hungarian self-purification, while Solomos called for a crusade of occidental powers against the Moslem "infidels." Above all, however, his stanzas breathed fire and raised the sword together with the cross.

If war was the activator of several of the anthems presented here, then the *Hymnos eis ten Eleutherian* (Hymn to Liberty) proved no exception. The Greek war of liberation from Ottoman rule—or misrule—had begun in March 1821. To all appearances, the struggle which was to last for nearly a decade constituted but another phase in the nineteenth-century drive of Europeans and Latin Americans toward national self-determination.

On three main points, however, the war of the Greeks differed from other liberation wars of that era: the severity of domestic rivalries, the perfervid passions of a religious conflict, and the extent of outside support for the struggling Greeks. Their cause had rapidly gained the enthusiastic backing of Western intellectuals and humanitarians, though not necessarily that of governments. Philhellenic groups were formed in many European countries and in the United States. Their inspiration and dedication were symbolized, perhaps even immortalized by George Gordon Lord Byron. Support for the Greek uprising came in many forms: contributions and subsidies, rallies and resolutions, advisors and volunteers, an undersupply of good weapons and an overflow of rhetoric. Not least in importance, however, was the poetry composed either by foreigners or collected by them from Greek verse.[1] Probably no other liberation effort in nineteenth-century Europe enjoyed such volume of lyrical output as did that of the Greeks.

They were widely regarded as the noble offspring of the founders of occidental civilization. The daring struggle now being waged in a border area between Occident and Orient was viewed by many Philhellenes as a fundamental cultural conflict between two worlds, and Greek leaders of the rising were not slow to capitalize on the achievements of classical Greece.

Something of a crusading spirit along with the remembrance of an inspiring past motivated not only the Philhellenes but also many of the Greek fighters. Fighting the "infidel" acquired the nature of a holy war. The latter did not lack in either ferocity or heroism; nor did it lack in high drama ranging from wholesale massacres in conquered towns or islands to daring raids by Greek fireships on Ottoman navy vessels or by small bands of intrepid irregulars on strong Ottoman fortifications.

What the Greek insurgents lacked most was cooperation and coordination. Distrust and disagreements among leaders or competing groups hampered their effort and at times it appeared as if they were more intent on fighting each other to the bitter end rather than putting an end to Ottoman rule. Nevertheless, the insurgents scored some noteworthy victories in the early stages of the war.[2]

But the Ottoman Turks and their Albanian, Algerian, and Egyptian allies were far from beaten, and the Sultan's government showed no intentions of surrendering the Greek mainland or islands still under its control. By 1823, the war had dragged on in a bewildering sequence of successes and defeats for either side, mainly incurred in local actions.

In May of that year, a young poet on the Ionian island of Zante made his first contribution to the embattled cause of Greece. Within a month, according to his principal biographers, he created a poem of Homerian sweep. It ran to one hundred fifty-eight quatrains. Had he known that his first major creation would become—by a curious concatenation of events—the Greek national anthem, he might have shortened it.[3]

But he had cast his *Hymnos* for a different purpose. Now that the war of liberation had entered its third year, with the outcome much in doubt, Solomos desired to hold up a vast mirror for the Greeks to see themselves in both timeless glory and just as timeless shortcomings. There was much to glorify in hard-won victories or hard-to-bear sufferings but also much to reproach: his fellow Greeks for their fratricidal strife and foreign governments for their inadequate support.

Solomos painstakingly crafted his verses in trochaic tetrameter whose long-short, long-short sequence of syllables gave the stanzas a marching rhythm conducive to rallying the Greeks to still greater sacrifices and acts of heroism. And the first stanzas sounded unequivocally the keynote of national resolve and resurrection.

> I know thee by the trenchant gleaming
> Radiant from thy battle sword,
> I know thee by that eye whose beaming
> Rules the earth as victor Lord.
>
> Sprung from hero bones that scattered
> Hallow every Grecian vale,
> With thy pristine soul unshattered
> Spirit of Freedom Hail all Hail!
>
> Buried in them thou didst languish
> Lost in shame and woe and fear,
> Waiting till to end thine anguish
> "Come to me" should greet thine ear.[4]

The next dozen stanzas depicted Liberty in search of help as she was hunted and shunted relentlessly while in flight, her garment stained by the blood of the enslaved Greeks and her eyes filled with tears. Bereft of her presence, the Greek people suffered grievously as they were made to bear the chains of oppression.

But lo! Stanza fifteen marked a turning point. The sons of Greece stood ready to battle, resolved to live as victors or to die in combat. And almost forty stanzas rhapsodized Greek triumphs, including the repulse of the first Ottoman siege of Missolonghi during Christmas 1822. These glorifying and edifying accounts were interspersed with reminders of Greece's heroic past such as the Spartans' stand at Thermopylae. Solomos' combative imagery reached its climax in verses such as

> I hear the musket's rolling clatter
> I hear the clash of sword and sheath
> The axe and club, the thud and spatter

I hear the grinding gnash of teeth.
Streams of lightning, groans of thunder,
Bursting through the midnight fogs,
Show the gates of Hell asunder
Waiting for the Othman dogs.[5]

If he praised his countrymen for conspicuous valor, he did not hesitate to
lambaste them for their equally conspicuous infighting. Nor was he any more
chary in his characterizations of Austria, its heraldic eagle's talons "crimsoned
in the blood of Italy,"[6] or of the British lion who "growls the utterance of his
wrath" when checked by Russia, archenemy of the Turks. By contrast, "the
land of George Washington" was lauded for the "bonds broken" and the "freedom she has won." In the final stanzas, Solomos once more turned attention to
foreign countries whose help he implored. Playing up the religious aspects of
the Christian-Moslem conflict, he asked rhetorically how Christian rulers could
fail to come to the help of those who fought for Christianity and liberty, and
he ended his magisterial poem with a beseeching appeal:

If this counsel you have taken
See before you stands the Cross,
Strike, ye monarchs, waken, waken,
Strike and rescue us from loss.[7]

The *Hymnos* thus completed had an extraordinary range of covering historic
and current events, along with emotional outpourings, lyrical interpolations, political exhortations, and religious appeals. To write such a monumental piece
within a single month is a baffling achievement. It becomes even more so if
consideration is given to the linguistic difficulties facing the author. A modern
literary medium still had to be developed, a task also faced by some other
anthem authors. What made that task unique for Solomos was that his own
medium of artistic expression and innermost thought initially happened to be
Italian.

Apparently, that factor did not hinder him in expressing Greek sentiments. In
1822 the statesman and historian Spyridon Trikoupis, who was to have a marked
influence on Solomos' Hellenization, remarked after their first meeting: "With
the few Greek words known to him he could express ideas . . . conceived in
Italian."[8] And Trikoupis forthwith undertook to teach the young poet Greek.

A year later Solomos had mastered poetic Greek sufficiently to accomodate
"an overflow of the soul" and to serve simultaneously "the cultivation of the
tongue."[9] These two motivations underlay the creation of the *Hymnos*. To give
voice to his own creative drive and to do so in the language of the Greek people
remained of equal importance to him.

For that purpose, he chose to write in the demotic style, the new literary
Greek. Classical or Attic Greek had been used for centuries by the educated

strata of the Greeks but proved less acceptable during the Enlightenment of the later eighteenth century. As a compromise, the *Katharevousa* was developed and found acceptance among the Greek Orthodox Church and many men of letters.

Solomos, however, disliked that artificial creation and insisted on making the *Demotiki* into a competitive and popular alternative. As yet, the only demotic literature was contained in the songs of the *Klepths*, the fighting outlaws in the Greek parts of the Ottoman empire. Using their speech and folklore, Solomos determined to integrate both with the existing vernacular and to blend them all into a popular language of literary quality.

But there were also other influences that shaped his writing skills and his conceptual creativeness. Among the most profound artistic and intellectual influences in his adolescence had been that of Dante Alighieri, who had achieved a national literary tongue.[10] One other great poet of much more recent vintage had a similar impact on the young Solomos.

Lord Byron's all-too-brief appearance on the Greek scene had a specific effect on the fledgling poet. Solomos used Byronesque concepts and flourishes, although the extent of Byron's influence on the *Hymnos* and other writings has been subject to scholarly debate.[11] Composition of the *Hymnos*, however, was certainly affected by the *Marseillaise* and by *Thourios*, the "War Song," fashioned after the French model by the Greek patriot Reghas Pheraios, who had also provided a translation of the French anthem. Solomos' stanzas, in turn, gained quick acknowledgment. His mentor Trikoupis exclaimed, "In no other country has liberty found such a worthy singer."[12] And a contemporary Greek poet exulted, "The dithyramb of Solomos flew like lightning to the comrades in Greece. In every mouth there were his patriotic phrases which fanned the flames in every heart."[13]

Such sweeping encomia doubtless require some modification. For one thing, the *Hymnos* lacked the principal means of rapid popularization, since it was not set to music for over two decades; for another, the Greek reading public was limited to a very small part of the population. A few lines or even some stanzas may well have been transmitted by word of mouth, but the young author remained largely unknown to his fellow Greeks until much later in the nineteenth century.

By contrast, the *Hymnos* acquired instant publicity elsewhere in Europe. The first extant edition, published in 1825, carried the Greek text on one page and an Italian translation on the opposite page. In the same year, Solomos' lyric was published in London and Paris, the logical consequence of popular Philhellenic sentiment. Copies reached such literary luminaries as Chateaubriand, Goethe, and Manzoni. Lord George Canning, who supported the Greek cause first as foreign secretary and then as prime minister, reportedly read the whole work and quoted from it.

Closer to home, Solomos' first major creation in Greek increased his reputation on the island of Zante, the *Zakynthos* of Homer's *Iliad* and *Odyssey*. He was born in the small island's capital by the same name in April 1798. Count Nicholas Solomos, father of the newborn and a rich tobacco trader, dated his title of nobility back a mere decade but then most of his fellow aristocrats on Zante had similar background to that of "Old Tobacco."

Dionysios' mother had a rather different lineage. Angelica Nikli had been taken into the count's house as a servant girl. Barely sixteen years old, she had but two negotiable assets: her looks and her age, and she was not slow in utilizing either to her advantage. Count Nicholas soon took a fancy to her, notwithstanding the presence of Countess Marnetta, his wife of many years and the mother of their six children. The results of that fancy showed—and not for the last time—in due course. Angelica gave birth to the count's son who was baptized Dionysios on June 8, 1798.

Zantiote interests, however, focused on other events. The previous August, French troops had landed on several of the Ionian islands and brought with them revolutionary ideas and institutions. All were welcomed by the peasantry and the few professional people but generally resented by the privileged aristocracy. The brief occupation or liberation by the French, depending on one's perspective, ended within one year. To the relief of the local aristocrats the *sansculottes,* with their long pants and dangerous slogans, were chased away by a Russian-Turkish naval force. Better still, the new interventionists permitted the establishment of an autonomous Heptanese—the seven Ionian islands—to be taxed by the Ottoman and protected by the Russian government.

In 1807, however, the French returned to incorporate the islands into the ever-expanding Napoleonic empire. But within two years they were ousted anew; this time by ships of the Royal Navy. British control, based on naval supremacy, was to endure for over half a century. Diplomatically, that control was secured under provisions of the Vienna peace settlement of 1814-1815. The United States of the Ionian islands were proclaimed a maritime republic under the protection of Great Britain.

Dionysios Solomos paid little attention to the kaleidoscopic changes in authority over the islands. There were far more pressing and tangible changes in his own life and that of the family. His father had passed away after having fathered another son by Angelica. Fortunately for his mistress and their sons he had legalized them all by marrying her on his deathbed, Countess Marnetta having died five years earlier in 1802.

Dionysios' inborn sensitivities were sharpened by the lack of parental care, his mother showing little interest in him. A guardian of the fatherless children and of the large estate assumed legal responsibilities and appointed an Italian theologian as tutor for Dionysios.[14] When that tutor returned to Italy in 1808 he took his ward with him.

Even though the Heptanese had been proclaimed an autonomous republic with its own constitution, legislature, and courts, reality proved different. The first Lord High Commissioner, Sir Thomas Maitland, governed autocratically and treated the islanders much like colonials in other British possessions. In February

1821, the leading Heptanese citizens petitioned King George IV for relief from "King Tom's" high-handed rule. Solomos affixed his signature to that petition, which the London authorities did not take lightly. They ordered the imprisonment of many of the petitioners, although Solomos was not among those detained.

He nevertheless remained critical of British policies. His animosity sharpened with the outbreak of the Greek war of liberation, since neither the London government nor the Heptanese administration endeared itself to the islanders by a policy of strict neutrality. There were even shooting incidents when British soldiers fired on a Zantian crowd about to lynch some Moslem sailors in October 1821.[15]

Anglophobe sentiments found expression in Solomos' first draft of the *Hymnos* but were later excised upon the urgings of such Philhellenes in the Heptanese as Lord Frederick Guilford, ultimately a close friend of Solomos who dedicated a poem to him. But the British Philhellene to become the subject of a long, admiring ode by the Zantian author was Lord Byron. His untimely death from swamp fever at Missolonghi in April 1824 shook Solomos as much as any of Byron's many admirers. He had just sent the most famous of all foreigners fighting for the cause of Greece a copy of the *Hymnos*. Upon learning from Trikoupis, who had hand carried the copy, that the intended recipient had died before he could reach him, Solomos broke into tears.

Within days he began to compose a major poem, designed not only to honor the fallen champion of Greek freedom but also to admonish the Greeks to live up to his example. The *Lyrical Poem on the Death of Lord Byron* exceeded the *Hymnos* in length but amounted to little more than a recapitulation of its main themes, apart from the praise of the Byronic example. But that praise along with the rest of the one hundred and sixty-six stanzas did not reach the public until 1857, the year that Solomos died. The perfectionist author never seemed quite satisfied with his work, the main reason for leaving much of it unfinished.

If his grandiose epic and prose projects were slowed down, if not halted altogether, by his laborious and didactic approach, this was fortunately not the case with his epigrams. In 1825, he finished his renowned *To Psara*. That small Aegean island which had furnished to the Greek cause some of the best sailors and their fireships had been laid waste by a Turkish naval force. Solomos caught both the sense of devastation and the spirit of heroism in a finely polished prism of six reflective lines:

On Psara's desolate, blackened stone
Glory silently walks, all alone
Meditating her sons noble deeds,
And wears a wreath on her hair
Made of such few and scattered weeds
On the desolate earth left to spare.[16]

The ongoing war would offer plenty of other opportunities to put reflective poetry into a national frame. In January 1826, Ottoman forces under the effective leadership of Ibrahim Pasha, oldest son of the powerful Egyptian viceroy Mehmet Ali, laid siege for a second time to Missolonghi. The strategic port where Byron had breathed his last a couple of years earlier was heroically defended. But after an abortive sortie of the starving defenders, the town fell to the Ottomans on April 24, 1826. Only three buildings were left standing, and most of the remaining population were slaughtered.

During that siege the hypersensitive Solomos could be observed leaving his comfortable and secure residence on the Akrotiri slopes just outside the town of Zante. The siege guns pounding Missolonghi, a dozen miles northeast at the entrance to the Gulf of Corinth, could be clearly heard. The poet stood with his arms raised while he exclaimed, "Hold out, poor Missolonghi, hold out."[17] Then, according to his manservant, he turned back toward the house with tears in his eyes.

It was this second siege of Missolonghi that moved Solomos to envisage a new epic. He intended to develop it into his magnum opus; instead it remained, like much of his major work, a fragment. What really mattered to him was the concept rather than the completion of a literary piece, the meaning rather than the message. As he himself put it unequivocally, "You must think profoundly about . . . the Idea before realizing the Composition."[18]

The Free Besieged, as he finally titled this grandly conceived project, was not merely about Greeks engaged in a life-and-death struggle marked by both endurance and valor. They countered deprivation, desolation, and decimation in an exemplary mood of sacrifice and self-denial. In so doing they rose above themselves, their surroundings, and even time. Thus, they became symbols of humanity's striving for enhancement, the triumph of the spiritual over the physical, the metamorphosis from the specific to the universal.

Such lofty interpretation of a desperate, down-to-earth, and no-holds-barred struggle Solomos could present only from the sidelines of a bloody arena. In the sanctuary of a British protectorate and as a British subject, he could afford to disengage from grim realities. Fortunately, relations between British authorities and the Heptanese elite had steadily improved since 1825, when the London government had shifted from a strict neutrality in the Greek-Ottoman conflict to diplomatic flexibility which benefitted the Greeks.

Lord George Canning consistently favored an autonomous and, more recently, even an independent Greece. Progress toward that goal was slowed by rivalry and, worse, suspicion among the major powers most directly interested: Great Britain, France, and Russia. Not until July 1827 did these powers agree on common steps to halt the fighting and to ensure Greek self-government. Joint intervention, as provided for by the Treaty of London, took place when the sultan refused to endorse an armistice. In October 1827, the last major naval battle in the age of sail ended in the destruction of the Ottoman fleet sheltering in Navarino bay at the western coast of the Peleponnesus.

Greek hopes for allied intervention had finally come true. Solomos, like many of his peers, began to view the British as allies. In December 1828, he moved to Corfu, home of the newly founded Ionian Academy and of the Heptanese central administration. Several reasons underlay his decision. Corfu's intellectual life attracted him while the narrow-minded materialism of most Zantiote society repelled him to the same degree. Above all, he chafed at the conduct of his own family. Feuds had become frequent, not least over property. Moving to Corfu, it was hoped, would leave the family quarrels behind. More agreeable still, he was feted and even lionized by the Corfiotes, especially their ladies, as the herald of Greek literary and intellectual revival. Best of all, he found acceptance among high British officials and even became a welcome visitor at the governor's residence.

His literary productivity, however, slowed down. As always, he projected and revised rather than created and completed. A monumental epic, *Lambros*, which he had contemplated for a decade, finally began to take shape. Not that it would ever be finished, with all its bizarrre twists and turns of murder, incest, self-sacrifice, and suicide. Solomos was the first one to acknowledge and accept that incompleteness. As he proudly explained, the project would remain unfinished "because the poem as a whole cannot match the sublimity of its parts."[19]

He had just readied for publication the first fifteen stanzas when misfortune struck in 1833. Disagreeable and soon highly disturbing family affairs had caught up with him. His mother's favorite son, perhaps on her urgings, had arrogated to himself the Solomos name without as much as a by-your-leave, calling himself Count Leontarakis-Solomos.[20] Dionysios Solomos, probably because of his own mixed parentage, was especially sensitive—not to say fastidious—when it came to the use of his aristocratic title and name.

He was shocked by Leontarakis' dubious claim, since he had generously contributed to the education of the litigant in Italy. But what affected Solomos most was the conduct of his mother who, for reasons best known to herself but not difficult to guess, supported the claimant. His lawsuit dragged on for half a decade until the supreme court of the Ionian islands finally dismissed the claim. Meanwhile, the high-strung poet had recourse to both solitude and drink, neither of these antidotes altogether new to him.[21]

His literary interests centered on large projects which remained just that. The Greco-Ottoman conflict furnished the background for several of them, although the war of liberation had ended with limited success for the insurgent Greeks by 1829.[22] After a couple of years an autonomous Greek state was given nominal independence and even a king by the grace of the protective powers. Solomos did not object to either; his overriding concern focused on corruption and division within the small kingdom. As if to compensate for the perceived flaws of a liberated if truncated Greece, he emphasized his attachment to the Heptanese with its well-regulated social and political order. Moreover, the traditional disdain shown by members of the Ionian intelligentsia for the assumed lower cultural level of mainland Greeks influenced the elitist Solomos. His own value scale as an aesthete, moralizer, and idealist added a touch of personal idiosyncracy. When he was urged in the early 1830s to visit at long last the liberated mainland, he declined with a laconic "I am afraid."[23]

That fear had first been expressed in the *Hymnos,* where he had warned against "Disunion and her wily offers" and "if a mutual hate they cherish, Liberty befits them not."[24] In the decade since, those admonitions had clearly failed and his refusal to visit the new kingdom hardened. He wanted no part of it. His visionary Greece was the noble embodiment of the Platonic ideal and of the Hellenist spirit.

Painfully aware of the dichotomy between the Hellenic Greece of his visions and the unpromising existence of the small kingdom of Greece, he remained unsure of the desirability of *enosis,* the union of the islands with the mainland. At best that union in his view was "difficult and premature"[25] and should be postponed until conditions on the mainland were more in line with his high level of expectation. In 1842 he commented bitterly, "What can I say of the present state of Greece? Corruption is so universal, its roots so deep that one can feel nothing but amazement. Only when those responsible are deracinated can a moral renaissance ensue. Only then can our Future be great."[26]

Turning his back to the country that was to make his *Hymnos* the national anthem, he immersed himself in Ionian culture with its British overlay. They provided him with poetic stimuli quite different from those of his patriotic poems. Some of his most beautiful verses related to British youths of both sexes whose looks and bearing he admired.[27]

But such admiration did not necessarily endear him to his Greek countrymen. They wondered why he stood aloof, and his didactic aloofness showed never more strongly than in his statement: "The Nation must learn to consider National whatever is True."[28] Truth like beauty or liberty remained spiritual absolutes in his Platonist mind.

Yet the patriotic ardor first fully expressed in the *Hymnos* did not leave him in later decades, nor did he have reason to disown it at any time. In 1849, King Othon bestowed the Gold Cross of the Knights of the Savior on the flattered poet. The high award was made because of "the Greek sentiments expressed . . . at the time of our country's struggle for independence."[29] Even though the German-born king probably had little knowledge and less understanding of Solomos' literary work, the *Hymnos* must have been in the minds of those who drew up the citation, and the recently created musical score for the *Hymnos* had enhanced their awareness of its significance.

In 1845, Nicolaos Mantzaros, a Corfiote teacher of music and part-time composer, had provided that score. He had known Solomos since 1828 when the author had moved to Corfu. There is no ready explanation as to why the musical composition of the *Hymnos* was delayed by nearly two decades. Mantzaros' prolonged stay in Italy, from where he did not return to his native island until 1840, may have been one of the reasons for the delay; the nature of Solomos' hymn, seemingly unsuited for singing if only because of its length, another. In any event, the conventional martial score which Mantzaros supplied facilitated the popularization of the *Hymnos*.

That the author had grown out of sympathy with developments and people on the mainland evidently had not militated against the award. Moreover, Greek defiance and valor still could stimulate him to strike off a paean or two in honor of these virtues. Curiously, some of his late poems—much like his earliest ones—were written in Italian, as if he wanted to complete the cycle of his artistic life. The use of Italian notwithstanding, these poems left no doubt as to Solomos' pride in the spiritual fibre of Greek patriotism.

La Navicella Greca saluted the courage of the master of a small Greek vessel who defied the flagship of a British squadron blockading Athens.[30] *La Madre Greca* depicted a Greek mother who in spite of the family's great losses in the war of liberation raises her remaining child in the tradition of Greek valor. She takes her young son to a battlefield so that he, whose father has fallen in battle, can breathe "the smoke and powder" and become a worthy heir of heroes.

Solomos did not put down his pen forever before one last salute in Greek to a Greek insurgent leading yet another effort to shake off Ottoman control.[31] But his creative powers declined along with his health. Alcoholism caused at times irrational behavior. He retreated ever more into himself and allowed access to only a few friends, much like Rouget de Lisle of *Marseillaise* fame. And much like him, he never married, causing speculation as to his sex life—or its absence.

In early manhood he had been strongly attracted by a Greek woman of great beauty, but she had married someone else who happened to translate the *Hymnos* into Italian. The bitter experience of rejection, coupled with his aetheticism and moralism, led him to worship womanhood, like nationhood, from a distance. Solomos came to despise physical love as animalist and bridled at seeing ladies engaging in such prosaic activities as eating bread.[32] Instead, he idealized young girls, particularly "vestalic virgins" in white dresses and carrying flowers. But such idealization also caused rumors of impotence, homosexuality, or—conversely—bastard children. There was even talk of an incestuous relationship with his mother. She was not present when he died but had included him in an earlier will.

Solomos' death in February 1857 evoked expressions of public sorrow that culminated in a state funeral. The Greek parliament recessed and a period of official mourning was decreed in both the Ionian islands and in the kingdom of Greece that he had consistently refused to visit. A still greater honor followed.

Eight years after his death, the *Hymnos* was proclaimed the national anthem of Greece. There were good reasons for that choice. The stanzas had been forged in the fires of the liberation war. Its author had been a pioneer in the creation of a national literature, and his verses still struck a responsive chord, since the Greek borders of 1865 left large areas of unredeemed Greece under Ottoman rule.

But there were other compelling reasons for choosing the *Hymnos* as the national anthem. In October 1862, the thirty-year reign of King Othon had come to an abrupt end. He had become increasingly unpopular, especially among a new generation of Greek leaders, because of autocratic measures and of his failure to expand the nation's territory. And as in 1832, the "protective powers" selected another foreigner for the Greek throne.

Their choice—rather than that of the Greek people—fell upon yet another prince, this time with a Danish lineage. More importantly, the prospective king was a son-in-law of Queen Victoria. What nicer coronation present from her than the cession of the Ionian islands to the new king of the Hellenes, George I![33]

France and Russia concurred quickly and the Ionian assembly voted unanimously for *enosis* in October 1863. On June 6, 1864, King George I set foot on Corfu, at last part of his smallish kingdom. What more opportune moment to integrate the Heptanese Greeks, traditionally separate in matters cultural and social, into the Greek homeland. On a proposal from his government the new king, with little knowledge of Greek, let alone Greek literature, proclaimed the *Hymnos* to be the national anthem.

The honor thus bestowed on both author and hymn was a logical choice from the political point of view. It was also commendable in view of Solomos' pioneering contributions to modern Greek literature. But on other counts the choice seemed more questionable. The author not only had sharply criticized conditions in the homeland but consistently refused to visit there. He never risked his life for Greek victory in the liberation war. Above all, he had expressed serious reservations about *enosis*.

As in the case of several anthems, other choices could have been made and Solomos acknowledged in the *Hymnos* one unforgotten predecessor: Reghas Pheraios who had lived and died for Greek independence. His *Thourios* matched the *Hymnos* in fiery patriotism, and *Thourios* had the advantage of being short and to the point.[34] It did not acquire a melody, however, and thus could not compete at any time for the honor of becoming the national anthem. Furthermore, the poem was confiscated in 1798 with other writings of the outlawed Reghas and did not reach the public until much later. He himself was put to death by Ottoman officials in Belgrade, some fourteen days after Dionysios Solomos was baptized in Zante.

Both authors led very different lives and met very different ends. Their personalities differed just as much when judged from their pictures. Reghas looked like a hefty rural innkeeper whose fleshy face displayed both energy and shrewdness. Count Solomos, by contrast, showed the finely shaped features of an aesthete poet with his high forehead, melancholic eyes, and disdainful lips. In most non-Greek books on the evolving Greek state, Reghas is given considerably more coverage, but conventional wisdom and an unchallenged tradition in Greece places Solomos first and foremost in the Parnassus of its literary founding fathers. And he remains "the national bard."[35]

His *Hymnos*, by the same token, remained through all the vicissitudes of modern Greece, whether kingdom, republic, or dictatorship, the unquestioned expression of national identity and aspirations. As such, it has not undergone any modifications in either text or status. It was sung during the harsh years of Nazi occupation[36] and in the hardly less oppressive era of the military junta which took over the government of Greece in 1967. Toward its very end in November 1973, a student uprising, centered on the Athens Polytechnic, was suppressed with much brutality. In circumstances of great similarity with the 1956 revolution in Hungary, the Greek students, like their Budapest counterparts, had recourse to the national anthem. It was in the one case as in the other the ultimate expression of the national will. And in the Greek case, at least, the surviving students and their supporters had the satisfaction to see their country freed from the dictatorship in just over six months (July 1974).

In the two decades since, use of the *Hymnos* has been largely limited to ceremonial occasions such as the national holidays of March 25, 1821, when the banner of rebellion against Ottoman rule was first raised, and October 28, 1940, when fascist Italy launched its abortive attack on Greece only to be repulsed within a month. The *Hymnos* was heard then triumphantly; nor has its appeal lessened since that time. Both anthem and author remain much revered. Solomos' ideas and work continue to be widely discussed, not least in the daily press.[37] And while they may be little known outside Greece, they are often cited in that country. Distant and discriminating as the author was in person, fragmentary as his literary output remained, and in two different languages at that, there is hardly a Greek who cannot cite a verse or two of Solomos, let alone the first few stanzas of the *Hymnos*.

NOTES

1. Among the most important collections of Greek freedom songs are Claude Fauriel, *Les chansons greque* (Paris, 1825); Charles Brinsley Sheridan, *The Songs of Greece from the Romaic Text* (London, 1825); and Wilhelm Müller, *Griechenlieder* (Leipzig, 1844). Over one hundred poems on the Greek war of liberation were written by Philhellenes in the United States.

2. In September 1821, Greek insurgents took possession of Tripolitsa, administrative capital of the Peleponnesus, and in the following spring they stormed the acropolis of Corinth.

3. The first three stanzas are commonly regarded as the Greek national anthem. High school students are required to know up to twenty-five stanzas of the *Hymnos*.

4. The translation used here is that by Arnold Green, *Greek and What Next?: An Address—Solomos' Hymn to Liberty* (Providence: Sidney and Rider, 1884), 35.

5. Ibid., 39, stanzas 44 and 46.

6. For references to Austrian dominance in much of northern and central Italy, see the chapter on the Italian anthem. Its author used almost identical terminology in his condemnation of Austria's presence. Whether he knew Solomos' lines remains uncertain.

7. Green, 51.

8. Romilly J. H. Jenkins, *Dionysius Solomós* (Cambridge: Cambridge University Press, 1940), 55.

9. Ibid., 73–74.

10. Solomos, not coincidentally, headed his *Hymnos* by a quotation from Dante's *Divina commedia*.

11. Jenkins's assumption that the Greek author was strongly influenced by Byron has been contradicted by Byron Raizis, *Dionysios Solomos* (New York: #193 Twayne's World Authors, 1972), 103 passim. Professor Raizis' biography of Solomos remains the most concise and thorough study of the Greek poet in English. More recently, Professor Raizis had made a strong case that Shelley rather than Byron substantially influenced the *Hymnos* through his lyrical drama *Hellas*. See M. B. Raizis's essay "Shelley and Greece's National Bard," in *Proceedings of the Shelley Symposium at Salzburg University*, ed. James Hogg (Salzburg: Salzburg University, 1993).

12. Polyhymnia Lascaris, *Solomós* (Chartres: Imprimerie Durand, 1940), 12.

13. Jenkins, 67.

14. Don Santo Rossi had left his native Cremona because of his liberal views. Solomos remembered him fondly until his own death.

15. Enraged Greeks had cornered the crew of an Algerian warship and were going to kill them when the British troops intervened, with both sides suffering casualties.

16. The Solomos epigram, *To Psara*, is reprinted with slight change, in English translation by M. Byron Raizis from his book *Dionysios Solomos*, p. 91. Copyright © 1972 by Twayne Publishers, Inc. Used by permission of Twayne Publishers, an imprint of Macmillan Publishing Company.

17. Jenkins, 111.

18. Vassilis Lambropoulos, *Literature as National Institution* (Princeton: Princeton University Press, 1988), 96.

19. Raizis, 38.

20. John Leontarakis was born almost nine months after the death of Count Nicholas Solomos. His natural father probably was Emmanuel Leontarakis, a goldsmith, whom Angelika Solomos had married in August 1807, but who had been her lover for some time. She gave birth to John in October of that year.

21. Solomos developed a penchant for solitude early in life, perhaps because of the lack of parental care. Some thirty years later he wrote, "There is no doubt that one can live well only alone." Raizis, 35.

22. Two major pieces, *Lambros* and *The Cretan*, had that conflict as background.

23. Jenkins, 122.

24. From stanzas 144 and 146 in the Green translation.

25. Jenkins, 180.

26. Ibid., 177.

27. In the epigram *To Frances Fraser* he adulated the daughter of a high British official as one of his "vestal virgins." In *Porphyras* he rhapsodized a handsome British soldier, swimming naked in the moonlit Ionian Sea, only to be devoured by a monstrous shark.

28. Raizis, 61.

29. Jenkins, 179. It was not solely for such past services that Solomos was honored. When Trikoupis visited with him in 1850, he mentioned to the author "the great success of his *Hymn to Liberty*."

30. In January 1850, Lord Palmerston, then British foreign secretary, ordered a blockade of the port of Piraeus. Greek authorities had failed to heed a request for compensation due to Don Pacifico, a British subject of Jewish religion and Maltese origins. His house

in Athens had been sacked by an antisemitic mob at Easter time in 1847. Palmerston defended his strong-arm action in a famous speech to the House of Commons where he argued that a British citizen, whatever the circumstances and personality, would be protected in any part of the world against "injustice and wrong" by British might.

31. In early 1854, Greek insurgents, taking advantage of the outbreak of the Crimean War, tried to wrest the Epirus region in northern Greece from Ottoman control. Their leader was Hadji-Petros to whom Solomos was going to dedicate the unfinished poem.

32. This story, probably apocryphal, has come down through the generations and still serves at present as an example of the spirituality of Solomos.

33. That title was agreed to by the king-elect and the protective powers as indicative of future Hellenic kings to be suzerains of all Greeks including those in the diaspora, mainly under Ottoman rule.

34. Its most evocative lines ran as follows: "How long, my Braves, shall we live in bondage . . . ? Better an hour to live free than forty years of servitude and imprisonment." A complete translation of the seven stanzas may be found in Ap. Dascalakis, *Les oeuvres de Rhigas Velestinlis* (Paris: Université de Paris, 1937), 188–89. The lines quoted here are from a partial translation by C. M. Woodhouse, *The Greek War of Independence* (London: Hutchinson's University Library, 1952), 40.

35. This epitaph has been used repeatedly by Professor Raizis not only as a mark of respect for the author, but as an acknowledgement of his place in Greek literature.

36. The *Hymnos* was struck up by large crowds when German troops entered Athens on June 1, 1941. It was again heard at the funeral of the popular poet Kostis Palamas in February 1943, this time not in protest but in reverence.

37. On the continued popularity of Solomos, see Linos Politis, *Around Solomos: Studies and Articles, 1938–1982* (Athens: Educational Branch of National Bank, 1985), 58–61 (title and text are in Greek). In January and February 1989, the important newspaper *Kathimerini*, for instance, carried several articles on Solomos' ideology and philosophy.

10

Belgium

La Brabançonne
(A. Dechet [Jenneval], C. Rogier, and R. Herreman)

In 1830, the year when the Belgian state was proclaimed, no less an experienced practitioner of foreign affairs than Prince Talleyrand observed that "there are no Belgians; there never have been, there never will be: there are Frenchmen, Flemings or Dutch (which is the same thing) and Germans."[1] Such caustic comment may be ascribed to the ulterior motives of French policymakers looking toward possible annexation of Belgian territory. But some eighty years later, a prominent Belgian deputy and future government minister outdid Talleyrand by an even more definitive, if less suspect, statement. Jules Destrée wrote, in a widely quoted *Letter to the King*: "Sire, there are no such people as Belgians; there are only Flemings and Walloons."[2]

These pronouncements might make one wonder whether such an uncertain nationhood required a national anthem and, if so, what its chances for survival might be. In fact, no fewer than three official Brabançonnes have followed one another, not to mention a plethora of unofficial ones. Bifurcated from its very inception as a state along ethnic and linguistic lines, the motto of the new state nevertheless affirmed that "union makes strength." And nothing characterized that union better than the title *La Brabançonne*,[3] a title that has remained unchanged throughout the transformation of Belgium from a centralized into a regionalized state.

That state emerged from the wave of national turbulence which swept Europe in 1830-31. In late August 1830, a feverish atmosphere of excitement and unrest prevailed in Brussels. The shock effect of the July revolution in neighboring

France made itself felt, and each successive day heightened tensions as well as expectations. Even a timetable in handwritten form had been posted at a few strategic places. If it was unofficial it gave, nevertheless, an accurate listing of forthcoming events: Monday, fireworks; Tuesday, illumination of the city; Wednesday, revolution.[4]

The fireworks scheduled in honor of the Dutch king's birthday, however, were cancelled on August 25 for fear of demonstrations, although the official explanation was possible rain. King William I was not overly popular in his southern provinces. In all eight of them, whether Flemish or Walloon, there existed resentment over the forcible union with the nine northern provinces. That union, resembling a shotgun marriage, had been consecrated by the peacemakers at Vienna as the kingdom of the Netherlands in 1815. Its newly elevated king, godfather and bridegroom at the same time, found himself in a rather uncomfortable position when trying to hold together the heterogeneous family members.

Their interests were as different as their history. The northern provinces relied, in matters economic, mainly on commerce and agriculture; those in the south, especially in the Walloon region, on a fledgling industry. The seafaring Dutch had built a large overseas empire while the almost landlocked Belgians at that time had no colonies. No less significant were the differences in matters religious: the Dutch were overwhelmingly Protestant and the Belgians almost exclusively Roman Catholic.

King William I had left unruly Brussels in mid-August 1830 determined to maintain the troubled union, whatever the costs. But as a gesture of goodwill, upon his departure he had ordered the restaging of Daniel Auber's opera *The Mute of Portici*. First performed in Brussels earlier that summer, the opera had inspired some demonstrative applause, primarily because of its revolutionary scenario. To avoid a repetition of such demonstrations the government simply had closed down the theater for the duration of the royal visit. Now that the king had returned to The Hague, a repeat performance could be chanced.

On the evening of the cancelled fireworks the *Théâtre de la Monnaie* was filled to capacity. Soon after the acclaimed tenor Jean François Lafeuillade had launched into the aria "Better dead than to remain miserable, break the yoke that weighs us down," thunderous applause erupted. It rose to a crescendo when he declaimed in the grand finale, "Sacred love of the homeland. Give us audacity and pride. To my country I owe my life. It owes me liberty."[5]

Not only members of the audience joined in but the resounding rendition echoed from a crowd assembled on the square. There cries denounced such hated personalities as the authoritarian minister of justice, the chief of police, and a newspaper editor in Dutch pay. Like burning oil, the agitated crowd spread menacingly toward their domiciles and set them on fire, the owners having fled.

Revolution was in the air. The next morning, pillaging took place in factories and shops; machinery was destroyed by dissatisfied workmen. The anti-Dutch rioting expanded into disorders of a socioeconomic character. A citizens' guard was formed to protect property and ensure order. But that guard also gave to the Brussels citizenry its first armed force to challenge Dutch dominance.

Among the proud volunteers was a bespectacled young man of serious mien who looked more like a scholar than a soldier. He may well have been present at the theatre demonstrations two nights before. As an actor of some renown he had free access to the *Théâtre de la Monnaie* where he had performed since 1828, mainly in tragic roles. He had come to Brussels that year from his native France. But now that the discredited Bourbon dynasty had been ousted there, he expected to return to Paris to perform at the *Théâtre National.*

The ultimate professional aim of Louis Hippolyte Alexandre Dechet was to be both an actor and a poet.[6] He had begun a stage career when barely twenty-one years old in Ajaccio, birthplace of Napoleon I. Since that profession scarcely pleased the family—his parents having intended him for the law—Dechet assumed a new identity as Alexandre Jenneval. Under that name he had attained a measure of recognition for his stage work, though not for his poetry, which was laced with references to liberty, brotherhood, and tyrannicide. His *Le Réveil du Coq* carried as its refrain, "The cock awakens, announcing the dawn. Do you hear its call for liberty?"[7]

Yet, in late August 1830, most of the people in the southern provinces were either hesitant about or opposed to breaking with the Netherlands. Perhaps the king would realize that the demands of his still loyal Belgian subjects were justified and would grant remedies. A petition to him asked for redress of major grievances: equality for Belgians and Dutch in appointments to high civilian and military positions, proportionate representation in parliament according to size of population in north and south,[8] the official use of French, freedom in religious instruction, and jury trial. In case of a royal refusal, however, the citizenry had to stand ready to defend their interests by force, if necessary.

Such views found spontaneous and suitable expression by one of the most literate members of the newly established citizens guard. Jenneval's emotions quickly shaped themselves into four stanzas. The first of these mirrored the hopes as well as the uncertainties of the patriots.

> Yes, worthy children of Belgium
> What a beautiful rapture has overcome us;
> To our patriotic impulses
> Great success shall be granted.
> Remain armed so that nothing will interfere.
> Preserve your spirit unchanged
> And you shall see the Orange bloom
> Upon the tree of liberty.[9]

Oddly, the second stanza rejoiced at the curbing of the rioters in Brussels "now cleansed of that insult which dishonored our city." But then the young poet-actor was a member of the guard which had been formed for the purpose of maintaining order and protecting property. The last two stanzas once more turned to the uncertain relationship with the Dutch ruler. If he granted his Belgian subjects their rights he would remain for them "the father" and "a model king." But if he pointed "the murderous canon at us . . . all would change" and "you shall see the Orange fall from the tree of liberty." These final lines, with their clever allegory linking the Orange-Nassau dynasty for good or ill with the tree of liberty, served as an effective refrain for all the stanzas.

Within ten days the patriots' hopes for Dutch concessions had sharply diminished. The Belgian delegation to plead with the Dutch king had returned empty-handed from The Hague. Worse, King William had ordered a substantial force under the command of his oldest son to restore Dutch authority in Brussels. But rather than forcing the issue, the crown prince preferred to enter the unruly city with only a small escort. What he saw there was not reassuring: barricades had been set up in some streets; groups of people seemed either sullen or agitated; the black-red-yellow colors of Brabant rather than the red-white-blue flag of the kingdom of the Netherlands fluttered from many a building. Worse still, solitary cries of "Vive le prince" were soon drowned out in a swelling chorus of "Vive la liberté." Even the strains of the *Marseillaise* could be heard in the distance.

After hurried talks with local dignitaries, the well-intentioned prince decided to present the critical situation to his father and encourage mediation. While the Dutch government stalled, activities in the south accelerated. On September 7, 1830, the nationalist *Courrier des Pays Bas* printed the *Brabançonne* for the first time in a slightly changed version. The first and second stanzas were now reversed. The "worthy children of Belgium" became "the proud children." There was, most importantly, no longer any reference to "their patriotic élan" or to "their determined courage," as Jenneval fully identified with his Belgian hosts and compatriots by writing "our élan" and "our courage." And now the "murderous Dutch cannon" did not merely point at the patriots but stood ready to fire.

Appropriately, this second version of the *Brabançonne* was also provided with a home-grown melody. Up to now it had been sung to the popular but borrowed tune of the *Lanciers Polonais*.[10] The composer François Van Campenhout, a Bruxellois by birth, gave the verses a national tune, changed little to the present day. The fast-paced melody with its allegro rhythm had drawn, consciously or inadvertently, on the *Marseillaise*,[11] a contributing factor to the immediate popularity of the *Brabançonne*. It was first aired with great effect by the tenor Lafeuillade on September 12, 1830, but Jenneval's creation had yet to reach its chrysalis.

The ongoing crisis in Belgian-Dutch relations intensified throughout September. In mid-month new riots occurred, and a committee of public safety was organized in Brussels to coordinate activities, including an anticipated secession. Clashes with Dutch troops took place in Liège, the most revolutionary-minded Belgian city, and elsewhere. In the disaffected towns the rousing tune most often heard was no longer the *Marseillaise*, as in August, but the new national song: the *Brabançonne*.[12]

If a majority of the population in the southern provinces, with significant exceptions in the Flemish ones, now favored separation, the king assuredly did not. At the opening session of parliament, the States-General, a stubborn William declared that he would not yield to "rioters." And as an earnest of his determination to preserve the union, he ordered his two oldest sons and their troops to march south once more.

This time around their presence was to be no mere show of force. Workers had rioted anew in Brussels where radicalized masses seemed in control. They had seized city hall on September 20 and dislodged the remaining authorities, including the civic guard and the committee of public safety. Political chaos prevailed. Social cleavages and confrontations rather than national interests reasserted themselves. The approach of the Dutch troops reassured many an uneasy member of the propertied classes. By contrast, some of the most determined radical patriots saw the moment as opportune to leave the city in the nick of time.

Many more among them, however, dug in behind hastily erected barricades. The majority belonged to the working class, though their leaders had professional or managerial background. Veterans from the Napoleonic wars leavened the civilian defenders with some military experience. All of them eagerly stood together in the attempt to ward off the restoration of Dutch power and control.

Dutch forces entered the city from various gates in the early morning of September 23 and gradually advanced toward its center, where the heaviest fighting raged around the main park. It was there that an enthusiastic Jenneval, armed with a carbine, saw action for the first time, and it was there that new verses came to his agitated mind.

The last chance for compromise between the Dutch monarch and his Belgian subjects melted away in the continuous firing. Only force could now decide whether the outcome would be subjugation or separation. For three days that outcome hung in the balance. But as September 26 dawned, the weary Belgian combatants in the park, to their surprise, sighted no Dutch soldiers. The king's troops had quietly withdrawn during the night. Jubilation soon became rampant among the defenders, and within twenty-four hours Jenneval poured his feelings into a third version of the *Brabançonne*.

It responded to the new situation like a sail catching a favorable wind, its artless simplicity and naïveté befitting more an exuberant freedom fighter than an accomplished poet. That naïveté found expression in the opening line, "Who would have believed it?" Jenneval, however, did not refer to the unexpected Dutch withdrawal from Brussels but to "the despot authorizing dreadful plans." And for good measure he added that the Nassau dynasty could no longer be negotiated with, let alone be trusted. Endowing his earlier allegory with a new punch line he exulted "The gun has smashed the Orange/From the tree of liberty." That simplistic if catchy wordplay served, with slight variations, as a triumphant refrain. But it was not only the Dutch dynasty that was denigrated. In the mind of such Belgian volunteers as Jenneval, the ongoing struggle involved two nations. His third stanza posited their conflict clearly by lauding "proud Brabanters, people of valor, whose bullets shall free them from the shameful rule of the Batavians." And the final stanza paid effusive homage to the fallen martyrs "sleeping in peace, far from the Orange, under the tree of liberty."[13]

This version of the *Brabançonne* differed from its two predecessors mainly in the awareness that the break between the northern and southern provinces was complete, perhaps irrevocable. The sharpened anti-Dutch theme could not fail to engross much of the Belgian public at this moment of truth. Campenhout, the composer of the martial melody and probably a better tenor than musician, took it upon himself to render the *Brabançonne* nightly to the acclaim of the throng gathered at the *Aigle d'Or* coffeehouse.

But there was no way of knowing whether this latest version would be the final one. What if the Dutch were to reconquer the Belgian capital? After all, the king's troops were far from being swept out of the country. On the contrary, they had taken up strong positions in the area around Antwerp, the key port city. Prolonged warfare loomed ahead.

In early October, Jenneval composed a quatrain for the patriots who had fallen in the crucial September days and were buried at *Place St. Michel*. They were, in his words, "plain citizens of whom one word speaks history. Fallen for liberty."[14] Little did he know how soon he would be one of them.

His influential friend Count Frédéric de Mérode, scion of one of the leading families, persuaded Jenneval to join the newly formed *Chasseurs Chasteler*, vanguard of the Belgian forces. They pressed on toward Antwerp and reached the fortified town of Lierre on October 16. The Dutch had evacuated the town but were ordered to retake it. Having failed to do so, they withdrew anew on October 18. To observe their retreat, a small group of scouts emerged from a town gate, Jenneval among them. Just as he aimed his carbine at Dutch artillery pieces in the distance, he was fatally struck by a splinter from one of their shells.

His sacrificial death accomplished what his verses alone might have failed to do. Not only did he acquire national renown, however fleeting, but his fate as "a martyr of liberty" propelled his latest version of the *Brabançonne* to anthem status. Although he was not given a state funeral—there was no Belgian state as yet in any event—he was buried with military honors in the center of Brussels.

Following his burial alongside those whose death he had glorified a mere fortnight ago, a benefit performance for the families of the dead combatants was staged. At its closing the *Brabançonne* was struck up, and the audience remained standing silently for a short while after the last notes had died away. Among the eulogies was one in verse form that ended

In his honor the song will live on
For the *Brabançonne* must live
Like our liberty.[15]

In reality the life span of Jenneval's best-known poem proved as short as his own life, barely three decades. The zenith of the anthem's popularity lay in the 1830s while anti-Dutch sentiments ran strong and Belgian independence remained precarious. When the newly elected King Leopold I, uncle of Queen Victoria, first set foot on Belgian soil, the roads along which he and his entourage travelled were crowded with "jubilant onlookers . . . the Brabant tricolore waved, and the *Brabançonne* filled the air."[16] And as the king entered his future capital, powerful fanfares sounded the tune triumphantly. The new state had a king, a constitution—the most progressive in the Europe of that time—a parliament, and an anthem.

Alas, that anthem soon lost much of its relevancy. If changing political situations had caused three versions of it within a single month, neither of the three could be expected to be timeless, and as the times changed, so of necessity did the national anthem. In 1860 a new national anthem displaced that of the half-forgotten young hero. The new *Brabançonne* differed from its predecessors in almost every respect. Only title and music remained intact like a still-serviceable old roof over a thoroughly remodelled structure.

Jenneval's combat death, ending a short life, had brought him to national attention, however ephemeral. Charles Rogier, author of the new anthem, stood in the center of that attention for much of his octogenarian life. He had been present at the creation of the Belgian state, playing a crucial role in the turbulent September days. On the day when Jenneval revised his *Brabançonne* for the first time, Rogier had led the Liège volunteers to the assistance of the Brussels patriots. Like the slightly younger Jenneval, Rogier's patriotism had been tested in battle, and like him, he had been born in France, though he was raised on Belgian soil.

There the similarities ended. While Jenneval turned to an artistic career, Rogier became a lawyer. Although he had written some youthful poetry, he soon found prose better suited to his political activism. Together with an older brother, he published the first journal of politics in the Belgian provinces. Within a few years it became the mouthpiece of opposition to Dutch domination. When that opposition burst into revolution in 1830, Charles Rogier emerged as one of its central figures. He coordinated resistance from the Brussels city hall and entered the provisional government. As an influential member of the first national parliament he voted for progressive domestic policies. In spite of his earlier republican leanings, he soon realized the need for a dynasty which could best ensure the long-term survival of an independent Belgium.

Always a realist, he voted for Prince Leopold to become king of the Belgians. The revolutionary tribune of yesterday had turned into an evolutionary statesman. He no longer coordinated militant action but instead promoted material progress. His efforts as a minister and twice as the senior cabinet member provided Belgians with the first continental railroad network, free trade benefits, secular schooling, and social aid. And he realized quickly that the well-being of his countrymen depended not only on progress at home but in equal measure on the promotion of good relations with all neighboring countries.

After all, Belgium owed its continued existence as an independent state to the concurrence of the five major European powers which had twice underwritten it.[17] And situated at the crossroads of northwest Europe its geostrategic position proved as much a liability in wartime as an asset in times of peace. External trade expansion was the corollary of internal development, but survival of the Belgian kingdom was by no means assured, even though it was nominally guaranteed. Any one of its guarantors might be tempted to violate Belgian independence. The very country which, at the dawn of that independence, had helped to secure it three decades later seemed on the verge of reneging. Imperial France under a new Napoleon vented annexationist desires.

In early 1860, the Belgian government looked for support beyond the national borders. If relations with the southern neighbor were uncertain, there was all the more reason to be certain of improved relations with the neighbor to the north. Rogier had already set in motion the complicated negotiations which would ultimately remove the last vestiges of former Dutch sovereignty by freeing the Scheldt river from tolls. Patriotism, pragmatism, and pacifism coalesced in his mind. The time had come to give expression to a new attitude among Belgians, face-to-face with a changed international situation. What better opportunity than the approaching anniversary of the accession of King Leopold I, symbol of Belgian statehood for three decades. As minister of the interior, Rogier held ultimate responsibility for the official celebrations, but he did more than just coordinate them.

His poetic inclinations and literary interests had never been entirely abandoned. Even at the height of his political involvement he had written an occasional poem. Now he determined to write a new national song for the royal celebration. No sooner was it finished when it displaced Jenneval's *Brabançonne*. Overnight, Belgium had acquired a new national anthem. Would it, in turn, survive?

The first of its four stanzas still carried with it some of the revolutionary and patriotic ardor of 1830.

> After centuries of bondage,
> Belgium, arising from its sepulchre,
> Has by its courage reconquered
> Its name, its rights, its flag.
> And your hand, sovereign and proud,
> Unconquerable people, henceforth
> Engraves upon the ancient banner
> The King, the Law, and Liberty.[18]

The second stanza triumphantly sounded the theme of progress; progress built on labor in town and country as well as in the arts. It was the third stanza, however, which differed diametrically from the earlier national anthem. Now Belgians and Dutch were called brothers; a brotherhood based on the line that "free peoples are friends." The final stanza echoed the patriotic élan of the *Marseillaise,* and such was its appeal that it alone survived to the present day as the official anthem—albeit only of French-speaking Belgium. Yet for Rogier its verses meant a trumpet call to all of his countrymen to stand together in defense of Belgium's independence and attainments:

> Oh, Belgium, oh beloved mother,
> To you our hearts; to you our arm.
> For you our blood, oh native land!
> We pledge to you our all; you shall live
> Always you shall live grandly and beautifully,
> And your invincible unity
> Will have as its motto:
> King, Law, and Liberty.[19]

Nowadays such lines may well sound maudlin and histrionic, and at least one prominent socialist has asserted that the last line, which also serves as a refrain for the whole poem, reminded him of a dog's barking, while men of letters complained about the mediocrity of the verses.[20] Yet most lines were in keeping with the spirit of the times and not uncommon among the authors of other national anthems.

What set Rogier's creation apart from many of them was the fact that it stemmed from a deliberate decision rather than from spontaneous inspiration. Immediate acceptance as national anthem must be credited to the political standing of the author, highest ranking official in the kingdom, rather than to any great literary merits. Not surprisingly, when first aired on July 21, 1860, the minister's *Nouvelle Brabançonne* gained general acclaim at a banquet honoring the king.[21]

Nor was this acclaim confined to Belgian citizens. Within a couple of days a Dutch author replied in kind and declared that "Holland has heard the song which has banished the old quarrels."[22] If Rogier's prime intent in its composition had been the displacement of an anti-Dutch anthem by one that was favorable to the Dutch and would promote good relations between the two countries, he had succeeded admirably.

But then the raison d'être of national anthems is home consumption and there the Belgian anthem soon encountered difficulties. One of these was the indisputable fact that the new words simply did not fit the old melody, a subject of much criticism. Far more weighty, however, were the ever-widening differences and rivalries between the two major ethnic population groups in the country. From about the time of the creation of Rogier's *Brabançonne,* Flemish sensitivities to Walloon cultural and political dominance were first articulated by individuals and then activated by corporate bodies. Rogier's francophone heritage and centralized administrative practices limited his understanding and even more so his sympathy for Flemish aspirations toward autonomy, not least in literary and linguistic matters. And in the eyes of some Flemish men of letters he remained Frenchified or simply "the Frenchman."[23]

Still, for a half century Rogier's *Brabançonne* remained the unchallenged if sparingly used Belgian anthem. The pragmatic Belgians did not overindulge in national effervescence. Regionalism asserted itself, ever stronger since the third quarter of the nineteenth century. It was hoped that the guaranteed neutrality of Belgium would keep the country free from attacks by its neighbors. For these reasons, Belgians tended to make little use of the national anthem. Their collective interests focused on domestic rather than on international issues.

Even in Rogier's lifetime there were few recorded occasions when his *Brabançonne* was struck up publicly. In August 1880—fiftieth anniversary of the independence struggle—he was greeted by thousands on his way to Parliament, over which he presided for that memorable event. The crowd broke into the anthem which he had re-created.[24] At the time of his death, in May 1885, there was an outpouring of encomia in Parliament and press alike. Rogier's many achievements as a founder of the state and promoter of progress for its citizens were fully recognized, but references to his composition were lacking. Obviously, it did not rank in the minds of his compatriots as a major attainment; a situation quite different from the eulogies and ceremonies upon the death of Jenneval, if only because the latter had little else to offer but the original *Brabançonne* and a patriotic death.

Rogier's revision was aired on such special occasions as the coronation of King Albert I, third of Belgium's long-lived monarchs, in 1909. On a still more crucial day a few years into his reign, the *Brabançonne* could be heard again. On August 4, 1914, the king and his family appeared in parliament where he announced the decision to resist the German invaders. All deputies rose and cheered, although detailed accounts make no reference to their breaking into the anthem. But Rogier's *Brabançonne*, much like other anthems in wartime, served as a powerful rallying cry of both defiance and pride. Nor was it sung only in the francophone part of the country, now almost wholly under German occupation. On national independence day in 1915, Antwerp citizens laid flowers at the monument of Leopold I and defiantly intoned the anthem.[25] The following year a visiting Hungarian journalist noticed that even remembrance of Jenneval had been reactivated. At his statue in Brussels, which was inscribed "Le poéte de la Brabançonne, mort pour l'independence nationale," a wreath of roses had been placed.[26]

Not all of these symbolic demonstrations of patriotism were collective in nature. In some instances the anthem served as the reassuring and ultimate identification of an individual with the country as a whole. Perhaps no more moving utilization of the *Brabançonne* may be found than that of a Belgian resistance fighter, a *franctireur*. On the eve of his execution in 1916 by a German firing squad, he wrote to his wife, "At the moment when I shall fall tomorrow morning under the German bullets you must play and sing to the children the *Brabançonne*."[27]

The anthem resounded triumphantly at the Grand Place of Brussels, along with the *Marseillaise*, with which it had so much in common, when the king and queen reentered their capital on November 21, 1918, in the wake of Germany's collapse. Alas, such moments of national jubilation were to be rare. The "knightly king" Albert shied away from public gatherings. His tragic death while rock climbing in 1934 deprived the country of celebrating the silver jubilee of his reign and numerous renditions of the *Brabançonne*. It found even less opportunity in the ill-starred reign of his son, the feckless and hapless Leopold III. There was not enough time to strike up the anthem when the Germans unleashed their Blitzkrieg in the West on May 10, 1940, and there was no king to salute when Brussels was liberated on September 3, 1945.[28]

But still weightier reasons underlay the waning role of Rogier's creation. Lack of synchronization and standardization remained formidable handicaps. In 1920, a commission was established to examine the structural faults of the anthem and all of its numerous variations, often local or regional. Two years later the findings were presented—only to point out that the best possible solution would be to return to the original stanzas of Jenneval and the original score of Campenhout! Failing that admittedly impolitic alternative, the adjustment of Rogier's verses to the unaltered Campenhout tune would be the next best thing.

Replacing the *Brabançonne* altogether was flatly ruled out by the commission. In the words of its rapporteur, the members had looked at proposals for a new anthem, but none equalled the *Brabançonne*'s capability "to rally all the hearts in a patriotic élan."[29] Such sweeping endorsement, however, did not ensure unquestioning acceptance or increased popularity. Efforts made since the early twenties to adjust the text to changing domestic conditions, including the upsurge of Flemish regionalism, came to naught. But if neither the stanzas nor the melody were readily changed, the verses of most common appeal, and thus least likely to cause objections, could be singled out. In 1926 the government ruled that only the last stanza of Rogier's *Brabançonne* would henceforth be sung on official occasions. After all, who could object to Belgium, the "beloved mother" to which hearts, arms, and blood were consecrated, to "invincible unity," and to the undying motto of "King, Law, and Liberty"?

But the survival of the *Brabançonne* depended on more than artistic harmony, textual modernity, and governmental authority. No one factor militated more against the status of the national anthem than the dualist development of the country. If, in 1847, an effusive patriotic poet could proudly declare that Fleming and Walloon were given names while Belgian was the family name, less than a hundred years later that situation was reversed. The emphasis now lay with the region rather than the nation.

As long as its public life was dominated by the francophone elite, the anthem—written in French by a French-born author—would prevail in whatever modified form. As the Flemish ethnicity movement gained strength, however, the position of that anthem was bound to be challenged. Even in the early stages of Flemish cultural revival in the mid-nineteenth century, several pieces created by its partisans were to rival Jenneval's *Brabançonne*. The deeply rooted tradition and pride of the Flemings in their municipal self-government, victorious defense against invaders, and great cultural achievements in bygone centuries almost of necessity sought regional self-expression. In not a few instances that urge was coupled with a challenge to the perceived francophone dominance.[30]

But the Flemish tongue did only gradually acquire legal equality with French. That equality was not attained until after World War I. One of the consequences of this at times painful evolution was the necessity to have an official Flemish text of the national anthem. Two versions appeared in the 1930s upon the request of such diverse ministries as those of public education and defense. Both versions were single stanzas, which ended with slight variations in the familiar Rogier refrain "for prince, liberty, and law." They stressed the traditional themes of liberty and unity, although only one specifically referred to Flemings and Walloons.

Linguistic equality, however, was but the first plateau of the long ascent to complete autonomy. A bicultural structure, once propagated by ardent francophones, now became the goal of the Flemish activists, the *Flamingants*. Its full realization had to await more propitious times than World War II. Only in the postwar era did the movement toward cultural partition gain its full momentum. It was not by happenstance that in 1954 a new Flemish poem appeared which proved acceptable as an anthem to a great majority of the Flemings.

Its author, Raymond Herreman, actually had better credentials as a poet than either Jenneval or Rogier. Herreman's poems combined earthly directness and contemplative introspection, an epicurean lust for life and a finely honed sense of human frailties, a striking simplicity coupled with deep emotions. His writings ranged widely but were always bounded by his awareness as a Fleming. And his *Brabançonne* was an outgrowth of his Flemishness.

> To you we dedicate our love and faith
> Oh, dear folk; oh, dear land.
> We shall build toward the future
> On the ancestors trust.
> Our heart is pledged to you in joy and sorrow,
> Grow and blossom to the weal of generations.
> We offer to one another a brotherly hand
> And consecrate devout thoughts
> To Liberty, Prince, and Fatherland.[31]

Herreman had created a text which was sufficiently regional without lacking a national commitment. But the only link with the French original, except for the title and the Campenhout melody, was the last line of the stanza, though "fatherland" had been substituted for "law." The two major cultural communities now had equal but separate status; symbolized as much by the Flemish lion and the Gallic cock as by two different anthems.[32] But the tribulations of the *Brabançonne* were far from ended. A commission formed in 1951 sat for seven years. It held numerous meetings, tested new proposals, commissioned textual and musical samples. Perhaps not surprisingly, its final recommendations tried to square the circle. "Since one cannot modify the *Brabançonne* without falling from one difficulty into another, it would be best to change nothing."[33]

Alas, the times had changed and so had the structure of Belgium. Neither the revised and reduced francophone stanza nor its Flemish counterpart could in the long run either jointly or even separately fill in as the national anthem. Rather than have two different renderings on official occasions such as Independence Day on July 21 or Armistice Day on November 11 or the late King Baudouin's 60th birthday, the ever-practical Belgians compromised on the highly sensitive issue. For some two decades now only Campenhout's music is being played nationwide while the words are omitted.

With the all-but-completed regionalization of the once centralized state, a vocal national anthem must be considered an oxymoron. Yet the search for a common and solemn national expression goes on. In 1985, upon a parliamentary interpellation, the premier ordered the interior ministry to study the possibilities of a "new look" for the *Brabançonne*.[34] It seems a reasonably safe prediction to make that for however long another commission may be in place, the findings would be much the same as those of its predecessors.

And why not? Regardless of all the changes, both in the state and in the numerous Brabançonnes,[35] the title, music, and last line have remained well nigh intact through almost one hundred and thirty-five years. The evolution of the Belgian anthem, with all of its variations and vicissitudes, is a true reflection of the country's evolution since the inception of the state and of the aspirations of its nationals. And the state's motto "Unity Makes Strength" might well be prefaced by "Diversity Makes Unity," as an indicator of Belgian regionalism even without a verbal, let alone uniform, rendering of its anthem.

NOTES

1. Reginald de Schryver, "The Belgian Revolution and the Emergence of Belgium's Biculturalism," in Arend Lijphart, ed., *Conflict and Coexistence in Belgium*, Research Series No. 46 (Berkeley: University of California, 1981), 14.

2. Richard Duperrieux, *Jules Destrée* ([Brussels]: Edition de "Savoir et Beautée," 1952), 41–42.

3. The title is derived from the province of Brabant, the center of the Belgian state.

4. Pryse L. Gordon, *Belgium and Holland with a Sketch of the Revolution*, 2 vols. (London: Smith, Elder & Co., 1834), 2:133.

5. Pierre Nothomb, *L'An I de l'independence*, in *Les Cahiers Historiques* (Brussels, 1969), 44.

6. His mother's statement to that effect is contained in *Notice sur Alexandre Jenneval*, which is the foreword to the only known collection of Jenneval's poetry and was published posthumously in Brussels in 1831.

7. *Études Poétiques de Jenneval [par sa mère]* (Poetic works of Jenneval) (Bruxelles: Laurent Frères, 1831), 8–10.

8. The Belgians, with over four million people in 1830, were twice as numerous as the Dutch.

9. Author's translation based on the authoritative study by Bernard Huys, "Historiek van de Brabançonne, haar editio princeps en andere vroege uitgaven," special reprint from *Academiae Analecta, Klasse der Schone Kunsten*, vol. 48, no. 1 (Brussels: Paleis der Akademiën, 1987). The three successive versions by Jenneval are reprinted there as Appendices I, II, and V.

10. This widely popular song, celebrating Napoleon's famous Polish lancers, dates to 1815.

11. Campenhout, who felt compelled to defend himself against charges of plagiarism, wrote in a letter of December 15, 1845, "This futile attack . . . discredits the hymn which has contributed by its moral influence to establish Belgian independence. . . . One should at the very least respect . . . the virginal purity of the younger sister of the imperishable Marseillaise." Camille Buffin, *La Revolution Belge*, 2 vols. (Bruxelles: Librairie Kiessling, 1912), 2:571.

12. Henri Pirenne, *Histoire de Belgique* (History of Belgium), 5 vols. (Bruxelles: La Renaissance du livre, 1972–1975), 4:308.

13. Huys, Appendix VII.

14. H. Boscaven, "La Brabançonne," in *Revue Trimestrielle* 28 (1860): 22.

15. Ibid., 34.

16. An eyewitness report by a Dutch officer. J. G. Kikkert, *Bericht van den Tiendaagse Veldtocht* (Report of the Ten-days Campaign) (Rotterdam: Ad. Donker, 1980), 85.

17. One of the two basic treaties which guaranteed Belgian independence, the Twenty-Four Articles of 1831, provided for that independence but divided the border provinces of Luxembourg and Limburg between Belgium and the Netherlands.

18. This author's translation from the French text which has been widely reprinted but not translated. The text used here is that in Huys, Appendix VIII.

19. Ibid.

20. One of the most pungent criticisms is contained in Ernest Closson's thoughtful article "Pourquoi la Brabançonne n'est pas devenue un chant populaire?" in *La Revue Belge*, vol. 3, no. 6 (September 1928): 539. But the author concedes that from such other points of view as patriotism and historicity, Rogier's version deserves higher marks. A more recent critic stated flatly that Rogier was even less a musician than a poet. Carl Bronne, "L'affaire de la Brabançonne," a four-part series tracing the evolution of the national anthem and published in *Bulletin d'information de la vie musicale Belge 3* (September 1969–April 1970): 3.

21. Within a short time the new anthem was distributed in three successive editions.

22. Ernest Discailles, *Charles Rogier*, 4 vols. (Bruxelles: J. Lebègue et Cie., 1893–95), 4:135.

23. That position, indicative of the deep ethnic division, is typified by Flemish nationalist writers such as Maurits Josson, *De Belgische Omwenteling van 1830* (The Belgian turnover of 1830) (Thielt: J. Lanroo, n.d.,) 20 passim.

24. Théodor Juste, *Charles Rogier, 1800–1885 d'après des documents inédits* (Verviers: Bibliothèque Gilon, 1885), 92.

25. Pirenne, V:229.

26. Ödön Halasi, *Belgium under the German Heel* (London-New York-Toronto: Cassell and Co., 1917), 51, 53.

27. Frans van Kalken, *Histoire de la Belgique* (History of Belgium) (Bruxelles: Office de Publicité, 1954), 693.

28. The controversial conduct of King Leopold III during the war made his return at its end inadvisable. He finally returned to Belgium in July 1950, but such was the opposition that he saw himself compelled to abdicate on August 1, 1950. During demonstrations against him in Brussels on July 27, both the *Marseillaise* and the *Internationale* were struck up but not the national anthem! E. R. Arango, *Leopold III and the Belgian Royal Question* (Baltimore: Johns Hopkins University Press, 1961), 203.

29. Sylvain Dupuis, *Commission de la 'Brabançonne' rapport*, published in *Bulletin de l'Academie Royale de Belgique. Bulletin de la Classe des Beaux Arts* 4 (1922):128.

30. In the late 1870s, the Flemish poet Albrecht Rodenbach parodied the *Brabançonne* in a quatrain, adding that until the moment of acquiring "our own song, we had to be satisfied with that foreign noise."

31. This translation was kindly provided by Mme. Bernadette Goovaerts Musselwhite of the Belgian embassy in Washington, D.C.

32. In July 1985, *De Vlaamse Leeuw* (The Flemish Lion) was officially recognized as the regional anthem of the Flemish population. The song dates to 1847 when an earlier poem was set to music.

33. Bronne, IV:3.

34. *La Libre Belgique*, January 30, 1985. The article, headed "La Brabançonne-est-elle démodée?" ended in the apotheosis that "in any event diversity must not make our unity less invincible since there is no question of renouncing our proud motto 'Union makes strength.' " Notwithstanding such affirmation, the question was raised in the same paragraph as to whether the "invincible unity, so dear to the *Brabançonne* of papa" still conformed to the regionalized Belgium of today.

35. Bernard Huys has appended no fewer than 21 versions of the *Brabançonne* to his comprehensive essay on the evolution of the Belgian anthem.

11

Norway

Sang for Norge
(Bjørnstjerne Bjørnson)

In Bjørnstjerne Bjørnson's name the word *bjørn* (bear) appeared twice and, like a bear, he embraced any cause he judged good, seemingly never running out of good causes. He deemed none worthier than that of winning Norway's independence, except perhaps, late in his long life, international peace. As has been rightly observed, "Bjørnson and Norway's full freedom and independence grew up together."[1] And although he contributed to that independence in numerous ways, his *Sang for Norge* (Song for Norway) remains the most constant reminder for many Norwegians of Bjørnson's patriotic devotion, as it also remains their most natural expression of commitment to the country.

The struggle for Norwegian national sovereignty took almost a century, but it was bloodless. For most of the nineteenth century and thus for the main part of Bjørnson's life, the sparsely populated country, with its hardy people, enjoyed a large measure of autonomy. True, Norwegians still owed allegiance to a foreign ruler, but that had been the case for centuries. The Vienna Treaty Settlement of 1814–1815 merely had exchanged ties with the Danish crown for those with Sweden.[2]

These new ties, however, did not relegate the Norwegians to an inferior status or bring on an inferiority complex. In 1814 Norway had preserved its Eidsvoll constitution, so named after the small town where it had been drawn up in April of that year. Under its provisions the country retained its own legislature—the *Storting*—with considerable powers. That assembly then proceeded to elect as king of Norway the sitting regent who administered the country on behalf of his cousin, the Danish king.

But another player in the triangular game had not been taken into account, and he soon made himself heard. Jean-Baptiste Bernadotte, a former marshal of Napoleon I and now crown prince of Sweden, had no intention of letting the Norwegians slip out of his reach. Had the peacemakers at Vienna not provided for the transfer of Norway to Sweden as Denmark's punishment for failing to join the anti-French coalition and as a reward for Swedish help? Had Bernadotte not earned his share of the spoils by joining the allies against his former master?[3]

The Norwegians did not think so, but after the briefest resistance they found themselves left with Hobson's choice: futile objection or unhindered cooperation. Given the long and peaceful tradition of the union with Denmark, that choice was a foregone conclusion. The Act of Union in July 1815 legalized the enforced marriage that had brought Norway and Sweden together the previous November. Henceforth the Swedish dynasty would rule the new dual kingdom. During the frequent absences of the monarch from Christiania (now Oslo), a regent was to govern the Norwegian part of the kingdom. Foreign policy would be conducted from Stockholm; command of the armed forces would rest with the Swedes, since they provided the bulk of the army and navy. And the crown retained veto powers over any legislation of the *Storting* or of Norwegian ministers in the union cabinet.

In spite of such limitations, some of which were gradually eased, the Norwegians found themselves in a more equitable constitutional position than the Belgians versus the Dutch between 1815 and 1830, or the Hungarians vis-à-vis the Austrians before the Equalization Act of 1867, not to mention the relationship between the southern Irish and the British. Even so, constitutional conflicts erupted repeatedly between Norwegian and Swedish authorities during the ninety years of union, and culminated in its breakup. For better than one-half of that time, Bjørnson took an active and often even a leading part in challenges to Swedish supremacy. But when first entering public life and intellectual combat he charged in a different direction.

The centuries of Norwegian linkage to the Danish crown had resulted not only in an administrative but in a more galling cultural predominance of the Danes. Whatever the institutional changes from Danish to Swedish control, the cultural life in the few larger cities of Norway remained under Danish influence after 1814. But the twin movements of liberalism and nationalism, undergirded by romanticism, which gave birth to so many anthems, made themselves soon felt in Norway, and the contest over a cultural and national identity spilled over into the political arena. There it took the form of an ideological conflict symbolized by the names of Henrik Wergeland and Johan Welhaven.

The radically progressive-minded Wergeland, being of peasant stock, championed a Norwegian culture based simultaneously on folklore and the vernacular and on the farmers and fishermen who carried that culture from generation to generation. Welhaven, by contrast, favored a continuation of Danish cultural influences, which had shaped his urbane scholarship and poetry. The conservative urban elite, opposed to Wergeland's views and to his largely rustic nationalist supporters, rallied around Welhaven.

Even though the first champion of Norwegianism had died in 1845 when Bjørnson was barely a teenager, Wergeland's patriotic and progressive concepts continued to motivate him strongly, not least in his ongoing battle for an idiosyncratic Norwegian culture. Bjørnson was twenty-five when he arrived in Bergen in 1857. Norway's second largest city provided a better base for such an undertaking than the capital, where Danish culture was still dominant.

Its tradition of commercial power notwithstanding, Bergen had recently developed ambitions of cultural leadership. In 1850, a theater had been established but had not quite measured up to the expectations of its founder, the musician Ole Bull. It was he who summoned Bjørnson to breathe new life into that theater as the artistic director and pathfinder toward a national culture. The buoyant nominee had accepted jubilantly. Here was the longed-for opportunity to promote Norwegian art and artists. Bjørnson brought with him not only a dynamic drive, always his modus operandi, but two historical plays, a couple of peasant stories, and some patriotic poems, all of them drawn from a Norwegian milieu. But his bursting activism did not limit him to the stage or the written word. Whether prose or poetry, politics or public debate, he would speak for Norway.

What better occasion to do so than the 17th of May! On that hallowed day in 1814, the Eidsvoll constitution had been promulgated. Since 1829, May 17 had been the unofficial national holiday in spite of Swedish efforts to suppress all celebrations on that day. Now on the thirtieth anniversary of that first public celebration, Bjørnson eagerly took up the invitation to be the principal speaker. "His speech rang out over the crowd, his blond head held high,"[4] one eyewitness noted that May 17, 1859. Nor did he fail in drawing thunderous applause when he expounded that "a national festival such as this is . . . like the constitution written over in fresh ink."[5]

He had already gone on record on where he stood on the subject of Norwegian nationhood. "The national instinct is the loftiest that a nation can possess . . . and woe to the man who doesn't possess it."[6] As for himself, that instinct found expression both in his writings and his speeches, fuelled alike by nationalism and progressivism. For him as for so many of his contemporaries, national and liberal movements were not divergent but convergent forces, and with typical nineteenth-century conceptualization, he had stated in 1855, "All nationality must be interpreted as an eternal progress."[7]

In anticipation of the May 17 anniversary he had not only prepared an oration but had written a patriotic poem titled *Faedrelandssang*. It depicted a country lying between snowbound mountains and the turbulent North Sea. This specific Norwegian setting was to reappear soon in another poem, destined to fame as the national anthem. Both poems, like sails in a favorable wind, were filled by a strong love for the land and visions of a forward movement.

In the early summer of 1859, Bjørnson vacationed at Hop, near Bergen. His mood was exuberant. A productive theater season under his direction had just ended. The long quest for Norwegian equality within the union seemed closer to realization now that a new Swedish king, Charles XV, had succeeded to the throne. Best of all, his wife of less than a year was expecting their first child.

Here at Wernersholm, a modest estate of friends, he enjoyed the rustic setting, so conducive to contemplation and imagination. The quiet cheerfulness of a June morning amidst a pastoral scenery with its stands of birches and firs, a placid brook meandering through the meadows, made the countryside so loveable. How good it felt to be part of it! And for that matter, of the whole country with its Norse sagas, valiant people, long history, and contrasting regions stretching from the southern uplands to the Arctic along deeply ribbed fjords.

Bjørnson felt strongly attached to that country, like a loving son to his mother.[8] That love now found its lasting expression in the poem just forming in his thoughts. He titled it in the first draft *Nationalsange* (National Song), but that title was changed in printed editions to *Sang for Norge*. It became widely known, however, much like the German anthem, by its opening line: "Ja vi elsker dette landet" (Yes, we love this our land).

Few other anthems have opened with a similarly appealing and affirmative declaration of love for the country, an appeal heightened by the unaffected simplicity of the words. The word "love" recurred in the first stanza and for good measure in the last of eight stanzas. Yet confession of and commitment to this patriotic love were neither grandiloquent nor hypocritical. The unadorned and unfeigned verses found a resounding echo among the Norwegian people precisely because they reflected their feelings, never showy or volatile.

> Yes, we love with fond devotion
> This our land that looms
> Rugged, storm-scarred o'er the ocean
> With her thousand homes.
> Love her, in our love recalling
> Those who gave us birth
> And old sagas which night in falling
> Brings as dreams down to earth.[9]

The next two stanzas glorified—as did so many other anthems—the past deeds of native heroes, mainly kings and chieftains. But Bjørnson, in an egalitarian spirit, also lauded peasants and women for having contributed so much to Norway's history and freedom. The fourth and fifth stanzas praised Norwegian staying power on the battlefield or during periods of dearth. Although few in number, Bjørnson commented proudly, Norwegians had shown their mettle and stood their ground in adversity.

A political note occurred in the sixth stanza where reference was made to the "three Scandinavian brothers," united after decades of hostility or animosity. The final stanza repeated the loving commitment to the country, adding that the victories won by the forefathers had to be secured—if possible by peaceful means.

> As our fathers' struggle gave it
> Victory at the end,
> Also we, when time shall crave it,
> Will its peace defend.[10]

Milieu and mood in which Bjørnson created his poem contributed to the peace motif. Yet the author himself pointed out in later years, "The Song is that of a peace-loving people . . . but if it is sung in the hour of danger, then self-assertion stands armored in every line."[11] That prediction was to prove correct when the Norwegian government and its supporters stood up to the Nazi invaders in 1940.

There were wellsprings other than peace and war that Bjørnson had tapped for his poem. The sagas, Norway's cultural treasure chest, enthralled him even before he could read. Likewise, the deeds of the warrior kings of medieval Norway had made a lasting impression on him, reflected in his historical plays. Equally important in both the making of the poem and the poet was Bjørnson's sense of self-reliance and independence of action. The Song's invocation of God in the seventh stanza as the ultimate guarantor of Norwegians' rights and fate seemed a logical corollary to their trust in themselves. And the Lutheran faith corresponded best to the spiritual needs of an austere and hard-working, inde-pendent-minded, and pragmatic people.

Bjørnson himself was the offspring of a stern and sturdy minister of that Church. Born at a frugal parsonage in the remote township of Kvikne to the southeast of Trondhjem, he soon learned to cope with the challenges of fierce winters and adverse conditions, much like his father handled rough parishioners from the neighboring copper mines. The roughness of life changed but slightly when the family moved to the more fertile and milder Romsdal valley. There Bjørnstjerne grew up and there he forged a close relationship with the under-privileged rural population, the *bonder*, whose life provided the substance of his early prose.

Other stimuli in his adolescence derived from the revolutions of 1848-1849. The updraft of drastic and progressive changes on the European continent had reached him in the form of news at the market town of Molde where he was enrolled in the Latin school. And for the first time, at age sixteen, he put his thoughts to paper. In a handwritten newssheet with the proud masthead *Frihet* (Freedom) he exulted, "Almost everyone in Europe has awakened from their deep sleep, reached for the sword and . . . made thrones shake and tyrants shiver. My thrilling call—freedom—is on everybody's lips."[12]

The crushing of national aspirations and liberal policies everywhere in Europe in 1849 did not overly deject him. There were battles to be fought at home, none more important than the one being waged for a Norwegian cultural identity.

When he went as a student to Christiania in 1850, Bjørnson soon became more attracted to the capital's theater than to its university. To his regret, the Danish influence in either institution had not decreased. He and his friends resolved to change that. Among these youths were several of Norway's future literary greats including Henrik Ibsen, Bjørnson's principal rival in the decades ahead. Before long the two luminaries were linked to one another in a curious relationship which fluctuated wildly between mutual support and unrestrained denigration. What joined them initially was their fascination with the theater and their readiness to supply it with their own handiwork.

While Ibsen worked on strengthening the Bergen theater, to which he had been called in 1851, Bjørnson aimed to undercut the Danish dominance at the Christiania stage. When the Danish director there did not hire a sufficient number of Norwegian actors, the resolute Bjørnson mounted a large and loud demonstration in May 1856, with the help of some six hundred tin whistles blown by youthful supporters.

Making plenty of noise but little headway in his struggle to shape the Christiania theater into a center of national culture, he gladly accepted the offer to take responsibility at Bergen after Ibsen's departure. The two years spent in that city offered numerous challenges beyond those of the local theater that he wanted to turn into a national one. In the spring of 1858, Bjørnson channelled some of his boundless energies into politics, appealing for support among artisans and laborers to replace Bergen's deputies to the *Storting* with candidates more to his liking because of their progressive views and a disposition to rein in Swedish administrative dominance.

He also engaged for some time in yet another struggle for the assertion of a Norwegian identity: the linguistic reform movement. Since the 1830s, efforts to give Norwegians a national language had gained momentum. Danish, with some Norwegian modifications, still remained the dominant tongue among the educated and in the few urban centers. The vernacular prevailed in the countryside. Like the authors of the Greek, Hungarian, Luxembourg, and Irish anthems, Bjørnson endorsed the development of a standardized and popular language with a native character. He had allowed some of his earlier work, which was written in Dano-Norwegian, to be recast in the *Landsmaal*, the rural idiom. Yet in the long run he thought it too limited, protesting in one of his many descriptive phrases that the *Landsmaal* proponents "want to sew us into skins again."[13] Just as well that he favored a compromise—the *Riksmaal*—under which urban speech had to be purged of excessive Danification while rural usage had to accept national standards; otherwise his *Song for Norway* might have lost out to a powerful poem written in the *Landsmaal*.[14]

The advancement of national art and literature preoccupied Bjørnson after his return to the capital in the fall of 1859. Together with Ibsen he founded the *Norske Selskap*, a society to promote Norwegian culture. As the new association became ever more politicized in its activities, the diminutive, introvert, and apolitical Ibsen disengaged himself. By contrast, the stocky, outgoing, and militant Bjørnson dominated its meetings as president. But the main outlet for his political partisanship was the liberal evening paper *Aftenposten*. In its columns he continued to challenge Danish literary predominance in the Norwegian capital, and it was that paper which first published his *Sang for Norge* in October 1859.

The following year he found a welcome opportunity to rebut Swedish claims to political superiority. A statement in the Stockholm legislature that Norwegian demands for equality resembled "a commoner's request for equality with the nobility" provoked the combative author into a rousing poem titled *Answer from Norway*. It opened with the challenging line, "Have you heard, young Norwegian man, what says the Swede now?" The answer, couched in no uncertain terms, came a few lines later.

> Shades of those from life departed
> Our forefathers single-hearted
> Who, when words like these were said,
> Mounted guard and knew no dread.[15]

So as to amplify the assertive verses Bjørnson asked his cousin Rikard Nordraak to set the poem to music. Only eighteen years old, the budding composer still studied music in Berlin. There he composed a tune inspired by romantic and national motivations and based on folk melodies. As it turned out, the festive melody, whose opening bars sounded a bit like "Deck the Halls," did not quite fit the defiant *Answer from Norway*.

In the spring of 1863, the two cousins met at the Nordraak home in Christiania. According to Bjørnson's account, he passed a copy of the *Song for Norway* to the young composer. The latter at once rearranged his earlier score to fit the mood and rhythm of the more contemplative poem. Soon afterwards he jubilated, "Now I have composed something that will resound from the North Cape to Lindesnaes."[16]

That ebullient assumption proved justified. Bjørnson's *Song*, vibrating to Nordraak's melody, soon could be heard throughout Norway. No less a composer than Edvard Grieg commented that the melody was "so infinitely moving because it matched the spirit of the poem to the point."[17] Nobody, however, could be more pleased than the author himself. Singing it, he said, was as uplifting as looking up to a mountain crest. And at the unveiling of a memorial for his cousin Nordraak, who had died in his twenties of tuberculosis, he attributed the powerful effect of the tune to its truly Norwegian character.

Initially scored as a quartet, the *Song* was first heard at a gathering of military officers in the early summer of 1863, a somewhat odd launching place for a hymn born out of peaceful ambiance. But acceptance by a wider public was to follow soon. The suitable moment came, appropriately, on May 17, 1864. The national holiday, so often heralded by a Bjørnson oration, had a specific signif-

icance that year. It was the fiftieth anniversary of the Eidsvoll constitution, still
the mainstay of Norwegian autonomy in the union with Sweden.

The rain which fell on Christiania most of that day did not dampen the festive
mood of the crowds or the buoyancy of the principal speaker. Bjørnson, in his
by now almost customary peroration, addressed a receptive multitude gathered
at the *Slotplats* in front of the royal residence, which stood empty much of the
time. He pointed out the symbols within sight or earshot: the unfinished monument depicting the goddess of freedom, the flags which were meant to represent
a union of equals, the music and songs which rose skyward as an expression of
national feelings. They all revealed, he said, the presence of freedom and progress—the two main themes of his speech. He ended it to strong applause with
the exclamation, "The deepest wish of patriotic love is for the future of our
beautiful Norway."[18]

At dusk people gathered at the steps to the university's auditorium and were
treated to musical entertainment. A choir rendered the entrancing *Song for Norway* to spontaneous acclaim. Such was the appeal of both words and music that
the existing national hymn *Sons of Norway, the Age-Old Realm* soon lost its
preeminent place. That hymn dated from 1820, one of many patriotic if conventional songs that had sprouted en masse in the Napoleonic era and its aftermath. And while Bjørnson's *Song* was never officially proclaimed as the national
anthem, its popularity and general use date to this fiftieth anniversary celebration
of the Eidsvoll constitution.

Yet the country still lacked full sovereignty, and in the decades ahead
Bjørnson would throw himself wholly and happily into every fight for it. His
ever-increasing role as a public figure, a powerful partisan of national self-
determination, and living symbol of Norwegian patriotism did not slow down
his voluminous literary creativity. To his earlier historical plays and peasant
stories he added from the seventies on dramas and novels with social and psychological themes. In so doing he challenged Ibsen's lead. Personality clashes
augmented their artistic rivalry. But where the two giants of Norwegian literature
differed most was in politics. These differences showed clearly in the highly
controversial flag issue.

By the late seventies Bjørnson had fully committed himself to the cause of
the "pure" Norwegian flag. He and other patriotic militants clamored for the
removal of the mark of union with Sweden, the joint red-white and blue-yellow
emblem in the Swedish flag. Ibsen, on the other hand, eschewed the flag controversy, arguing that what really mattered was the independence of the
individual rather than that of the state.

Agitation both for and against a purely Norwegian flag increased sharply.
Ever active in the cause of nationhood and reforms, Bjørnson not only contributed a rousing poem[19] but mounted the rostrum on more than one occasion. In
March 1879, he addressed a large and noisy crowd. For once his stentorian
voice did not prevail, and he had to cut short his speech in favor of a Norwegian
flag. There were even accusations of unpatriotic behavior levelled at him. The

irate author questioned in a newspaper article how anyone who knew his poetry could possibly doubt his patriotism. An answer of sorts came unexpectedly but not entirely to his displeasure.

An unruly crowd of hostile demonstrators had gathered near the lodgings of a *Storting* member who had offered a motion to give Norway a separate flag. The mob, suspecting Bjørnson's presence in the house, began hurling stones at its windows until they were chased away. When the author was asked in later years on what occasion he had most enjoyed being a poet, he reportedly replied, "After they had finished their assault . . . they felt that they had to sing something and . . . began to sing 'Yes, we love this land of ours'—they couldn't help it. They had to sing the song of the man they had attacked."[20]

According to other accounts of the episode, it was partisans of the "pure" flag who sang the Bjørnson piece in his honor. But no matter which group did the singing, the upshot was the same. His *Song* had become so widely accepted by the end of the decade that different groups would identify with it. Its creator might well take satisfaction from that incident. And he could be more pleased still when the *Storting* finally passed a law establishing a separate Norwegian flag in 1893.

Now that the Swedish blue-yellow emblem was removed and Norway had its own colors—could independence be far behind? As it turned out, independence and union were not compatible. The stress test came in the form of Norwegian demands for a separate diplomatic and consular service. Consular representation was of specific importance to the Norwegians, not only because of the ever-expanding commercial interests abroad, but also because the Swedish government espoused protectionism, anathema to the free traders of Norway.

Bjørnson lost no time in joining the fray, leading into the final round for Norwegian nationhood. So intense became his involvement in the issue of a separate Norwegian foreign service that he declared in 1891 he would for the time being be "only a politician."[21] But, in fact, his artistic productivity flourished alongside his political engagement. His literary work made him the foremost Norwegian author of the era, a standing attested to by the Swedish academy's award of the Nobel prize in literature in 1903, the only author of a national anthem to be so honored.

It was the ultimate acknowledgment of the totality of his written work, which in volume and variety exceeded that of any other Norwegian writer, including Ibsen. But there may have been additional reasons for the award by the Swedish Nobel committee. In the final and most sensitive phase of the breakup of the union, the ever-combative award winner for once had reined in his temper and tongue. Bjørnson did not waver in his support for an independent Norway, yet he steadfastly maintained that the union should be dissolved peacefully.

In the 1890s, there was talk of war and preparations for it on both sides of the mountainous border between Sweden and Norway. But military conflict was the last thing the towering warrior of any good cause wanted to see. Even if the union ended, Scandinavian unity had to be preserved. Negotiations, perhaps through Danish mediation, had to continue until a peaceful separation could be arrived at.

In the spring of 1905, public pressures in Norway reached a climax when the *Storting* passed a bill establishing a Norwegian consular service. The bill was vetoed by the king, who also refused to accept the subsequent resignation of his Norwegian ministers. The ultimate showdown was at hand. Unlike earlier constitutional crises, such as the flag controversy which had lasted over two decades, this crisis spurred the *Storting* to action without delay.

On June 7, 1905, the Norwegian parliament unilaterally declared the union with Sweden dissolved. As *Storting* members left the building where they just had voted unanimously for Norwegian independence, applauding crowds repeatedly struck up "Ja vi elsker dette landet." Like most of his countrymen, the aging author was jubilant. The goal which he had so passionately striven for in countless speeches, articles, and not least in his poetry had been attained at long last: an independent Norway and an equal partnership with its Scandinavian neighbors.

Separation still had to be ratified by both former members of the union. There were some misgivings on the Swedish side, but common sense prevailed mainly because of the reasonable attitude of the king. If the Norwegians would make some concessions and gestures of goodwill, such as dismantling the recently constructed frontier forts, they were free to go.

To the Norwegians nothing was more important than independence, which Bjørnson asserted to be "the desire of all."[22] The proof of that assertion came with the plebiscite of August 13, 1905, to ratify the action of the *Storting*. On that Sunday the author and his neighbors in the Gausdal valley, where he now owned an estate, spontaneously joined in singing his *Song for Norway* as they gathered to cast their vote. Quite naturally, Bjørnson was given the honor of casting the first ballot. And just as predictably, the poll in the Gausdal valley with a lopsided vote of 533 to 1 in favor of the union's dissolution approximated that of the country at large.

It had been an easy choice to make, but a second plebiscite loomed ahead and Bjørnson, among others, found it more difficult to make the choice this time around. The issue to be decided in November 1905 was the constitutional form of the new sovereign state. For decades nationalism and progressivism had fused, not least in his dynamic mind, and propelled him toward republicanism.

He had frontally attacked royalism in his play *The King* and risked imprisonment in 1877.[23] But toward the end of the century his pragmatism had caused him to reconsider his republican predilections. His pleasant visit with the Swedish king on the occasion of the Nobel prize award even made him consider the possibility of a Bernadotte on the future throne of Norway.

The second plebiscite did not show the same unanimity as the first. A sizeable minority of over twenty percent held out for a republic. Bjørnson, however, was not among them. Realizing that a Norwegian king with strong dynastic connections would be in a firmer position internationally than an isolated republic, he opted for the monarchy.[24] His change of position caused resentment among many of his friends, but he could take comfort in the continued popularity of the anthem he had created.

It now served as the first collective greeting to the newly elected king. Prince Carl, second son of the reigning Danish king, had accepted the call to the Norwegian throne. As a symbolic gesture and token of his new responsibilities as Norway's monarch, he adopted the name of Haakon VII.[25] Approaching the Norwegian coast, in November 1905, he and his family transferred from the Danish royal yacht to the Norwegian warship *Heimdal*. As they came aboard the crew greeted them with the *Song for Norway*. It resounded again as the royal procession made its way through snow-covered streets to the palace.

Bjørnson stood with Edvard Grieg as they applauded their new sovereigns, symbols of Norwegian sovereignty. Pride surged in the author of the anthem when it rang out to celebrate this thrilling moment in Norway's history. He had given to his countrymen a collective voice to express their feelings, and he was equally proud of the characteristics of that anthem.

Comparing it to that of other nations, Bjørnson argued with much perspicacity. "Other anthems either make a melancholic impression or else they breathe insurrection, or alternately they are pure idylls. But this national anthem of ours, free and open like the day soars upward without a threat. It shows determination without boasting."[26]

If these were the characteristics of the *Song for Norway*, they corresponded closely to the character and attitudes of the Norwegians. Poem and nation had come together in the anthem and had done so not by happenstance. The new nation in the aggregate was neither showy nor effusive but unpretentious and moderate. There is little aggressiveness recorded in Norway's modern history; yet its people have shown a good deal of individual and collective determination. Their lives in a rugged countryside or on the high seas were certainly far from idyllic. Yet hardship motivated many of them to better themselves and to endorse all kinds of progressive movements.

If the anthem typified Norwegian traits, its author was just as typically Norwegian. By temperament and tradition he was linked to a Viking heritage, but his weapon was the word rather than the sword. He had taken up every fight, joined every struggle for a worthwhile cause: the underprivileged at home and the oppressed abroad, national independence and international conciliation, self-determination and self-restraint, liberalism and socialism. Much of the last decade of his life he had dedicated to the international peace movement, a favorite subject among fellow Scandinavians. Ironically, he had done so with the same militancy with which he had joined any other cause.

It seemed altogether fitting, therefore, that he would make his last voyage aboard a Norwegian warship. Equally appropriate was its name: *Norge* (Norway). The flagship of Norway's growing navy had come to France in April 1910, when the young state had reached out to the old warrior to bring him home with the honors due Norway's foremost public figure. *Norge* was to carry

Bjørnson's body home from a French port to Christiania. He had died earlier that month in Paris during the last of his many stays abroad.

But wherever he had gone on his travels, he had never left Norway in spirit. In April 1880, he had written to his friend George Morris Brandes, the leading Scandinavian literary historian and critic of the era, "I shall sing . . . and die in Norway. Be certain of that!"[27] Although the second part of that prediction did not come true, much of his voluminous work had been written on native soil and nourished by it. Larger than even his literary output, however, loomed his part in the evolution of Norwegian nationhood. He embodied it, and his *Song for Norway* had given voice to the innermost sentiments of his countrymen. As Brandes was to observe correctly, "Bjørnson in his own person comprehends the nation."[28] And the nation surely comprehended his significance both as a writer and a patriot. On that spring day when he was laid to final rest, thousands lined the way to the cemetery and across the whole country flags were flown at half-staff.

His literary reputation remained formidable, even though Henrik Ibsen has long since overshadowed him as the greatest figure in Norwegian literature and in international theater. But Bjørnson's name will always be linked to the Norwegian anthem which was heard annually at the 17th of May celebrations, a tradition in which he had so often played a leading part. That tradition was brusquely, if temporarily, broken after more than a century in April 1940, when German invaders struck.

The Nazi occupiers disallowed the national holiday within a month after their invasion, but such prohibition only triggered spontaneous demonstrations. In Karl Johan Street, Oslo's main thoroughfare, an impromptu parade took place with people defiantly singing the *Song for Norway*. Such was its continued appeal that not even the pro-Nazi Quisling regime dared to ban the anthem. It was even struck up officially in Berlin when Vidkun Quisling, foremost traitor and nominal prime minister of the occupied country, paid a "state visit" to his Nazi overlord in April 1942. But the true users of the Bjørnson-Nordraak creation were the patriots of the resistance movement who made *Ja vi elsker dette landet* their fight song.[29]

Ultimate triumph of that resistance came only with VE-Day. A month later King Haakon VII and his family returned after five years from self-chosen exile in Britain. For the second time in forty years the king entered the capital in solemn procession, and for the second time he did so to the strains of the national anthem. Neither words nor melody had changed in the intervening decades. But on this occasion the four hundred thousand voices merging in the anthem rose from a quite different experience than that in November 1905. This time around, joy was tempered by the recollection of five years of oppression and suffering. Never before had Bjørnson's words of freedom, victory, and peace been sung with so much understanding of their meaning as on that ultimate day of liberation.

Not once in the half century since have any demands been heard or proposals made to change even a single word in the anthem. Unlike several other anthems, it remains unchallenged. Probably the most compelling reason for this preeminence was alluded to by Bjørnson in his comparison with other anthems. The characteristics of the *Song for Norway* fully reflect those of the people who made it their anthem.[30] Thus, the life of the anthem is closely bound up with the life of the nation and a timeless expression of unsentimental and unpretentious love for a country of austere beauty wedged between mountains and sea.

NOTES

1. Arthur H. Palmer, *Poems and Songs by Bjørnstjerne Bjørnson*, in series of *Scandinavian Classics* (New York-London: Oxford University Press, 1915), xxxi.

2. Norway had been joined to Denmark since the Union of Kalmar in 1387 which also briefly included Sweden. The Danish kings were represented in Norway by regents and by a host of Danish officials. Norwegians had their advisory council but otherwise little self-government. Danish dominance was most marked in cultural affairs.

3. J. B. Bernadotte had one of the most extraordinary careers in recorded history. An ambitious and quick-witted Gascognard, he had been a sergeant before 1789. The French Revolution and Napoleon in particular had greatly benefitted him. He not only married into the Napoleonic dynasty but rose to the rank of marshal and prince. That did not keep him from accepting, with Napoleon's concurrence, an offer to become successor to the ailing and aging Swedish king. Bernadotte acted as regent until 1818 when, as Karl Johan, he succeeded to the throne and thus became founder of a dynasty lasting to the present.

4. Quoted in Christian Gierloff, *Bjørnstjerne Bjørnson* (Oslo: Gyldendal Norsk Forlag, 1932), 109.

5. Ibid., 159

6. Harold Larson, *Bjørnstjerne Bjørnson: A Study in Norwegian Nationalism* (New York: King's Crown Press, 1944), 95.

7. Bjørnstjerne Bjørnson, *Artikler og Taler* (Articles and stories), eds. C. Collin and H. Eitrem, 2 vols. (Kristiania-Kjøbenhavn: Gyldendalske Boghandel, 1912), 1:71.

8. Bjørnson used this metaphor in the *Faedrelandssang*.

9. This translation is that of Professor Palmer, 230–31.

10. Ibid., 231.

11. Halvdan Koht and Sigmund Skard, *The Voice of Norway* (New York: Columbia University Press, 1944), 247.

12. Gierloff, 52.

13. Larson, 48.

14. Even though the *Riksmaal*—literally Language of the Realm—prevailed and Bjørnson used it along with his own variations which he called "Breast-Norwegian"—the *Landsmaal* had its supporters among men of letters. One of them, the poet Arne Garborg, wrote *God Bless Norway's Land*, which might have been a very serious competitor as a potential anthem had it not been written in *Landsmaal*.

15. Palmer, 230–31.

16. *Richard Nordraach: Hans efterlatte breve* (R.N.: His posthumously printed letters), ed. Wladimir Moe (Kristiana: Jacob Dybwads Forlag, 1921), 12.

17. Larson, 75.

18. *Artikler og Taler*, 1:243–44.

19. Titled *The Pure Norwegian Flag*, it climaxed in the lines:

Tri-colored flag, and pure
Thou art our hard-fought cause secure.
Thou liftest us high when life's sternest
Exultant, thou oceanward turnest
The colors of freedom are in earnest.

Translation is that of Palmer, 185–89.

20. William Morton Payne, *Bjørnstjerne Bjørnson, 1832–1910* (Chicago: A. C. McClurg & Co., 1910), 42.

21. Larson, 113.

22. Ibid., 122.

23. A charge of high treason had been initiated against Bjørnson and he had left the country for some time afterward. The charge, in turn, was dropped.

24. In justifying his volte-face, Bjørnson referred to the example of Giuseppe Garibaldi who in spite of his republican convictions had embraced, quite literally, the future king of Italy in October 1860. See Chapter 13 for additional reference.

25. King Haakon VI, the last Norwegian king, had died in 1380 after which Denmark, Norway, and Sweden had been brought together under the scepter of his wife, the Danish Queen Margaret, upon the death of their son in 1387.

26. Koht and Skard, 247.

27. Georg M. Brandes, *Henrik Ibsen: A Critical Study: With . . . Essay on Bjørnstjerne Bjørnson*, reissued (New York: Benjamin Blom, Inc., 1962), 132.

28. Ibid.

29. On May 17, 1944, a speaker at the Grini detention center outside Oslo, where many Norwegian patriots were in custody, pointedly reminded his listeners of the close ties that existed between Bjørnson, the *Song for Norway*, and the national holiday. Finn Jor, ed., *17 Mai* (Oslo: J. W. Cappelens Forlag, 1980), 172.

30. The sturdy and steadfast self-reliance of the Norwegian people found its most recent expression in the vote of November 28, 1994, against European membership; two other Scandinavian countries, Finland and Sweden, had previously voted for it.

Unification Anthems

12

Germany

Das Lied der Deutschen
(August H. Hoffmann von Fallersleben)

Probably no other national anthem still in use has been more controversial than
the German one. Generally known by its first two lines as *Deutschland, Deutschland über Alles—über Alles in der Welt* (Germany, Germany above all else—
Above all else in the world), the song has been and still is sometimes regarded
as symbolic of German nationalistic behaviorism and expansionism. Nor have
the vagaries of modern German history and of the anthem's fate helped much
toward a fuller understanding for the song or the author's motivations. As one
thoughtful commentator has put it in recent years quite succinctly, "The changing history of the song ... casts a significant light upon the difficulties of the
Germans on the road to democracy."[1]

Such observations, however justified, refer solely to the anthem rather than
to the author whose life and views reflected these difficulties as much as the
Lied der Deutschen itself. When he wrote its three stanzas in 1841 there was
no Germany but only the Germanies and, strictly speaking, no Germans but
Bavarians, Prussians, Saxonians, and nearly three dozen other populations in
thirty-nine states of widely varying size, history, and importance. Politically,
this congeries was held together, ever so loosely, by a cumbersome confederation: the *Deutsche Bund*, dominated by imperial Austria. Culturally, a common
language, albeit with regional variations, and analogous customs served as a
natural rather than a national bond.

The urge to see these variegated components melded into an entity made itself
increasingly felt in the aftermath of the Napoleonic era. But the brightly burning

hopes were quickly dampened and finally doused in most of the German states whose conservative governments held on tenaciously to the status quo. The foremost spokesmen for German union and domestic reforms—mainly university professors—were either reprimanded or removed, and the principal carriers of the national reform movement—student associations—dissolved in 1819.

The obnoxious persecution of "Demagogues" drove the reformers temporarily out of public life but did not drive their aspirations out of existence. Nor did the appeal of their convictions lessen. While the *Wartburgfest* in 1817 had drawn fewer than five hundred patriotic students, a national festival in 1832 had brought together some 30,000 patriots from various regions and backgrounds.

Two years later a partial German customs union (the *Zollverein*) linked for the first time about one-half of the German states. But that limited economic and fiscal togetherness did not go far enough toward national union for such dynamic patriots as August Heinrich Hoffmann von Fallersleben, who had welcomed the *Zollverein*.[2] With greater hopes, however, he had greeted the accession to the throne of a new Prussian king in 1840. Frederick William IV reportedly had romantic inclinations and might be amenable to making Prussia a prime mover toward a union of German states. Years later Hoffmann was to recall that he had discussed the king's possible role in such a union while he himself was heading for a vacation on Heligoland.[3]

The island off the Hamburg coastline had become a favorite spot for him. The Heligoland air had a salty freshness. The red sandstone cliffs, jutting above the white beaches, gave the little island an appearance of towering defiance that appealed to him. The natives were hardy and healthy fisherfolk who spoke a low German vernacular that Hoffmann, as a renowned philologist, found attractive.

True, the island had been British since 1807, but so in a way was Hoffmann's birthplace. The market town of Fallersleben, whose name he had added to his own, lay in the electorate of Hanover, itself linked in personal union with the British crown from 1714 to 1837.[4] Thus, Hoffmann's vacation place did not differ much in terms of sovereignty from his erstwhile residence. But nominal sovereignty mattered little to him. What counted were the people and their language; together they constituted the true nationality. By his reckoning, Heligolanders and Hanoverians, like the inhabitants of other German lands, were Germans.

That conviction stayed with him whether on visits to Hanover from his position as professor of philology at Breslau University or on vacation in Heligoland. Why should Germans view their fellow-citizens across unwanted and unnatural borders as foreigners? And why should not all Germans benefit alike from long-overdue reforms such as the franchise and a free press?

On the way over from Hamburg to Heligoland the passengers aboard the ferry included reform-minded Hanoverians whose cause Hoffmann had made his own.[5] Some of them had read with enthusiasm the poetic professor's first collection of poetry. Part I of his *Unpolitische Lieder* (Unpolitical Songs) had been published in 1840 and quickly gained in popularity, not least because of the political meaning that could be read between the lines. It did not take much astuteness to do so, least of all on the part of the ever-watchful censors, since many of the poems dealt with current events and institutions; nor did the forthright author take much trouble to disguise his democratic and nationalist points of view as he flailed away lustily. After all, the first song in the collection carried the telling title ''Cudgel out of the sack.'' And he had no intention of putting that cudgel back into its cover. On the contrary, Part II was about to appear!

Both parts stood to gain in readers and approval, not solely because of the author's criticism of public institutions and sectors of society but because of the humor that marked many of the poems. That humor ranged from innocuous banter through sharp sarcasm to caustic caricature. The latter, though comparatively rare, included antisemitic pieces that showed unequivocally the narrow limits of Hoffmann's reform proclivities, rooted as they were in nationalist rather than rationalist conceptions.

As he himself was to observe, ''the greater my knowledge of German conditions, the greater the urge to express myself poetically. Once I had found the right mood . . . the songs came to me on their own.''[6] That mood stemmed from his passionate concern with the future of the Germanies and the union of their populations.

On the morning of August 26, 1841, he strode with his determined step along the island cliffs. The rhythmic pounding of the North Sea waves against Heligoland's rocky coast sounded to him like a drum call to action. Sky and sea merged in the distance into a grey horizon. Beyond that horizon stretched the Germanies from the coasts of the Baltic and North seas to as far as the Rhine in the west, south to the Alps, and east to the borders with Russia. His thoughts encompassed all of this vast expanse which he had envisioned as an entity from youth on.

Now that vision flooded his agitated mind with full force. A solitary customs guard, according to one account, watched from afar as Hoffmann gesticulated intermittently and strongly as if to wrestle that vision into instant reality. Even though it remained a vision for the next thirty years, it was preserved in lasting form that same afternoon. Shortly after Hoffmann had returned to his rented room, he began to write in his neat Gothic script. The three stanzas of the *Lied der Deutschen* quickly took shape in the summerly stillness.

> Germany, Germany above all else,
> Above all else in the world,
> If it always stands together
> Fraternally in defence and defiance,
> From the Maas to the Memel,
> From the Etsch up to the Belt
> Germany, Germany, above all else,
> Above all else in the world!

Unity, and justice, and freedom
For the German fatherland!
Let us all strive together
Fraternally with heart and hand!
Unity and justice and freedom
Are the guarantors of happiness
Flourish in the luster of this happiness,
Flourish you German fatherland![7]

Although the last stanza alone has been the German national anthem since 1952, the first stanza and, more specifically, its opening lines have stood out for a far longer period like a lightning rod in drawing negative comment, not least outside Germany. "Germany . . . above all else in the world," repeated for good measure at the end of the stanza as if to open the *Lied* with a double salvo, may well lend itself to such censure. Were these lines an unmitigated expression of chauvinism and expansionism or merely a passionate plea for a united Germany to which all other regional and special interests had to be subordinated? Was a supremacist arrogance or a fervent love for the fatherland the catalyst? That has remained the much disputed question to the present day; nor is it likely to be answered conclusively.[8]

What meaning Hoffmann wanted to convey must remain indeed a matter of conjecture. That a unified Germany meant more to him than anything else, however, is a plausible assumption to make. He was infatuated with the yearning for a united and powerful Germany, a yearning made ever more intense because of the seeming impossibility to attain its fulfillment. By the same token, it appears questionable to impute any supremacist aspirations to these two lines—if only because there was no Germany or German leader in the 1840s to espouse or embody such aims. With these conditioning factors in mind a case could be made that it was not the idea of dominance in the world but rather the dominance of an idea, that of a unified Germany, which inspired these lines.

Moreover, the phrase "above all else in the world" was one that the author had borrowed rather than created. Its origins date as far back as 1684, long before modern nationalism of any kind made its appearance. An Austrian nobleman had published a tract that year advocating fuller cooperation within the Habsburg empire, to secure for it economic independence under Austrian leadership.[9] "Austria above all else" came to life again in the same monarchy in 1809. This time around, it acquired a military connotation as the first verse of a poem which, like the others in the same collection, called for valor and steadfastness on the part of Austrian conscripts in the defense of their country against Napoleonic France.[10] Such obviously rousing lines as "Austria above all else" soon were readily picked up in the Germanies, the appellation Austria suitably substituted by either Germany or Prussia.[11]

Two more lines in Hoffmann's first stanza gave rise to charges that the *Lied* and its author provided ample proof of German aggrandizing, if not supremacist

proclivities. The Germany of his vision was indeed one of pan-Germanic proportions, reaching from the Maas (Meuse) river in the west to the Memel river
in the east and from the westernmost Danish narrows—the Little Belt—to the
Tyrolean Etsch (Adige) north to south. Generations of commentators, only occasionally contradicted, have asserted that these boundaries coincided with that
of the German Confederation. Yet it may be reasoned more convincingly that
for Hoffmann, the German philologist, the boundaries of his visionary Germany
were linguistic rather than geopolitical in nature. He had travelled the length
and width of these borders, first as a student and later as a recognized scholar:
French, Swiss, Belgian, and Dutch in the west, Russian and Polish to the east,
Italian to the south, and Danish to the north. In any event, there is in the *Lied*
no indication of expansionism or aggression. The militant stance, far less pronounced than in a half-dozen other anthems, is one of standing together for
protection and defiance.

The second stanza shaped itself into an ethnocentric paean of German womanhood, wine, loyalty, and song. Retaining their qualities along with "their good
old name" showed Hoffmann to be far more traditionalist than any police reports, and there were plenty, seemed to suggest. Such reports may have had
more pertinence in relation to the third stanza. "Unity and justice and freedom"
smacked indeed of dangerous demagoguery if not outright subversion to those
keeping up the surveillance. For Hoffmann and his fellow patriots, however,
that triad had quite a different connotation, one of a unified Germany where
justice could be had for its citizens and where they could express themselves
freely. He had carried that image, overlaid with a hefty touch of nationalism
and ethnocentrism, since his student days.

They had led him to Jena, center of the new *Burschenschaft* movement of
reform-minded students caught up in the whirl of romanticism and nationalism.
Almost at once Hoffmann fully identified with their yearning and agitation for
a unified Germany with representative institutions. As he was to record later on,
"I was thrilled, body and soul, by the thought of a barely attainable German
freedom. Soon . . . I began to write of freedom and fatherland."[12]

In 1819, Hoffmann transferred to the newly founded Bonn University. One
of its professors had just been suspended because of his outspoken championship
of German union and reforms. Ernst Moritz Arndt had long propagated in essays, lectures, and poems a unified and powerful Germany based on national
pride and public support. Arndt's Gallophobia affected Hoffmann just as
strongly as did his forceful, nationalist poetry. It was Arndt who rhapsodized
"the fatherland of all the Germans"—yet to be created—and who sang long-
ingly of "freedom, fatherland, and justice."[13]

These catchwords embedded themselves deeply in the mind of the vivacious
young Hoffmann. They were to resurge prominently in his later poetry, not least
so in the *Lied der Deutschen*. After graduation from Bonn University with a
degree in comparative philology, he secured employment as an assistant curator
at the library of Breslau University. There he used his literary and linguistic

qualifications with good effect, gaining eventually a professorship in German literature. But he was soon manifestly at odds with officialdom, both at the university and beyond. In a letter of October 1831, Hoffmann complained to his brother about "the despotic character of our police . . . and of surveillance. Everything suffocates the last bit of confidence in the government and embitters one toward the officials."[14]

He almost certainly shared the aspirations as well as the frustrations of those German patriots who yearned for a thorough change. Yet he did eschew revolution, a word which never appeared in his poetry. Nor did he belong to those who, in their despair of ever seeing the desired changes toward a unified and progressive Germany, preferred emigration over stagnation. In the mid-1830s, the restless professor-poet was offered, as were other German democrats, a grant of 300 acres in the new free state of Texas. Hoffmann, with his flair for contemporary verse, wrote several *Texanische Lieder*, one of which began: "On to Texas, on to Texas where the star in the blue field does herald a New World."[15]

But he never could bring himself to forsake his beloved German soil forever. On the contrary, his deep attachment to land and people became more pronounced as he returned from foreign travel. Already, in 1834, he had written, "Only in Germany do I want to live always." And on returning from a trip to France, which he held in low esteem, he jubilated in 1839, "Be you greeted with heart and hand, Germany, you my fatherland."[16]

The magic pull of a conceptualized Germany also made itself felt in the first part of his *Unpolitische Lieder*. Part I had to be reprinted quickly since the first printing, much to the delight of the publisher, had been sold out. That unexpected success also buoyed the author, now in his forties. His patriotic aspirations soared along with his literary inspiration. They were enhanced further by an unexpected if also unintentional boost to German nationalism at the turn from 1840 to 1841. Great Britain and France, rivalling colonial powers for so long, had stood eyeball-to-eyeball again in the Near Eastern crisis of 1840.[17] France had blinked and now was rumored to be planning a descent on the Rhine so as not to lose face altogether. Anticipation of such a move triggered an outburst of resentment on the eastern side of the river, echoed in other parts of the Germanies. A surge of anti-French sentiments coupled with an affirmation of German togetherness culminated in several strongly nationalist songs.

The two most famous, not to say notorious, were *They shall not have it, the free German Rhine* and the equally powerful *Watch on the Rhine*. As it turned out, the latter poem with its resounding refrain "dear fatherland do calmly rest, firmly and faithfully does stand the watch on the Rhine" proved more popular than Hoffmann's *Lied der Deutschen* for well over a half century. And more likely than not these songs fertilized his own.

On August 28, 1841, two days after its completion, the publisher Julius Campe arrived from Hamburg on a visit to Heligoland. The next morning an ebullient Hoffmann told him, "I have created a *Lied* but it will cost [you] four Louisd'or."[18] He read it to Campe, who had published the *Unpolitische Lieder* at a substantial profit and looked for more of the same. Even before Hoffmann had ended, the publisher placed the requested amount on the author's wallet. Moreover, Campe did take the poem with him on the return trip to Hamburg. A few days later he was again in Heligoland bringing the news that Hoffmann's poem would be published forthwith as a song. Its melody would be that of Franz Joseph Haydn's *Gott Erhalte Franz den Kaiser*, the Austrian national anthem since 1797. Most likely, the astute publisher figured that there could be no more appealing or fitting tune; better still, he wouldn't have to pay royalties to the deceased composer.

Hoffmann declared himself well satisfied with that arrangement and left the island on September 4, 1841. Upon arrival in Hamburg he was told that 400 copies of the *Lied* already were on the way to Breslau in advance of Hoffmann's return to his academic post. That piece of good news, however, was soon overshadowed by a report from the publisher that copies of the second part of the *Unpolitische Lieder* had been confiscated by officials in Breslau who considered the verses "subversive in orientation."

Before setting out for Breslau with some misgivings, the author did have the satisfaction of hearing his *Lied* sung publicly for the first time. On October 5, 1841, the Hamburg gymnastic association, the *Turnerbund*, gathered in front of a hotel to serenade the liberal leader Professor Friedrich T. Welcker, one of Hoffmann's friends. A torchlight procession provided a suitable background for the rendition of the solemn song as it rang out from a hundred young voices. Alas, quite a different reception lay ahead for the creator of the song.

When Hoffmann arrived in Breslau in late October 1841, he soon was questioned as to the suspected political meaning of his poetry. After additional hearings, the author of *Unpolitische Lieder* was suspended from his academic appointment early in 1842. Not until more than a year later did the Prussian ministry of religious and educational affairs announce final disposition of his case. Hoffmann was dismissed without a pension.

Henceforth he had to fend for himself and for almost two decades relied on his pen for a meager income. Poetry remained his primary form of expression and travel his main activity. He roamed the Germanies from east to west and north to south like a minstrel, a Whitmanesque figure not only in looks and lifestyle but also in his earthiness and vitality. The one state that he avoided was his native Hanover, from which he had been banned since 1842 unless he were to take up permanent residence. But wherever he wandered or briefly stayed, more poetry sprang from a versatile mind: ballads, political satire, folk songs, love poems, and children's rhymes. Of the latter alone he composed over five hundred, some of which became widely known and lastingly popular. Much of his poetry was steeped in Germanic folklore and under the persistent influence of the brothers Grimm, whom he had befriended in his youth. Jacob Grimm in particular stayed close to him, especially after the investigation and during the years of academic banishment.

While the roving life suited Hoffmann's temper and habits, it hardly lent itself to the acquisition of professional and social prominence, let alone prosperity. To the detriment of the latter, not even royalties were coming in. The publisher informed Hoffmann that the *Lied der Deutschen* "has not made it; I cannot recover the costs."[19] While a good bit of his poetry, mainly for political reasons, found quick acceptance and wide circulation among Germans, the *Lied* did not. The most obvious reason was that as yet no German *Reich* or nation existed with a clearly identifiable structure or a corresponding need for national symbols, including an anthem.

A first chance to gain such an identity came in 1848. The March revolution radiated from Berlin to many parts of the country, mainly the south and southwest. Now that the long-frustrated hopes and aspirations for a democratic and unified Germany appeared close to realization, Hoffmann could hope for redemption and restitution. After all, he had striven for that realization since adolescence and could rightfully claim to have sacrificed his career in its behalf. He certainly had given unique expression to the ultimate attainment of this most precious goal in the stanzas of the *Lied der Deutschen*.

Yet when the opportunity arose to make his way to the forefront of political action and transformation, Hoffmann held back. He stayed aloof from the public arena, be it in Frankfurt, where the first German parliament met, or Berlin, where a Prussian reform-minded assembly was in session. In all probability he could have been elected to either, but he refused nomination, and that at a time when friends and fellow poets eagerly took their seats in the famed Frankfurt legislature.

Instead, Hoffman focused his activities on academic rehabilitation and possible compensation. After a brief stay in Berlin, brimming with revolutionary ardor, he retreated to the rural quietude of Mecklenburg, where he concentrated on putting together a collection of folk songs. He did, however, notice with satisfaction that some of his earlier political poems had reappeared on placards and broadsheets. The *Lied der Deutschen*, however, was not among them! But in the one and only piece of political writing that he contributed from his pastoral retreat there recurred the noble call for "Germany's unity, freedom, and happiness."[20]

Even though that inspiring triad still reverberated in his mind, it did not necessarily echo elsewhere. Curiously, the unification song, with its democratic undertones which had so readily and powerfully emerged from his inspiration a mere seven years before, failed to be heard in the Frankfurt *Parlament*. Here, where the enthusiastic and patriotic deputies from all over the Germanies and parts of the Austrian empire talked first and foremost about the new *Reich*, that song of nationhood and brotherhood was not struck up once!

The most obvious reason for this lacuna was the deep and lasting division between the *Kleindeutsche* who wanted German unification without the Austrian empire, and the *Grossdeutsche* who wished to include at least all those of German speech and ethnicity. Hoffmann, as a cultural pan-German, sided with the latter group, and that made the rendering of his hymn in Frankfurt even more unlikely, since the *Kleindeutsche* prevailed.

On his part Hoffmann proved hardly more interested in the national assembly than its members were in the *Lied der Deutschen*. When the author finally did get to Frankfurt in April 1849, he recorded that "the whole of this parliament's history does not make an enjoyable impression on me."[21] And he left the city within a week. But if he and his hymn went almost unnoticed during the eighteen months of abortive efforts at forging a democratic German nation, the author did come away with some personal gains. While not restored to his academic position, he was at least granted a partial pension. More rewarding still was his being accepted in marriage.

In spite of his adulation of German womanhood, not least in the *Lied*, he had not been very successful in his wooing of women. The *Wanderjahre* after his dismissal from Breslau University were hardly conducive to settling down in marriage. Yet Hoffmann's vitality and determination prevailed. Ida vom Berge was not only almost thirty-five years younger than the bridegroom but—more surprisingly—was his niece! This peculiar but lawful situation did not, however, preclude the couple from a happy relationship and successful procreation. Family responsibilities weighed ever more heavily on the roving scholar and author. His search for regular employment was hindered in the years of political reaction after the mid-century revolutions. In spite of the fact that he had not been involved in any revolutionary activities, he remained a suspect, a fate dating back to his dismissal in 1843, if not indeed to his student days.

On more than one occasion in the early fifties he found himself harassed by local police regardless of where he stayed or what he was doing. According to one expert on Hoffmann's life and work, the author was altogether expelled from various German states thirty-nine times.[22] Since this was exactly the sum total of all the states in the German Confederation, he averaged one expulsion from each of its components; in reality, however, he was expelled from several locations in the same state at different times. Fortunately, one state, politically one of the most progressive and culturally the most advanced in the Confederation, offered hospitality: Saxe-Weimar. It was the artistic and literary center of a Germany still to be formed. The grand duke graciously received the scholarly author on several occasions. Moreover, in 1853 he granted a subsidy for a new biannual yearbook of German language and culture which Hoffmann was to edit.

Unfortunately, that editorial work came to an abrupt close. By 1857 the *Jahrbuch* ceased publication and the grand ducal subsidy ended even earlier. Almost sixty years of age and with a family to take care of, he was again at loose ends. Fortunately, a friend of his wife secured for him an appointment as librarian to the Duke of Ratibor. In 1860, Hoffmann assumed his final employment and, as it turned out, final residence in Schloss Corvey at Höxter, near the border between Lower Saxony and Westphalia, haven at last for the remaining fourteen years of his life.

The Storm and Stress themes of earlier decades now lay behind him. German unification, of which he had sung so fervently for so long—and seemingly in vain—came ever closer to realization. Curiously, he did not particularly care for its principal mover and maker. In the late sixties, he frankly admitted that he did "not belong to those who excessively praise Bismarck as our redeemer."[23] Perhaps he resented not being reinstated in his academic rank, for which he still hoped by 1870. But the outbreak of the Franco-Prussian war that year greatly thrilled him. Always an ethnocentric and assertive German with a strong bias against the French and to only a slightly lesser degree the British or Italians, he wrote on August 27, 1870, "May God grant . . . that we will emerge from this heavy struggle against the depraved French race victoriously and render humanity the great service of letting my, our *Deutschland über Alles* become a reality."[24]

A few days earlier he had written to a friend who, on his own, had reissued a one-page reprint of the song. "It would please me . . . if now finally my song . . . would gain general acceptance, thus becoming . . . a song for the whole of Germany."[25] Predictably, Hoffmann greeted the proclamation of the German *Reich* on January 18, 1871, with jubilation, and he acclaimed the new German emperor with equal enthusiasm. But unlike the author of the *Marseillaise,* who had the satisfaction to see in the final years of a long life his hymn become once more the official anthem of France, Hoffmann died without such an awareness. Quite the contrary! In one of the last poems before his death in 1874 he remarked bitterly:

> And I sang again of Germany,
> Did sing in joy and hope;
> Yet my "Germany above all else"
> Meant only so much pulp.[26]

That pessimism, so strongly at variance with the buoyancy which carried him through the many vicissitudes of his life, proved unwarranted. It was precisely the *Deutschlandlied,* as his poem became ultimately known, that preserved his name and fame through the generations. By contrast, many of his most appealing poems have long since become folk songs without attribution to their author.

During the decades following the author's death, his *Lied* had to compete for anthem status with the always popular *Watch on the Rhine* and *Hail Thee in Victor's Wreath,* which became the imperial hymn. The new German empire and its successive crowned heads obviously were in no hurry to adopt the work of a reputedly militant democrat as a precious symbol of their own power and glory. There may have been a tragic irony in the fact that neither poet nor poem were accorded special status in the unified and strong Germany, the apotheosis of several of Hoffmann's most powerful verses and in particular of his *Lied.*

The first time that it was officially intoned came, appropriately, on the day when Heligoland was transferred from British to German sovereignty in October

1890.[27] Suitably, too, within less than two years the unveiling of a Hoffmann bust took place near the main thoroughfare of the island. Yet formal recognition as the national anthem remained in limbo. Moreover, each of the component states within the German empire continued to have its own preferred hymn. Nevertheless, in the opening decade of this century, the *Deutschlandlied* was widely, if unofficially, acknowledged as Germany's anthem.[28]

But as in the case of several other national anthems, notably the *Marseillaise* and the *Brabançonne*, it took a war to make the *Lied* spontaneously the song of the nation. A bulletin by the German High Command headquarters reported on November 11, 1914: "West of Langemarck young regiments [mainly student volunteers] advanced toward enemy positions and took them while singing *Deutschland, Deutschland über Alles.*"[29] After three-quarters of a century, Hoffmann's poem had finally received its baptism of fire in circumstances hardly foreseen by the author but most likely to be acceptable to him.

Yet official recognition of the *Deutschlandlied* as the German anthem came about in a strikingly different situation: not in the triumph of war and the glory of German power but in defeat; not by order of a crowned head but on recommendation of an elected president. That this official was a Socialdemocrat of humble background, though as patriotic as any man in Germany, only added to the contradictions associated with the anthem.

On August 11, 1922—the third anniversary of the constitution drawn up in Weimar—President Friedrich Ebert proclaimed with as much conviction as patriotism, "In fulfillment of his [Hoffmann's] longing the song of unity-justice-freedom shall under the black-red-gold flag become the expression of our patriotic feelings."[30]

While Hoffmann von Fallersleben might have readily concurred in this proclamation and perhaps taken pride in it, his hymn had also been appropriated by totally different political groups, and their interpretation and utilization of the *Deutschlandlied* differed accordingly. It was sung by the ultranationalist Erhardt Brigade, one of the several free corps that haunted the Weimar Republic. A little-known Munich versifier added, in 1923, a fourth verse of defiance and reassertion, culminating in the lines "Germany, Germany above all else and in its misfortune even more so now."

The newly recognized anthem became "the battle hymn of German chauvinists."[31] Not unlike the *Marseillaise* when used by opposing French political camps in 1871, the *Deutschlandlied* was thus turned into a symbol of domestic partisanship rather than union. Yet, in a curious contraposition, the French anthem, composed by a moderate royalist, moved steadily leftward while the German anthem, created by a nationalist democrat, moved toward the rightist side of the political spectrum.

The fact that the Nazi government of the Third Reich reaffirmed official status of the first stanza only added strength to that drift and to the negative image of an aggressive Germany. In 1867—decades before the *Lied* became the official anthem—a French deputy, at a moment of Franco-Prussian tension, remarked that a nation with "such a song shows a lack of modesty." And no less an author than George Bernard Shaw commented early in World War I that it was "an imperial hymn of conquest."[32]

While such scathing comments must be ascribed at least in part to the circumstances in which they were made, it hardly served the reputation of either author or hymn that the latter was utilized by the Nazi regime. To make matters worse, there were two injunctions under which the *Lied* had to be sung: only the first—and most controversial stanza—could be sung publicly and then only in tandem with the Nazi hymn, the *Horst Wessel Lied*.

That unsavory connection was buttressed by sustained propaganda efforts to fit Hoffmann von Fallersleben into the ideology of Nazi Germany. He was depicted as a spokesman of pan-Germanism, ethnic purity, assertive militancy, and antisemitic proclivities. It proved not very difficult to adduce supporting evidence for that kind of interpretation, which nevertheless presented only a one-dimensional picture of the man. And such oversimplification of documentary evidence led to an equally stereotyped judgment among those who interpreted his best-known poem as a symbol of German chauvinism, expansionism, and racism.[33]

The collapse of the Third Reich in May 1945 did not by itself change such assumptions and interpretations. For quite some time into the postwar era, the German image remained tainted in the eyes of many non-Germans or former German citizens. Their suspicions had by no means all been dispelled when the Federal Republic of Germany was established in May 1949. It was one thing to reinstate the often abused black-red-gold colors as the republic's flag. But it was quite another to reintroduce the *Deutschlandlied* as the national anthem. Theodor Heuss, first president of the newly created *Bundesrepublik Deutschland* and a life-long democrat, was fully aware of the negative connotations of the *Lied*. He had, therefore, considerable misgivings about its restoration to anthem status. Rather than opt for that alternative, he commissioned a well-reputed poet to write a new anthem.[34] Yet, as in other such cases, it failed to be accepted when first aired publicly on New Year's eve 1950.

Meanwhile, the newly elected chancellor, Konrad Adenauer, had moved on his own. During a visit to West Berlin in April 1950, he had encouraged the singing of the third stanza of the *Lied* at a public meeting. Not all of those present joined and several Socialdemocrats actually left in protest. But the chancellor, no less committed to democratic institutions than President Heuss and as thoroughly anti-Nazi, believed that it was in the best interest of the infant republic to revive part of the anthem.

In a celebrated exchange of letters between these two leaders, the issue of reinstatement was squarely joined. In April 1952, Adenauer wrote to Heuss that the question of a national anthem had been discussed between them repeatedly during the preceding two years. He pointed out that the president's reservations regarding the use of the former anthem were justified. Yet considerations of the international position of the *Bundesrepublik* made a decision in its favor urgent.

Cleverly, the conservative chancellor referred to the "statesmanlike decision" of President Ebert in proclaiming the *Deutschlandlied* as the national anthem, and he closed his letter with the statement that its third stanza alone should be intoned at all official gatherings.

On May 2, 1952, President Heuss replied to the chancellor's request in an equally careful and thoughtful letter. He stated that his earlier efforts in behalf of a new anthem were predicated as much on the awareness that Hoffmann's song had been so badly abused, most recently by the Nazis, as on the realization that the new republic needed new symbols. He had, however, understood by now the strong traditionalism of many Germans and the importance of emphasizing its positive values. After all, "Hoffman von Fallersleben was a Black-Red-Gold [supporter], even slightly miffed that his poem did not find [official] acceptance after 1870."[35] The letter concluded with the admonition that all those who argued in favor of Hoffmann and his poem, including the chancellor and his cabinet, should see to it that the true meaning of the third stanza be fully understood and supported. Both the republican flag and Hoffmann's words had to be given more than just nominal and official sanction.

And thus, the most viable and progressive of Hoffmann's three stanzas was accorded unique recognition. Other anthems had to wait longer for official acceptance, or underwent textual changes, or were disestablished altogether. None, however, served a dictatorship with one stanza and the succeeding parliamentary republic with another! Hoffmann von Fallersleben probably would have been annoyed with either arrangement. After all, the three stanzas of his *Lied* had been conceived as an entity and were written with a vision of a unified Germany.

Assuredly, he would have been crestfallen at news of the post–1945 division of the *Vaterland*. For over forty years Germany remained divided, as if to deny the very existence of his anthem, a division which was symbolized by the existence of two German anthems.[36] German reunification in 1990, however, required but a single anthem, and it stood to reason that Hoffmann's third stanza would be the logical choice, if only because it had been West Germany's anthem since 1952, and West Germany formed the core of the reunited state.

The *Deutschlandlied* had already been heard for a year or so on the eastern side of the former border, largely from protesters in the closing days of the communist regime. On October 3, 1990, the familiar tune rose triumphantly in Berlin, the traditional capital of Germany, in celebration of formal reunification. At noon it was sung by the members of the all-German parliament, at last assembled in the partially restored *Reichstag* building. Twelve hours later, "unity, and justice, and freedom" reverberated from the throats of nearly one million people just before the fireworks were set off.

The official proclamation of the *Deutschlandlied*'s third stanza followed in August 1991 through an exchange of letters between the federal president and the federal chancellor, similar to those exchanged initially between the two former heads of government and state in 1952.[37] Yet, while in both instances the third stanza alone was given pride of place, the other two stanzas pop up from the dim past on occasion. Not only has "Germany, Germany above all else" been belted out defiantly by neo-Nazis in recent years; at least two state governments have made available to the schools under their jurisdiction the text of all three stanzas, with the explanation that pupils may wish to know the whole poem.

Whatever the intention of these propagators, it is most unlikely that the first stanza in particular will regain the honor of anthem status in the forseeable future. And whatever the author's intent when writing it, the current course of German history seems to rule out such a revival. A European-oriented Germany will almost certainly not turn back the clock and run the risk of reactivating unsavory ghosts and unwelcome images, least of all at a time when the country moves ever closer, along with other countries, to an effective European Union. But such are the fluctuations of German history and mentality that if this Union should fail and Germany, like a loose cannon, be left to its own devices, a supremacist resurgence might one day restore the controversial first stanza of the *Deutschlandlied* to anthem status.

For the present, the domestic controversy over the merits or faults of the anthem's stanzas continues, at least among intellectuals. There are those who argue that "despite all the wrong interpretations, despite all ill-uses, it is a democratic song."[38] Others take the opposite view by asserting that "the Deutschlandlied from the beginning, all asseverations notwithstanding, was never the song of 'all the Germans' " and that "in reality . . . [it] is the expression of an unbroken history of an aggressive German nationalism."[39]

Such diametrically different interpretations may be traced back in the final analysis to the author of the *Deutschlandlied* himself. August Heinrich Hoffmann von Fallersleben was both a nationalist and a democrat. He, like many of his generation, had no difficulty in amalgamating both concepts. The dichotomy, so clearly reflected in the diverse opinions regarding the anthem, evolved with later generations unable to find the delicate balance between the two interacting dimensions.

NOTES

1. Ingrid Heinrich-Jost, *August Heinrich von Fallersleben*, in series *Preussische Köpfe* (Berlin: Stapp Verlag, 1982), 65.

2. August Heinrich von Fallersleben, *Unpolitische Lieder* (Unpolitical songs), hereafter cited as *Lieder*, Parts I and II (Hamburg: Hoffmann und Campe, 1842), 46. Hoffmann wistfully wrote, "Wool, soap, yarn, and beer . . . A thousand thanks to you/What no great mind has yet achieved/You alone have accomplished."

3. August Heinrich von Fallersleben, *Mein Leben* (My life), hereafter cited as *Leben*, in *Gesammelte Werke* (Collected works), ed. Heinrich Gerstenberg, 8 vols. (Berlin: F. Fontane), 7:289–90.

4. Since Queen Victoria, upon assuming the British throne, could not as a woman succeed to that of Hanover, her place was taken by the third son of King George III, Ernest August Duke of Cumberland.

5. The autocratic Ernest August, by his high-handed measures, had made himself no more popular among his Hanoverian subjects than his father had with the American colonists.

6. Heinrich-Jost, 71.

7. This author's translation. To the difficulties of anthem translation alluded to elsewhere in these pages there has been added in this case the very controversial nature of that poem's first two lines. About one-half of the linguistic experts consulted have opted for "Germany, Germany above all" while the other half favored "Germany, Germany above everything else," which has a less assertive ring to it. Since these two translations have resulted in different wording, which could quickly lead to different interpretations, I have chosen a combination of the key words "all" and "else." The second stanza has been omitted here.

8. Most German commentators from the 1920s to the present have argued that the true meaning of Hoffmann's opening lines was his unshakable conviction that the whole of Germany mattered more to him than any part thereof, and that the striving for and love of a united Germany mattered more to him than anything else. A minority, however, holds the view—not uncommon among foreigners—that these lines clearly suggest an expansionist nationalism.

9. That tract was written by Philipp Wilhelm von Hörnigk right after the lifting of the siege of Vienna, beleaguered by the Turks. The title read, "Austria above all else if it only wills it so."

10. The collection was the work of Heinrich Joseph Collin and titled *Songs for Austrian Militiamen*. "Austria above all else" was one of sixteen patriotic songs in that collection.

11. A patriotic German editor in 1813 included that poem in his songbook "Germany above all else," and four years later a Breslau University professor whom Hoffmann may have known in later years when living in that city published a pamphlet with the title "Prussia above all if it wills it so." The catchy phrase thus had made the rounds long before Hoffmann used it. This significant aspect has not been taken into consideration by critics of Hoffmann's nationalism. See, for instance, Benjamin Ortmeyer, *Argumente gegen das Deutschlandlied* (Arguments against the *Deutschlandlied*) (Köln: Bund Verlag, 1991), who omits all references to the antecedents of that turn of phrase.

12. Hoffmann, *Leben*, 8:39.

13. This was the final line in Arndt's *Lied vom Stein*. His most famous poem, titled *Was ist des Deutschen Vaterland?* (What is the German's fatherland?), ended in the apotheosis "it shall be the whole Germany."

14. Hoffmann, *Leben*, 7:186.

15. Heinrich-Jost, 105.

16. Hoffmann, *Unpolitische Lieder*, Part I, 159.

17. The French were backing the Egyptian viceroy Mehmet Ali, who had challenged the sultan, his overlord, for control of Syria. Sultan Mahmud II, in turn, enjoyed the support of Great Britain. After a bombardment of Beirut by a British naval squadron in the fall of 1840, the viceroy's son Ibrahim was forced to withdraw from the region since expected French help was not forthcoming.

18. Hoffmann, *Leben*, 7:291.

19. Adolf Moll, *Deutschland, Deutschland über Alles* (Leipzig-Wien: J. Günther, 1938), 75.

20. This was the last line of an appeal to the Frankfurt parliament that Hoffmann and his host, a republican-minded estate owner, had jointly drafted.

21. Hoffmann, *Leben*, 8:238.

22. Fritz Andree, *Hoffmann von Fallersleben*, 2d ed. (Fallersleben: Just & Seiffert, 1960).

23. Hoffmann, *Leben*, 8:238.

24. Ibid., 239.

25. Moll, 75.

26. Hoffmann, *Gesammelte Werke*, 6:271. Translation by this author.

27. In a territorial swap Great Britain acquired Zanzibar, the island off the East African equatorial coast, in exchange for Heligoland.

28. Hermann Kurzke, *Hymnen und Lieder der Deutschen* (Hymns and songs of the Germans) (Mainz: Dieterische's Verlagsbuchhandlung, 1990), 55, points out that the well-reputed *Brockhaus* encyclopedia, 14th edition, which appeared in 1907 and dealt with national anthems in vol. 17, mentioned that the *Deutschlandlied* was often used as the national anthem. Yet the most authentic German study of European national anthems in the same time period does not once refer to Hoffmann's *Lied*. Emil Bohn, *Die Nationalhymnen der europäischen Völker* (The national hymns of the European peoples) (Breslau: Verlag M. & H. Marcus, 1908).

29. Moll, 80.

30. Hans Tümmler, *Deutschland, Deutschland über Alles* (Köln-Wien: Böhlau Verlag, 1979), 11.

31. Ronald Schlink, *Hoffmann von Fallersleben* (Stuttgart: Akademischer Verlag, 1981), iii. Schlink's monograph is one of the most thoughtful and objective on the subject of the German anthem.

32. Ibid., 54, 59.

33. Volume and thrust of partisan literature provide a noteworthy indicator, not only of the controversial character of the *Lied*, but to what degree of a priori reasoning both it and the author are subject. In the Nazi era they were made honored precursors of "Germanhood" and a greater Germany. In the era of the Federal Republic the bulk of the Hoffmann literature attempted to clear them of such charges or, to the contrary, link author and anthem to Nazism so as to discredit both.

34. The author of the *Hymn to Germany* was Rudolf Alexander Schröder, whose poem studiously avoided any reference to German power aspirations.

35. The exchange of letters was first printed in the *Bulletin* of the Press and Information Office of the Federal Republic on May 6, 1952.

36. An East German anthem, composed by the well-reputed "worker-author" Johannes R. Becher, was proclaimed the anthem of the German Democratic Republic in November 1949. In spite of communist approval and the socialist antecedents of the author, the three stanzas carried undertones of nationalism and used some of the *Deutschlandlied* terminology. It even had the same title!

37. The exchange of letters between Federal President Richard von Weizsäcker and Federal Chancellor Helmut Kohl has been made public in *Bulletin* of the Press and Information Service of the Federal Republic, August 27, 1991. In his letter President von Weizsäcker stated that "the third stanza of the Hoffmann-Haydn *Lied* has proven itself as a symbol. . . . It gives expression to those values to which we as Germans, Europeans, and partners in the world community subscribe." On his part, Chancellor Kohl pointed

out that "the desire of all Germans to accomplish the unity of their fatherland in freedom has been expressed emphatically in the *Deutschlandlied*."

38. Guido Knopp and Ekkehard Kuhn, *Das Lied der Deutschen: Schicksal einer Hymne* (The song of the Germans: Fate of an anthem) (Frankfurt: Verlag Ullstein, 1988), 20. This is one of the most thorough and balanced studies of the troubled history of the German anthem.

39. Ortmeyer, 22–23 and 25.

13

Italy

Inno di Mameli
(Goffredo Mameli)

After the establishment of the Italian republic on the ruins of the discredited fascist state in June 1946, the new leaders had to reach back over nearly a century to find a suitable anthem. The song selected had first inspired a generation of Italian patriots who strove—in vain—for their country's independence and unification. And the author was a young man whose life and death symbolized that striving.

In 1846, the hopes for a united and free Italy, never quite quenched, stirred once again in some of the peninsula's nine states of widely different size and structure. They ranged from the Austrian provinces of Lombardy-Venetia and the small kingdom of Savoy-Sardinia, commonly known as Piedmont; its still smaller neighbors the duchies of Parma and Modena which were under Austrian influence, through the extensive if poorly administered Papal States; the moderately affluent and stable grand duchy of Tuscany; the minute duchy of Lucca and the even smaller but ancient Republic of San Marino; to the large but backward Kingdom of the Two Sicilies in the south.

The hopes of patriots in most of these states for an Italian entity with representative institutions had been dashed at seemingly regular intervals since the early 1820s. But a quarter of a century later, a break with the forbidding past appeared possible at long last. The accession of a new pope in June 1846 had brought some modest changes in the deplorable administrative and judicial conditions within the Papal States reaching from Bologna in the north to just south of Rome. Better still, the newly elected pontiff, Pius IX—known throughout the

Italian states as *Pio Nono*—had endeared himself to Italians beyond the confines of his territories when denouncing foreign arbitrariness and expansionism in the northern part of the peninsula.

There the Austrians chose to show their dominance by encroaching upon papal lands when they unilaterally took control of the city of Ferrara in August 1847. The Pope's strong protest had given his countrymen hope that he might speak for all of them by assuming the guardianship of Italian interests, perhaps even the leadership of an Italian federation. In any event, his first year of the pontificate had heightened anti-Austrian and pro-reformist sentiments, which activated a formidable if as yet uncoordinated movement for sweeping changes in existing patterns of government and borders that kept Italians from nationhood. Unrest spread like a firestorm, engendered by discontent with the existing order and frustration of ardent hopes for decades on end. By early October that unrest had reached Turin, capital of Piedmont. There, however, demonstrations were suppressed by a strong government under the watchful eye of the conservative, if vacillating, King Charles Albert, appropriately nicknamed *Re Tentenna* (the wobbly king).

A different situation prevailed in the port-city of Genoa with its proud history of self-government and self-reliance based on ancient republican institutions and traditions. To these components there had been joined a new impulse: nationalism. It had found its most eloquent and persuasive expression, along with republicanism and liberalism, in the person and pronouncements of Giuseppe Mazzini, a Genoese by birth and destined to become the foremost apostle of a unified and republican Italy, free from all foreign controls.

In early November 1847, Charles Albert had arrived for a visit in Genoa to reassure himself of the loyalties of his subjects, which were at best superficial unless he were to take the lead in rejecting Austrian dominance and in bringing together Italians in some form of federation. During his brief stay, demands for reforms sharply increased, with calls for a free press, formation of a citizen guard, a ban on the Jesuit order—considered strongly authoritarian and in league with reactionaries—and not least the freeing of Lombardy-Venetia from Austrian control.

Similar demands had been heard in other parts of northern Italy, and some had already been implemented. In Tuscany and Lucca demonstrations and even riots had caused the respective governments to grant constitutions and civic guards. The just-formed customs union by Piedmont, the Papal States, and Tuscany gave rise to expectations that this might be the first step toward an Italian federation.

Few among the Genoese were more thrilled by these events and more eager for further action than students at the university. And one of the most passionate, eloquent, and committed among them was twenty-year-old Goffredo Mameli. His physiognomy had the intensity of a charcoal fire. The somber appearance, accented by mournful eyes and a full black beard, could not hide the inner glow of inspiration coupled with an equally driving determination. But inspiration and determination did not solely radiate from his looks and personality. He had written passionate poetry since he was in his teens. Increasingly, however, that youthful poetry had turned from sentimental love poems and romantic elegies to historic themes and patriotic exhortations. The writing of poetry had become for him a call for action rather than a substitute for it.[1]

Now, in early November 1847, with the king still in seething Genoa, the moment had come—at least in the excited minds of Mameli and his fellow students—to arouse Italians to stand together and fight for union and independence. Agitation for action ran high in the patriotic societies, most notably in the *Entelema*, formed by students, where Mameli held sway.[2] In between making speeches, partaking in debates, and recording petitions, he had dashed off a new poem.

Such was his eagerness and hurry that he did not even bother with full punctuation. But what did it matter! This was a fighting song. Its purpose was to galvanize his fellow Italians into action and to vocalize their yearning for unity and liberty. He probably wrote the incandescent five stanzas, marked by few erasures or emendations, in the house of the French consul,[3] which may account for some similarity with the *Marseillaise*, a comparison made repeatedly.

On November 6, 1847, he showed the five stanzas to a couple of friends, but was in such a haste to move on that he did not even wait for their response. That response came the same night, when they made copies to be distributed the following day. Some twenty-four hours later Mameli's stanzas were heard publicly for the first time. The activist young author and his close friend Nino Bixio had arranged for a mass demonstration to celebrate the three-state customs union, and Mameli's stirring verses reverberated first near the lodgings of the Tuscan consul and then at those of the papal nuncio.

> Italian brothers
> Italy has arisen,
> With Scipio's helmet
> Crowning her head
> Where is victory?!
> She offers her long, flowing hair.
> What a slave of Rome
> God has created.
>
> Let us gather in legions
> Ready to die
> Italy has called![4]

If the first two lines in a vision as sweeping as an embrace, compressed into a mere five words, called into being both Italian brotherhood and nationhood, the last line had Italy—as yet only a patriotic image—call its citizens, presumably to arms. The middle part of this stanza, however, is far less self-explanatory. Not only does the upbeat of the first four lines contrast sharply with the next four and their note of dejection, but it must remain uncertain which Rome Mameli had in mind: papal Rome or ancient Rome, which had gradually subjected the tribes throughout the peninsula in the fifth and fourth centuries B.C.

There were no such ambiguities either in the evocative refrain, reminiscent of that of the *Marseillaise*, or in the other four stanzas. The second stanza effectively contrasted the status of the "downtrodden and derided" population, not yet a people because divided, with a brighter future. "One flag, one hope" would bring them together. The third stanza proclaimed that under the guidance of God the union would be a fraternal one. And once united, the native soil would be freed and the nation would be unconquerable.

To inspire his compatriots, Mameli reminded them of past glories and victories, a ploy similar to that used by other authors of national anthems. In the same fourth stanza he envisaged a triumphant Italy to reach from the Alps to Sicily.[5] His final stanza focused on the archenemy Austria. He left no doubt among his fellow citizens about his contempt for that enemy. The Austrians were denounced for drinking "the blood of Italy." But there was no reason for further worry! The Austrian eagle, the young author asserted, had not only "burnt his gut" but also lost his feathers.

The perfervid patriotism that ran through all of the stanzas could hardly fail to generate an enthusiastic response in the highly charged atmosphere of an impending upheaval. Less than a week after its creation, the *Canto Nazionale*, more often called by its first line invocation *Fratelli d'Italia* (Italian brothers) and ultimately known as *Inno de Mameli* (Mameli's Hymn), was sung passionately throughout Genoa. On November 10, 1847, a Genoese patriot wrote to a friend in Paris that the Genoese "are singing hymns to Pio Nono, to Italy, to union but the most popular one is 'Fratelli d'Italia' whose author is Goffredo Mameli."[6] And before year's end Mameli's admired champion Mazzini himself requested that among the popular songs that of young Mameli should be copied for him.

As yet, however, the words lacked a suitable melody. They were probably sung to a just-created tune which glorified the Piedmontese king, who still had to prove his readiness to seek Italian unification and liberation. Shortly after the return of Charles Albert to his capital in early December, Mameli's poem reached Turin where it fortunately as well as fortuitously came to the attention of Michele Novaro, an established composer. After briefly perusing the stanzas, he exclaimed, "A stupendous thing."[7]

The much impressed Maestro forthwith supplied a lilting melody that not only suited the spirit of the poem but made it even more widely popular. The Piedmontese now had a powerful song that vocalized their sentiments and spurred their aspirations into likely action. For that very reason Turin authorities first looked askance at the inflammatory verses and in mid-December 1847 banned the poem, a measure which had the predictable opposite effect. Lyrics and melody were published in Genoa on December 10, 1847.

The same day a unique opportunity occurred to vent anti-Austrian sentiments

at the centenary of the Austrians' expulsion from Genoa.[8] The city was astir
with demonstrations, speeches, banquets, fireworks. Mameli not only had the
satisfaction of hearing his *Canto Nazionale* vibrantly resound in the packed
streets, but he already had composed a new poem for this special occasion, both
marked by a cutting bias against Austria.

Yet his anti-Austrian and pro-reformist positions had been long in the making.
Born on September 5, 1827, into an upper-class family, partly Genoan and partly
Sardinian, he had been raised in a patriotic and progressive environment. Much
as his mother and some Piarist fathers had shaped his thinking, the most profound influence had been that of Giuseppe Mazzini. His apostolate of total commitment to a united and democratic Italian nation-state, resting securely upon
republican institutions, found in the young Mameli one of Mazzini's most faithful disciples.

Aside from the influence of individuals, there were the collective experiences
of Italian patriots of whose hopes, deeds, and sufferings the sensitive youngster
first heard from his mother. It was she who told him of the abortive uprisings
in 1821 and 1831; the ephemeral *Giovine Italia* (Young Italy) association
founded by Mazzini; the imprisonment or exile of many worthy men aspiring—
and conspiring when need there be—to realize the vision of a free and unified
Italy.

Now, at twenty, Goffredo Mameli stood in the forefront of a new generation
of Italian patriots ready for action. There was little doubt in his mind as to who
would win out. On January 2, 1848, he addressed a Turin banquet where he
urged his receptive audience "to smash the Austrian enemy like a vase."[9] And
it was not long afterwards that initial blows were struck. Ironically, the first
rebellion of 1848—the Year of Revolution in Europe—broke out in one of its
most backward and remote areas—Sicily. The population in some of the island's
larger cities demanded greater autonomy and traditionalist privileges, curtailed
by the absolutist government in Naples. Before long the shock effects made
themselves felt throughout much of the peninsula. Clashes soon took place far
to the north between Austrian troops and patriots. At Pavia half-a-dozen students
were killed and the incensed as well as compassionate Mameli at once arranged
for a memorial mass that took the character of a powerful demonstration.

His *Canto* continued to be heard throughout Piedmont. A Turin paper could
state without much exaggeration: "The voice which interprets the sentiments of
all is that of our Mameli; the hymn *Fratelli d'Italia* . . . is sung throughout the
city by the whole population."[10] Genoan activists, with the students in the vanguard, certainly missed no opportunity to clamor for reforms at home and war
against the Austrians. But the Turin government hesitated on either issue, although the ban on Mameli's hymn was lifted except for the last stanza with its
blistering attack on Austrian "bloodsucking." Not that the Piedmontese government had any great sympathy for the Austrians, but it wanted to avoid pro-
voking them into a preventive intervention.

That probably was the very hope of Mameli and his friends. Genoa was atwitter with revolutionary talk, even rumors of secession. The young author, turned agitator, used his poetry to incite his listeners; nor did his prose fail him in fierce harangues. The king, he asserted, was left with the choice of granting a constitution or bombarding Genoa. To the relief of the patriots, ever-wavering Charles Albert at long last opted for the first alternative. On March 4, 1848, his government promulgated the *Statuto*, the much desired constitution. But its salutary effects were almost at once eclipsed by even more welcome news.

On March 19, fighting broke out in Milan, capital of Lombardy-Venetia, a region effectively if undemocratically governed by Austria. Effective or not, however, the Milanese considered the Austrians as domineering foreigners. Taking their cue for action from the American colonists, boycotting British tea imports, resentful Milanese had decided to boycott tobacco goods, a state monopoly.

Foregoing such pleasures voluntarily, they were incensed when Austrian soldiers in the streets of Milan ostentatiously smoked pipes and cigars, probably blowing the smoke into the faces of the citizenry. The latter set upon their challengers with whatever weapons they could lay hands on. To the surprise of everyone involved, after five days of severe street fighting the imperial Austrian forces withdrew from Milan.

Their retreat toward the *Quadilateral*, the formidable defense position based on four fortresses along the line separating Lombardy from Venetia, coincided with the news that a revolution had broken out in Vienna itself. Better still, the Venetians at the eastern pivot of Austria's dominion of northern Italy had risen in arms. The days of the Austrian empire appeared to hurtle to their end while those of Italian redemption seemed near.

Even before this exciting news had reached Genoa, Mameli and his fellow militants jumped into action. In the evening of March 19, he addressed a tumultuous crowd. "Citizens! At Milan they are dying; we . . . shall leave tonight and cross the border [into Lombardy] tomorrow. Who among you wants to do the same!"[11] His fervent appeal met with a gratifying response. Some three hundred men volunteered their services. By taking command of these eager volunteers, the budding poet now turned to soldiering. He formed the men into a company appropriately named after his role model: Mazzini.

Not unexpectedly did the men cheer themselves and their goal by singing their commander's *Canto*.[12] But it was one thing to muster enthusiastic volunteers and quite another to bring them into action. Only after the Turin government—within days—had declared war on Austria was Mameli able to lead his company across the Ticino which marked the border of Piedmont and the Austrian provinces of Lombardy-Venetia. To the regret of the volunteers, they did not reach Milan until after the fighting there had ended. But their commander at least had the pleasure of meeting for the first time the venerated Mazzini, who had returned from exile to the Lombardian capital.[13]

Later that spring Mazzini asked his young friend to write an Italian *Marseillaise*. In spite of assertions by renowned historians, such as the Frenchman Jules

Michelet, that Mameli's *Canto* constituted the *Marseillaise* of Italy, Mazzini apparently did not think so. He even undertook to ask Giuseppe Verdi to provide a melody for the newly commissioned hymn. Five weeks later Mazzini acknowledged receipt of Mameli's *Inno Militare* with the statement that "it pleased me well."[14] The newest creation of the passionate activist that Mameli was could indeed rival the most martial lines of the *Marseillaise*.

In Mameli's excited mind, no less than in his exulted words, the trumpet sounded to battle against the Austrian occupiers. The sword would not be sheathed as long as they enslaved even one corner of Italian lands. If thousands were to fall for an Italy free from the Alps to the seas, twenty times as many would take their place, a line that owed much to the *Marseillaise*. Alas, the *Inno Militare* failed to inspire victory. A week after Mazzini's graceful acknowledgement of receiving the poem, the Piedmontese army was routed by the Austrians at Custozza. The Mantua column, to which Mameli had added the remnant of his Genoa volunteers, retreated into neutral Parma.

The disappointed but not disheartened poet-soldier returned to Genoa. There he resumed political and publishing activities, centering on a rejection of the armistice that the Turin government had concluded with the victorious Austrians in August 1848. He was pleased to hear his *Canto* sung freely and frequently, now that the authorities had withdrawn their ban of the last stanza. Better still, it was heard in other parts of the peninsula[15] and especially in the newly proclaimed Republic of St. Mark's, bravely resisting Austrian efforts at subjugation.

His prose, as the editor of a new journal, was fuelled by the same burning patriotism that marked his poetry. He published as his first article a piece with the heading "Citizens, load your guns." But his principal effort focused on the establishment of a constituent national assembly, popularly elected, as the foundation for an all-Italian state that could conduct all-out war against the Austrian enemy.

By the fall of 1848, however, the forward momentum of the revolutionary year had slowed considerably. Moderate and conservative forces, soon to give way to outright reaction, reasserted themselves in Berlin, Paris, Vienna. In Rome, by contrast, a very different development took place. The Eternal City became more radicalized.

Pope Pius IX had foregone—some like Mameli said forsaken—his earlier role as a potential national leader. To the great disappointment of patriots throughout the peninsula, he had not only refused to enter the first independence war in the spring of 1848 but had issued an encyclical renouncing war against Austria. Worse, he had ordered papal troops marching to the assistance of the Piedmontese army to turn back. From that time on the devout Catholic Mameli had turned his back on the papacy.[16]

Papal efforts to maintain a modicum of reforms came to nought when the principal minister was assassinated in November 1848. After random shots were fired at the *Quirinale*, the Pope's residence, the enraged rather than frightened Pius IX took refuge with the reactionary king of the Two Sicilies. The ensuing political vacuum in the patrimony of St. Peter's soon attracted the Mazzinians. Mameli quickly observed that "the events in Rome will have a great impact," adding that it was essential "to make it our center." [17]

Vibrating with new hopes the young firebrand rushed to Rome at the end of November. There he helped lay the groundwork for a national constituent assembly which, when it met in January 1849, amounted to little more than a city council. The union envisaged in his *Canto* was no more than a mirage; many regions throughout his visionary Italy being either unable or unwilling to send delegates.

But to his delight a Roman republic was proclaimed on February 9, 1849. Now the ultimate opportunity to create a free, democratic, and unified country was at hand. Logically, the faithful disciple immediately called for the arrival of its principal apostle. Mameli's call to Mazzini came in the same dramatic and laconic form that characterized his political appeals in crisis situations and stood in sharp contrast to the effusiveness of much of his poetry.

Roma! Repubblica! Venite! (Rome! Republic! Come!). The master thus summoned did respond, arriving from Marseilles in early March. Almost at once he was elected one—and the most important—of the triumvirs who were to govern the city-state that hopefully would soon become the core of the new Italy. The Piedmontese government was on the verge of resuming war against Austria. Coordination was vital to avoid the calamities of the previous year when Italian states or regions had gone off on their own like a string of firecrackers—only to be subdued one after another.

Alas, the second war of independence waged by Piedmont had an even worse and quicker ending than the first. Within two weeks its army was defeated by the indomitable Field Marshal Joseph Radetzky at Novara, deep in Piedmont territory, on March 23, 1849. The hapless Charles Albert abdicated and an armistice was agreed on. Piedmontese hopes were shattered. Yet Mameli hardly had expected a very different outcome. As early as January 1849, he had forecast that "the royal war cannot save Italy." [18] In his more and more outspoken view only a national war of the Italians could, and only a republic could sustain their aspirations.

To canvass those possibilities Mazzini despatched Mameli and his friend Bixio to Genoa in early April. The two emissaries, returning to their native city, found it in a revolutionary mood. The *Canto* still played its part in it but an Italian brotherhood standing together for the attainment of nationhood now seemed further away than a year and a half earlier when Mameli had created his poem. Genoans who attempted to emulate the Republic of St. Mark's separate resistance to Austria were quickly subdued by the Piedmontese government.

The most resolute patriots had to flee the city which the young poet-soldier, the sobriquet by which Mameli became known, never was to see again. If the Piedmont monarchy had failed the Italy of Mameli's hopes, the Roman republic, hopefully, would not. He and his friend Bixio were among those now conveyed by sea to that republic's principal port of Civitavecchia; albeit the ships that took them there flew the Stars and Stripes. The *USS Princeton* and the *USS Allegheny* had been assigned to help the Genoan refugees find a safe haven, and Mameli recorded with gratitude that "the Americans showed an incomparable courtesy."[19]

Ominously a mere ten days after the Genoans had been put safely ashore at Civitavecchia from where they made their way to Rome, a large French squadron together with numerous transports cast anchor in the same port. Some 10,000 soldiers disembarked, but their commander, General Charles Oudinot, a son of one of the marshals of Napoleon I, gave no indications as to their objectives. Yet it quickly became obvious that one of them would be the restoration of Pius IX to the patrimony of St. Peter's.

On April 26, Mameli wrote to his mother back in Genoa, criticizing the French for their planned intervention. He assured her that "we are preparing to resist. God wants us to save our honor so that foreigners cannot say that Italians are cowardly."[20] And five days later he jubilantly told her, "Yesterday the French attacked at three points and have been beaten back. In many a year this is the first day of glory for Italy."[21]

Much to the surprise of almost everyone present on April 30, 1849, Oudinot had been compelled to withdraw his troops toward Civitavecchia. A motley force of artists, students, *Trasteverini* from the working class sections of the city, foreign volunteers— all stiffened by some regular troops—had successfully withstood the French assault. Much of the effective resistance effort was due to Giuseppe Garibaldi, at forty already a living legend of the Italian fight for unity and freedom. Within days Mazzini appointed him to command the armed forces of the republic, and Garibaldi's *Legione* sang or whistled Mameli's *Canto* proudly and defiantly.[22]

Mameli, always the militant, soon served with great pleasure and expectations on Garibaldi's staff. In that capacity he partook in a sortie directed at Neapolitan troops sent by their reactionary king to close the ring around Rome. At Palestrina in the Alban foothills, the Neapolitans were routed and the Roman republic had scored its second victory in as many weeks. Had Mameli seen Garibaldi's assessment of him, he would have been very proud.[23] Suffering from a fever did not keep him from following his inspiring commander in pursuit of the Neapolitans. They were driven from the territory of the Roman republic after the brief engagement at Velletri where Mameli was slightly wounded. That minor wound gave him more pleasure than pain; he could now think of himself not only as a veteran but one who had been bloodied in a noble cause.

His feverish exultation and inexhaustible optimism alike led him to write that the victory at Velletri might trigger an uprising in Naples. Better still, it might lead "within the next few months to an expansion of the Republic from Sicily to the Po."[24] Little did he anticipate that this republic might very shortly disappear into the Elysian fields of history.

Just as fleeting as Mameli's vision of a unified and democratic Italy was his expectation of a French withdrawal. Far from it, General Oudinot presented an ultimatum to the government of Rome; unless the city was surrendered to him within three days his troops would take it by force. Mazzini and his followers, not to mention Garibaldi, had no intention of yielding. Mindful of the repulse of the French just over one month ago, they thought a repeat performance likely. Rejecting the ultimatum, Mazzini and his colleagues in the triumvirate ordered the forces of the Roman republic to be combat-ready by June 4.

Unfortunately, the French commander stole a march on the defenders. Before dawn on June 3, the troops of the Second French Republic fell upon them and quickly carried the outposts. A further advance, however, was checked for much of the day by Garibaldi and his largely volunteer force. In the late afternoon the reinforced French renewed their drive, advancing to the very walls of Rome. It was then that Mameli, who had acted for much of the day as one of Garibaldi's adjutants, pleaded with his chief to let him help turn the fleeing men once more toward the enemy.

Garibaldi, who sensed Mameli's impatience and determination, allowed him to go forward. Shortly afterwards the young poet-soldier was carried back on a stretcher. By his own account Garibaldi was deeply moved at that sight.[25] Yet the leg wound appeared to be superficial. A buoyant Mameli informed his mother on June 12 that "a bayonet worked by a *Bersagliere*"[26] had wounded him in the left calf. He hastened to reassure her of his quick recovery. Once again his inborn optimism was to prove in excess of given realities.

He was overjoyed when informed in hospital that his bravery in action had earned him a promotion to staff captain. His friend Bixio, who also had been wounded and taken to the same hospital, heard him say, "Our primary need is to fight, fight, and fight."[27] Mameli's physical condition, however, did not match his eagerness for combat. His left leg developed gangrene and after a week of much pain and uncertainty had to be amputated.

That amputation gave Mameli and his friends new hope. Yet at the end of the month his condition took a turn for the worse, and so did the desperately struggling republic. The French had breached the city walls at several points and were closing in on the remaining strongholds. On the night of July 3, 1849, the intrepid and inexhaustible Garibaldi evacuated Rome and began an escape of legendary proportions.

The next day French troops took possession of Rome. No record exists of how the dying rhapsodist of an Italy yet to be created reacted to this final blow at the Mazzinian republic. His hyperactive patriotism and unbridled optimism may have led him to believe that somehow the Italy of his passions, dreams, and not least writings would live. If anything, the *Canto* would arouse his compatriots to stand together as brothers and make that Italy a reality. Then neither his life nor his death would have been in vain.

On July 6, Nino Bixio recorded: "At half past seven o'clock in the morning Mameli yielded up his great soul."[28] The youthful poet-soldier "who lived between a song and a battle"[29] was lamented by many, Mazzini and Garibaldi foremost among them. Nor was he forgotten by succeeding generations, remembering probably his sacrificial if somewhat less than heroic death better than his flamboyant poetry and prose. In 1871 a group of Genoa students sponsored the erection of a plaque at Mameli's birthplace, and in July 1891 the municipality of Rome had a monument raised over his grave. That monument depicted a dying soldier, resembling Mameli, and carried an inscription which read: "Lyra and sword remain the proper symbols of his life."

But being remembered in stone was not tantamount to being recited frequently and passionately. Mameli's poetry, while not lacking in literary quality and certainly not in forceful appeal, formed either around historical or current events. As the latter receded into the past and new situations took their place, some of his poems lost in relevance. His *Canto* was no exception. The 1850s brought a somber reassessment of the ebullient hopes of 1848-1849; the territorial status quo ante prevailed; in addition to the restored Austrian dominance in much of northern Italy, a French garrison now secured the returned Pope Pius IX in Rome where he set a reactionary cause outdone only by the even more reactionary king of the Two Sicilies. In short, it was a very unpropitious time to sing of unity and liberty.

True, by the end of that decade there were great changes in the wind. A seasoned statesman not only had planned them but set them in motion. Count Camillo Benso di Cavour, now chief minister in the kingdom of Piedmont, was no visionary like Mazzini or Mameli but no less a patriot than either of them. Having laid the diplomatic groundwork very skillfully Cavour invoked French military help in 1859 and wrested Lombardy from Austria. But he had larger plans, and to realize them had taken Garibaldi, just returned from self-chosen exile, into his confidence. The most popular personality in the peninsula had responded enthusiastically.

Garibaldi, leaving nothing to chance, had already commissioned a new marching song for those who were going to fight with him yet another round, perhaps the decisive one, for a free and united Italy. Although the veteran fighter still extolled Mameli, he did not utilize the *Canto* of the heroic days in the previous decade. Perhaps he wished to have his own battle hymn, or maybe he felt that young Mameli, in spite of his liking for him, was too close to Mazzini with whom he, Garibaldi, had quarreled repeatedly.

In any event, Mameli's *Canto* was left aside in favor of the newly commissioned *Cacciatori delle alpi* (The Alpine Huntsmen) by Luigi Mercantini. At the outbreak of war with Austria in late April 1859, the proud *Garibaldini*, who were all volunteers, many of them veterans who had fought alongside their admired leader for two decades, eagerly sang what soon became known as the *Inno Garibaldi*.[30] It was to echo throughout the new Italy in the making, after the *Garibaldini* first freed Sicily and then the Neapolitan mainland.

However popular the *Inno Garibaldi*, it could not entirely displace the *Inno di Mameli* as the *Canto* gradually became known. In late 1860, it had been proclaimed the anthem of the steadily expanding kingdom of Piedmont joined voluntarily by neighboring Italian states. The proclamation had been initiated by a friend of the Mameli family who had been appointed chief administrator of the Marches, formerly the northeastern part of the Papal States, whose population had just voted for inclusion within Piedmont. This proclamation, however, did not guarantee that the *Inno di Mameli* would be the national anthem once the nation-state had been created in its entirety.

On the contrary! When the kingdom of Italy, still in embryonic form, was established in March 1861, neither the *Inno di Mameli* nor the *Inno Garibaldi* was given the honor of anthem status. Instead, the *Marcia Reale*, the royal Piedmontese march dating to 1832, became the official anthem. Not surprisingly, there was no room at the top for any song connected with republicans and republicanism. Even though Garibaldi, for reasons of state, had cooperated with the dynasty, he had personally remained a republican. As for Goffredo Mameli, he not only had fallen in the defense of the Roman republic but he had sharply criticized the Piedmontese king. Much the same as in the newly established German empire, there seemed to be no need to take as anthem a piece created by a citizen of dubious antecedents. Thus, the *Marcia Reale* remained the national anthem after the completed unification of Italy in 1870 and to the end of the monarchy in 1946.

During those seventy-five years, the *Inno di Mameli* led a twilight existence neither fully accepted nor fully rejected. The proud heritage of the *Risorgimento*, the Italian national renascence, was neither forgotten by successive generations of Italians; nor did succeeding regimes disown that welcome heritage. In 1872, the mayor of Turin requested the inclusion of the *Inno* in a collection of memorabilia of the *Risorgimento*. A few years later an exhibit at Bologna featured in its illustrated catalog a facsimile of Mameli's draft.[31]

Yet there is no evidence that his poem, sometimes euphemistically praised as his most remarkable, was widely used in the era of the Italian monarchy. Almost certainly, the *Inno Garibaldi* enjoyed a greater degree of prominence and utilization. After all, Garibaldi's name and deeds were household words, while remembrance of Mameli was generally confined to the first verses of his *Inno* and a vague awareness of his role in the first war of independence. Anti-Austrian sentiments, which culminated in World War I, did their part in keeping the Mameli piece in good standing and, if anything, they sharpened in the postwar years, not least over the troublesome and controversial Alto Adige–South Tyrol issue.[32]

Nor did the advent of Benito Mussolini and the fascist regime prove detrimental to the *Inno di Mameli*. A fascist songbook included it as the fourth item, even though the *Marcia Reale* and the party song *Giovinezza* (Youth) took precedence. Such fascist ideologues as Giuseppe Bottai showed their unlimited admiration for Mameli.[33] And the fascist youth organization *Balilla* took its name from the youngster whom Mameli, in the fourth stanza of his *Inno,* had singled out for his courage in throwing the first stone at an Austrian officer in the ousting of the Austrians from Genoa in 1746.[34]

After the fall, first of fascism and then of the monarchy, a much battered Italy transformed itself into a republic by the summer of 1946. Along with a new constitution and flag, the latter being no different from the green-white-red flag that Mameli long ago had waved triumphantly at a student demonstration in December 1846, there arose the need for a new anthem. The *Inno Garibaldi* seemed a natural choice. For one thing, Garibaldi's lustre as the ultimate hero in the struggle for independence had not tarnished, and his image proved as acceptable to rightist as to leftist parties. Moreover, the hymn bearing his name had all the ingredients of a strong and sound patriotic appeal: the call to arms, the link with the martyrs of the past, the solidarity of the compatriots, and the freeing of the land. But there was one catch. For the sake of a future Italy the convinced republican Garibaldi had joined forces with the Piedmontese king in October 1860. By contrast, the republican government of 1946 would brook no deals with the discarded dynasty.

If the *Inno Garibaldi* was unacceptable, there fortunately was another *Inno*, composed at the dawn of an awakening Italy by a young patriot who not only was a bona fide Mazzinian but had given his life to the cause of a Roman republic. And thus, without any opposition Premier Alcide de Gasperi's cabinet proclaimed the *Inno di Mameli* to be the anthem of the first Italian republic as of October 14, 1946.

For the larger part of the following half century the anthem remained unchallenged. Pupils learned it routinely in elementary schools; it was played on official and public occasions, such as the republic's national holiday on April 25; the opening bars of the *Inno di Mameli* are still heard daily when the RAI—the state broadcasting network—begins its external programs.

Yet, as in some other countries, most notably in neighboring France, the relevance of the anthem has been increasingly questioned from the 1980s on and for reasons readily explained. The heroic age of Italy in the making recedes ever further into a distant past. Moreover, the great majority of Italians center their thoughts and efforts on the joys—and problems—of living rather than on sacrificial death. Even more important may be the fact that the Italian people are among the most ardent supporters of the transnational European Union. Never one of the very nationalist or ethnocentric peoples, notwithstanding the fascist era, Italians learned over the centuries how to accommodate foreigners, or accommodate to them, first as their overlords and then as their visitors.

Last but not least, there were the specific circumstances in which the *Inno di Mameli* had been proclaimed the national anthem in 1946 as well as those which had led to its creation in 1846. During the intervening century much had changed for and in Italy. Most of the stanzas were outdated of necessity in 1946, and in particular the first stanza, the only one now to be heard on national occasions. After all, Italy had ended up, as in 1918, in the victors' camp, if only by a repeat volte-face; thus, there was no compelling reason to ask, "Where is victory?" And as for that confusing and controversial line of being "the slave of Rome," the Italians had just voted into power their first ever republican government in the hope that it would lay from Rome the foundations for a new and better Italy.

It was that government which by decree had given a national anthem to the Italian people, rather than have one come up from the people. While a century earlier the *Inno* had been enthusiastically acclaimed by those many for whom it spoke, popular acceptance in 1946 was more of a formality. Thus, the newly accredited anthem was not as deeply embedded in the public mind or made all but sacrosanct by tradition as, for instance, the British, Dutch, and Polish anthems.

Small wonder, then, that the *Inno di Mameli* has in recent years come in for its share of criticism and calls for replacement. Proposals have been made to have the opening lines of Verdi's highly evocative opera *Nabucco* (Nebuchadnezzar) as a new anthem. Some public opinion polls have suggested—perhaps playfully—*O' sole mio* as an alternative. Doubtless, there will be other suggestions. Few critics of the current anthem have been as outspoken as the head of the *Northern League*, now a sizeable party in the political arena. Umberto Bossi stated unequivocally in 1990: "The anthem . . . is out of touch with the collective conscience of the times and no longer can be useful in mobilizing the country. . . . I shall limit myself to underscoring the necessity to finally have a better anthem, one that is more representative, more appropriate for our era."[35]

To be sure, the anthem still has its defenders, none more prominent than the recently retired president of the republic. The outspoken if controversial Francesco Cossiga, in a spirited defense of Italian patriotism and its symbols, declared in March 1991: "I would never change the *Inno di Mameli*. I would play it both at the beginning and the end of [daily] broadcasting."[36]

Whether Mameli's hymn will follow that president into retirement is an open question for the time being. Similar efforts elsewhere, most noteworthy in France, have yet to succeed. But if any anthem among those dealt with in this book is a prime candidate for displacement it may well be the *Inno di Mameli*, the only anthem presented here to carry its creator's name in the title.

NOTES

1. One biographer of Mameli has summarized, "Goffredo Mameli's life is a record simply of his songs turned into action." Evelyn (Countess) Martinengo-Cesaresco, *Italian Characters in the Epoch of Unification*, new ed. (London: T. Fisher Unwin, 1901), 198.

2. Mameli became the Society's secretary and, in spring of 1847, a member of its executive committee. His dedication and drive made him "quickly the soul" of *Entelema*. Domenico M. Seghetti, *Goffredo Mameli* (Genoa: F. Ceretti, 1950), 38.

3. Domenico Pastorino, *Mameli* (Milano: Garzanti, 1946), 102.

4. The official translation, as provided by the Italian embassy in Washington, D.C., has not fully satisfied some of my colleagues and students. Differences of interpretation center on lines six and seven and the meaning of Italy being "the slave of Rome." Italian commentators generally regard that reference as antipapal, but I am inclined to accept the other interpretation that Mameli had imperial Rome in mind. When he wrote

his *Canto Nazionale* in 1846, the then Pontiff Pius IX was still viewed by Italian patriots as their potential leader. I have therefore availed myself of the translation prepared by Dr. Douglas Wertman and David A. Bustamante. The offering of the hair was the traditional gesture of submission to the mastery of Rome. The reference to "Scipio's helmet," on the other hand, is clear. It is Publius Cornelius Scipio "Africanus," the latter name bestowed on the Roman consul for his final triumph over the Carthaginians in the second Punic war.

5. That line, recurring in Mameli's poetry, doubtless would have provoked the author of the German anthem, whose first stanza referred to the borders of a united Germany as reaching "from the Etsch to the Belt." The river Etsch is the Italian Adige, flowing into the Adriatic from the southern reaches of the Alps, and gave its name after 1945 to the province of *Alto Adige*, which borders on Austria. Had the two authors known each other or at least of each other, they would have been natural enemies, a striking illustration of the built-in conflict between competing yet similar national aspirations.

6. A. Codignola, *Goffredo Mameli: la vita e gli scritti* (Goffredo Mameli: Life and writings), 2 vols. (Venezia: La Nuova Italia, 1927), 1:96. This is the standard work on Mameli.

7. *Dizionario del Risorgimento Nazionale* (hereafter cited as DRN), 4 vols. (Milan: Dottor Franceso Vallardi, 1931–1937), 2:441.

8. Genoa had been under temporary Austrian occupation in 1746 when rioting began. According to tradition, a boy, Giuseppe Balilla, heaved the first stone against the Austrians who subsequently evacuated the city. Not only did Mameli single him out for praise but he gloried in the success of the rebellion.

9. *Pagine Politiche de Goffredo Mameli*, ed. Aldo Borlenghi (Milano: Universale Economica, 1950), 13. This collection, hereafter cited as *Pagine Politiche*, contains most of Mameli's flamboyant prose articles.

10. Codignola, 1:211, quoting *La Concordia*, February 12, 1849.

11. Pastorino, 146.

12. DRN, 1:519–20.

13. Although Mameli and Mazzini had been in correspondence for over one year, this was their first face-to-face meeting of which there is a record.

14. Pastorino, 107.

15. DRN, 1:519.

16. Mameli's biographers have always stressed that he was deeply religious but had been increasingly bitter about papal policies since the spring of 1848. Codignola, 1:353–54; Pastorino, 82.

17. Codignola, 2:376.

18. Ibid., 282.

19. Pastorino, 242.

20. Ibid., 245.

21. Codignola, 2:386–87.

22. DRN, 1:520.

23. Garibaldi commented in a report on the action, "Mameli, this fine and candid youth . . . has demonstrated at one and the same time the sagacity of a commander and the ebullience and dash of the valorous soldier." Pastorino, 265.

24. Codignola, 2:389.

25. Some fifteen years later, Garibaldi wrote to Mameli's mother. "I had kept him by my side . . . as my adjutant . . . but his position near me seemed to him inglorious. In

a few minutes he was carried back past me . . . his face shining because he had shed his blood for his country. We did not exchange a word but our eyes met with the love that had long bound us together." George M. Trevelyan, *Garibaldi's Defense of the Roman Republic* (London: Longmans, Green, and Co., 1907), 186.

26. Codignola, 3:395. The *Bersaglieri* were regular troops who made a good record for themselves in the first war of independence and as the core unit in the defense of Rome in 1849. In later times they were a crack regiment of the Italian army.

27. Pastorini, 268.

28. Martinengo-Cesaresco, 244–45.

29. This striking phrase was coined by Mazzini when he wrote from renewed exile in Switzerland in October 1849. His commemorative piece on Mameli has been reprinted in *Poesie di Goffredo Mameli* (Milan: Carlo Brigola, 1878), 7–10.

30. Text and score of the *Inno Garibaldi* may be found together with an English translation in George Macauley Trevelyan, *Garibaldi and the Making of Italy*, new impression (New York: Longmans, Green and Co., 1928), 229–30.

31. DRN, 2:441.

32. The Italian claim to "the crest of the Alps" as the natural border between Italy and Austria, a claim first advanced by the Mazzinians, was fulfilled at the end of World War I—over the objections of defeated Austria. South Tyrol came under Italian sovereignty but the majority of the Südtiroler strongly opposed that transfer. In turn, Italian animosities toward Austria, which backed its former nationals, increased.

33. Giuseppe Bottai, a member of the Fascist Grand Council and a leading theoretician in the fascist party, was one of Mameli's most fulsome hagiographers. See his *Köpfe des risorgimento* essay, trans. Adelaide Morandotti (Berlin: Junker & Dünnhaupt, 1943).

34. The relevant lines read: "The children of Italy are all called Balilla."

35. *La Repubblica*, September 13, 1990.

36. Ibid., March 22, 1991.

Anthems of Contentment

14

Sweden

Du gamla, du fria
(Richard Dybeck)

The Hymn
(Carl August Vilhelm Strandberg)

DU GAMLA, DU FRIA/RICHARD DYBECK

On the international scene Sweden has lain becalmed ever since the end of the Napoleonic wars, the one European country free from war, domestic or foreign, since that time. The lionesque power of the north, whose strong claws had ripped deep into central Germany in the seventeenth century and even deeper into tsarist Russia in the eighteenth century, had pulled in those feared claws. In 1815, Sweden also abandoned title to its remaining continental possessions in the northern part of Germany, thus turning its back seemingly for good on the European continent. Henceforth it would enclose itself, together with the newly acquired Norway, inside the Scandinavian peninsula—not much caring to be a player on the international scene unless for the sake of peace.

Domestically, the large country with an incongruent small population re-mained hierarchical in its social structure and overwhelmingly agrarian for much of the nineteenth century. Encased in its traditional form of government—dom-inated by the king, administered by the nobility, and represented by a national assembly of four estates[1]—there seemed to be little immediate need for far-reaching changes. Nor was King Carl XIV Johan, the erstwhile French profes-sional soldier and founder of the Bernadotte dynasty, in any hurry to modernize Sweden's institutions or surrender any part of his extensive powers, notwithstanding his own revolutionary background. The shrewd if temperamental Jean-Baptiste Bernadotte carefully avoided any unequivocal commitment that might limit his options or undercut his uncertain hold on the Swedish throne to which he had ascended in 1818.[2]

For much of the following quarter century, during which he not only reigned but ruled, Bernadotte found it more opportune to side with the conservative groups, notably the clergy and most of the aristocracy, than with the reformers among the bourgeoisie and the peasantry. They increasingly agitated for press freedom, detailed accounting of government expenditures, limited ministerial responsibility, and—most important—the transformation of the estates into a parliamentary system. Most of these demands were blocked or side-stepped by the wily first Bernadotte king.

It was probably not just by mere chance that in 1844, the year of his death, there appeared two songs destined to national prominence and ultimately to quasi-anthem status. Sweden, like Denmark, was to have two anthems: one royal and one common.[3] Unlike their Danish counterparts, however, neither of the two has ever been formally recognized as the Swedish anthem. Though both originated in the same year, they differed as widely in theme and thrust as their respective authors differed in experience and interests. The author of *Du gamla, du fria* (Thou ancient, thou free) centered his concerns and creativity on the far-distant past of prehistoric and Viking Sweden. By contrast, the creator of the *Hymn*, later more commonly known as the *kungssången* (The king's song) was deeply engaged in contemporary affairs as a political partisan. While a pithy melody for his poem was quickly supplied by a professional composer, the melody of *Du gamla, du fria* went in search of an author, thus making the Swedish national anthem one of the very few whose tune preceded the text.

That tune belonged to one of the numerous folk songs which abounded in largely rural Sweden. Not all of them were of a purely Swedish origin. *Du gamla* may well have sprung from a mixed parentage of German and Swedish background. Yet there was certainly enough of a national heredity to make it "typical of Swedish folk songs."[4] As such, it came to the attention of a young Swede, himself deeply rooted in his country's past. It seemed inevitable that Richard Dybeck and the euphonious melody would be drawn toward one another, much like the magnet and the metal.

Dybeck probably had heard that happy little tune as a boy, but it did not attract him fully until he saw its score as a young man. He was not, however, an accomplished musician or, for that matter, a prolific poet. His real interests lay in the collection of every kind of Swedish relic that he could lay his hands on. The deeper he could reach into the remote past, the more satisfaction he felt at being Swedish. In his twenties the budding ethnologist had literally walked the width and breadth of the Swedish countryside, collecting, as he went, artifacts, ballads, legends, and songs. He had come to love the deep forests, numerous lakes, rushing rivers, luscious meadows. And he heard the ancient

melody that seemed to call for more weighty words than those which had accompanied it for so long.[5]

Still other influences impacted on the young Dybeck, most notably romanticism. The very movement that had such a profound bearing on many an anthem
author had made its way into Scandinavia after flooding the European continent
in the early nineteenth century. The most formidable Swedish literary voice of
romanticism, that of Esaias Tegnér, had stirred numerous Swedes, not least
among them Richard Dybeck.

Dybeck, who looked like the quintessential romantic artist with his gentle
features, dreamy expression, and curly hair, took a very active part in the organization of folklorist groups. Eager to share their findings, he and his friends
sponsored an evening of folk music in Stockholm on November 18, 1844. Dybeck perceived that public meeting as a welcome opportunity to air a traditional
song for which he had recently written suitable words. At the finale of the
concert, with the author present, a professional tenor rendered the *Song to the
North* for the first time in public.

> Thou ancient, thou fresh, thou mountainous North
> In beauty and peace our hearts beguiling,
> I greet thee, thou loveliest land on earth,
> Thy sun, thy sky, thy verdant meadows smiling.
>
> Thy throne rests on memories from days of yore,
> When worldwide renown was valor's guerdon.
> I know to thy name thou art true as before.
> Oh, I would live and I would die in that North.[6]

Spontaneous and prolonged acclaim greeted these two innocuous and enthusiastic stanzas, making them in time the shortest anthem among those presented
here. As yet, Dybeck's eight-liner was just one more patriotic song, but one that
moved the listeners to tears on that November night in Stockholm.[7] And the
most prominent personage present, the highly regarded historian and writer Erik
Gustaf Geijer, jumped up from his seat while exclaiming, "That's what I call
poetry, music. More of it Dybeck."[8] A month later the little song with the telling
effect even caused the newly crowned King Oscar I, present at the second concert of folk music, to applaud heartily.

But the flattered author did not deceive himself as to the literary quality of
his two stanzas. In a frank evaluation, unique among anthem authors, Dybeck
commented in 1845: "At best mediocre, these words" were of transitory value
and "not meant for publication."[9] This remarkable self-criticism notwithstanding, the verses reflected a good bit of his personality and proclivities.

Not incidentally did the opening words read, "Thou ancient. . . ." His view
of and sentiment for his native country reached over two millenia to its very
beginnings. Hardly less important a catalyst was Dybeck's love for the Swedish
countryside. As he put it succinctly in a comment on "unassuming tunes" like

Du gamla, "I intend to have people benefit . . . who have felt at home in the Swedish woodlands at least once."[10] And he rhapsodized the unspoiled beauty as well as the salutary quiescence prevailing in much of Sweden in his time. Yet he was not unmindful of Swedish power and glory in recent centuries when Gustavus II Adolphus had led a feared and formidable army into central Germany, where he fell in battle, and Carl XII had penetrated deeply into Russia, making a legend of endurance and daring.

Dybeck's intellectual drive and creative urge alike, from youth on, had two principal goals: the rediscovery and the revitalization of Sweden's far-distant past. His native province of Västmanland had given him the first impressions of pre-Christian, even prehistoric Sweden. That province—stretching to the west of Stockholm—proved to be a rich lode for Dybeck's eager archaeological research, and he quite literally considered it his birthright to draw from that wealth of artifacts, inscriptions, and structures.

Trained in the law, he soon left a judicial career. A few years later he gave up office as acting mayor of a sizeable town. Not only did he dislike officialdom but he wished to indulge his passion: ethnology. Free from boring responsibilities, Dybeck searched full-time for the Swedish past, building up collections of relics, data, and folklore items.[11]

A crippling stroke slowed him down less than a year after he had written the *Du gamla* stanzas. That handicap did not keep him from revising them repeatedly. He doubtless thought of improving their literary quality, but the changes made over the years were mainly semantic, except for one which was to cause both controversy and confusion. The change occurred in the opening line of the song.

To be sure, Dybeck never had second thoughts as to the validity of "Thou ancient. . . ." After all, that was the bloodline linking generations of Swedes through the centuries with himself as the principal recordkeeper. Rather it was the second adjective which underwent a substantial change. Some time between late spring 1857 and March 1858, the author substituted *fria* (free) for the original *friska* (fresh). That substitution certainly looked insignificant, not least because of the similarity of the two words. Yet the reason for this replacement lay deeper than in a mere semantic perfection.

The mid-1850s had brought Sweden precariously close to losing its precious and comfortable cover of nonalignment. During the Crimean War, the Swedish government had allowed British and French warships, operating in the Baltic against Russia, the use of port facilities. Moreover, the Swedish king openly favored "slashing the throat" of the tsarist empire at St. Petersburg rather than peripheral operations at "the giant's toe" in the Crimea.[12]

Anti-Russian sentiments had lingered, at least since the disastrous campaigns which pitted Carl XII against Tsar Peter the Great. They peaked after the loss of Finland to Russia in 1809. Apolitical as Dybeck's overall orientation was, his very Swedishness, strengthened by his passionate and deep reach into the remote past, made him view the contrast, perhaps even a potential conflict between Sweden and Russia, as one between free and unfree people. To emphasize that difference he chose to replace "fresh" with "free."

The latest change in the *Song to the North*, however, lacked in general acceptance among the public for several generations. More often than not the original line, "Thou ancient, thou fresh, thou mountainous North," was heard for most of the next half century, even though printed texts henceforth carried the revised line. Several reasons underlay this discrepancy. Popular songs in particular may prove difficult to revise, especially when they come down through the generations by word of mouth. Dybeck's song owed much of the initial popularity not only to its emotional appeal but above all to the efforts of a single devotee. The widely known opera singer Carl Frederick Lundquist for years on end closed his solo performances with a powerful rendition of *Du gamla* in the original form.

Moreover, most Swedes did not think their freedom was endangered by either foreign invasion or domestic upheaval. There was no compelling need, as existed in some other countries, to make the struggle for freedom a major theme.[13] To savor the beauty and freshness of the unspoiled and pristine Swedish countryside was a far more immediate concern of many a Swede, and in his first version of *Du gamla, du friska* Dybeck had given visceral expression to that blissful feeling.

He had neither intention nor gumption to act as the literary drummer goading his countrymen into action for greater glory or a better future. All he wanted was to make them aware of the Swedish past. The very nature of his work attested to that preoccupation. In the first half of the 1860s, he published five collections of folk songs, three brochures, and no fewer than ten pieces on runic writings, but only a couple of poems.[14]

As a poet he hardly left a mark in Swedish literature and remains unnoticed in most Swedish standard works on that subject. For good reason! There is not even a collection of his few poems. Just one of them in addition to *Du gamla* is widely known and heartily recited to the present day. Its verses not only revelled in the glorified courage and virility of Swedish youth but seemed to compensate Dybeck himself for the disability suffered from his stroke.

> Courage, manhood, daring!
> Still can be found in old Sweden
> Strength of arm, and strength of heart,
> Youthful warmth in battle cry!
> Blue Eyes,
> [Like] tiny flowers,
> Twinkle in the fresh air.
> North, you the strength of life and limb
> North, you home of gentle hearts![15]

These and similar lines proved so popular that several versions came into existence, all set to a rousing march melody. Notwithstanding such popularity,

Dybeck's true literary medium remained the antiquarian magazine *Runa*, which he first issued in 1842 and to which he contributed numerous articles and remarkable drawings over nearly three decades.

The death of his wife, after a few years of happy marriage, ended his most productive period and plunged him into deep gloom by 1865. For the remaining dozen years of his life he kept adding to his numerous collections and ethnographic work. But declining health and vigor along with exhausted funds, to which both government and private sources had contributed, forced severe curtailment. Dybeck's death in 1877 was hardly noticed by the public, and the funeral was attended by no more than a dozen people. Worse still, his burial place at Stockholm's North Cemetery was a pauper's grave, soon to lose its identity. Much of his work, its pioneering features notwithstanding, was shelved and all but forgotten in libraries, museums, and antiquarian societies. Only his collections of more than five hundred folk songs retained their use as living entities. Yet *Du gamla, du fria* did not hold a special position among them.

A decade after its author's death, however, an elementary schoolteacher and part-time organist argued warmly in behalf of Dybeck's song. He reasoned, in a spirited talk, that "since we Swedes are the only ones among the nations to lack a national anthem, I venture to suggest . . . that *Du gamla, du friska* [*sic*] is sung jointly with the refrain as a duet."[16] What that ardent proponent of an anthem for Sweden did not take into account was that the never-ostentatious Swedes felt secure and separate enough in their peninsula to forego any collective manifestation of either national identity or power. Until an external crisis arose there would be no need for such a manifestation.

The growing tension, however, between Norway and Sweden in the 1890s, when Norwegians pushed for the breakup of the union that had existed since 1814,[17] brought about an occasion to demonstrate Swedish unity and resolution. If the Norwegians asserted their national interests and identity, not least by singing their anthem, why should the Swedes not do likewise?

It was precisely at the turn of the century that *Du gamla* could be heard more and more often, acquiring unofficial anthem status. And it probably was no coincidence that the word "fria" now came into general use, replacing the older "friska" for good. The expanding use of Dybeck's placid and pleasing song seemed to ensure its role as a quasi-anthem. Not only was it advanced to that position by popular choice and public sentiment, King Oscar II, the royal patron of Swedish art and artists, stood up when hearing *Du gamla* at the graduation exercises of Lund University in 1893. Benefitting from such an endorsement, the Dybeck piece henceforth was placed first in musical presentations.

Its position, however, was by no means uncontested. Early in the twentieth century, a music director commented frankly that to have *Du gamla* as the national anthem would be "absolutely absurd."[18] He based that sweeping judgment on the contention that the two stanzas were no more than a drinking song and one that was altogether artless, and capping such a censure, he faulted Dybeck's verses for not having mentioned Sweden at all.[19]

Weightier challenges came from potential competitors whose poetry was no less patriotic but perhaps more elaborate and in some cases more sophisticated. The most serious contender in the long run was a poem that not only reached the public in the same year as that of Dybeck but remained in place as the royal anthem to the present day.

THE HYMN/CARL AUGUST VILHELM STRANDBERG

Carl Vilhelm August Strandberg's Christian names sounded more German than Swedish, a fact that may have been coincidental. There was, however, incontrovertible evidence that Strandberg had been influenced by German philosophy and poetry.[20] Dybeck, by contrast, had drawn his inspiration almost entirely from Swedish sources. While he remained aloof from the contemporary political scene, Strandberg, on the other hand, had been, in his formative years, a militant activist at Lund University. As such he had sported a radical republicanism and adopted in the mid-1830s a combative pen name, *Talis Qualis* (I am what I am). That self-designation notwithstanding, Strandberg did change ideological hobbyhorses within a decade and became a moderate monarchist, a change that was to culminate in the creation of his *Hymn*, a poem occasioned by the accession to the throne of Oscar I in March 1844.

Like his father, the ex-sergeant and ex-marshal, Oscar was born in France but had come to Sweden as a child, learned Swedish, and given his future subjects the feeling that he identified with them in the advancement of national interests. For Strandberg and other young liberals the new king "embodied the democratic ideal of kingship."[21] And the budding poet soon cast that image into the ornate form of the *Hymn*.

His idealized vision had been shaped in part by his German models, not least among them the magisterial Prussian court philosopher of international renown, G. W. F. Hegel. The Hegelian theorem of the strong monarchical state, overarching the generations and serviced by sovereign and subjects alike for the good of the nation, had triggered a resounding echo in the Swedish author's mind. In like measure, Strandberg was influenced by German radical or liberal poets whose work he translated. None impacted more directly on him than the author of the future German anthem, H. A. Hoffmann von Fallersleben, whose *Lied der Deutschen* was among those that Strandberg translated.[22]

Hoffmann's ebullient image of a free, proud, and strong Germany resembled that of Strandberg's Sweden. The concept of the *Volkskönig* (the people's king), which Hoffmann had rhapsodized, found its counterpart in the *Hymn*. But Strandberg also added his own ingredients, most noticeably martial and religious themes. The resulting compound, the *Hymn*, replaced or rather displaced a Swedish translation of *God Save the King*, which hitherto had served as Sweden's anthem.

From deep within Swedish hearts there comes
A unifying and simple song,
That is offered to the king!
Be faithful to him and his [house],
Make light the crown on his head
And put all your trust in him,
You people of renowned lineage.[23]

The closeness of sovereign and people is woven as the basic theme throughout the five stanzas, marked by neo-Gothic imagery. Ruler and ruled support one another in victory as well as in defeat. If the need arises, the king, "sword in hand," will clothe himself in the national colors of yellow and blue and lead his "faithful folk" into battle, perhaps even to doom. Their blood would "weave a royal purple, warm and true" to protect the king. The final stanza not only invoked God's help but the ancient fighting spirit that had joined together the Swedish kings and their men.

Notwithstanding such enraptured visions, melodramatic phraseology, turgid style, and martial gore, Strandberg's poem met with strong approval when first heard publicly at his alma mater in Lund, on December 5, 1844.[24] The warm applause was as much due to the high expectations placed in the newly crowned king as to the sweeping rhythm of the *Hymn* set to music by Otto Lindblad, a skilled composer and male choir pioneer.

Enthusiasm for Oscar I waned during the following decade, not least so in Strandberg. Fortunately, his *Hymn* had not been written for a specific king but rather for the Swedish monarchy as such. Soon he became a sharp critic of the royal government. His patriotism and liberalism, however, remained unchanged, as did his martial spirit. Strandberg's first collection of poetry, which included the *Hymn*, carried the characteristic title *Songs in Armor*.

Because Scandinavian solidarity had more political meaning to him than to Dybeck, Strandberg backed the Danes when resisting German encroachment on North Slesvig in 1848. Strandberg's bête noire, however, continued to be the Russian bear, not solely as Sweden's traditional enemy but because of the reactionary nature of the tsarist government. His unvarying liberalism found expression in the translation of Lord Byron's poetry and in such poems of his own as "Our Free Speech," and it showed in some stanzas of the *Hymn*.

Ironically, that poem came to be viewed by a new generation of Swedish students as the work of a traditional royalist and soon was contraposed to Dybeck's *Du gamla*. Both authors died in 1877, a third of a century after they had created their respective poems, with neither man anticipating the future role of these poems. As yet there was no indication of their rise to anthem status. Indeed, Sweden had long remained one of the few European countries without a national anthem, for reasons indicated earlier.[25]

The crisis in relations with Norway, however, activated a search for such an anthem. In 1899 a competition was announced and drew more than one hundred entries. But, as in similar cases elsewhere, none of these entries gained enough support to make the grade. Thus, both the Dybeck and the Strandberg poems slipped into the twentieth century as the unofficial contenders for pride of place. Yet *Du gamla* had the edge.

The most obvious reason for the widening margin was that Dybeck's piece remained as timeless as Sweden's forests, streams, lakes, and mountains. His little poem was bucolic, homelike, peaceful, and thus more acceptable to Swedish mentality in the modern age than Strandberg's poem with its accents on war, monarchy, and self-sacrifice. The interpretation of the *Hymn* as conservative and out-of-date by the very groups who espoused *Du gamla* as the song of the dominant liberals further lessened the general appeal of the Strandberg song.

It was *Du gamla* that could be heard along with the Danish and Norwegian anthems in meetings of student associations in Uppsala and Lund. In 1914 Strandberg's "democratic royalism" held little attraction for these groups as they backed the liberal prime minister in a showdown with the king over ministerial responsibility and parliamentary authority.[26] *Du gamla, du fria* now acquired a domestic political meaning with emphasis on the word "free," while the *Hymn* found itself bereft of its original meaning, the union of king and people.

Although the country was affected by a constitutional crisis, it was spared involvement in the impending World War I. No declaration of war or general mobilization, no armistice or victory parades offered opportunities for singing the anthem, nor would a second world war be much different in that respect.[27] That did not mean that the two authors, let alone their songs, were consigned to oblivion. Remembrance of Dybeck and his work in particular enjoyed a marked revival.

In late July 1917, a stele shaped like a runic stone was unveiled in his native Odensvi on the fortieth anniversary of his death. The massive stone carried the first two lines of *Du gamla* like an arc around its upper edge. A similar memorial was erected eleven years later over his presumed grave. On that occasion a choir presented several of Dybeck's songs, while the principal speaker quoted from *Du gamla* verses, "acknowledged by millions of Swedes."[28]

While this may have been true, these millions thought of Dybeck's unpretentious song as more of a folk song than an anthem. In that former capacity it is an inalienable part of the Swedish cultural heritage and an endearing reflection of the unspoiled beauty of the Swedish countryside. Not by chance did the author's paean earn him new esteem in the 1970s. The veteran ethnologist came to be viewed also as an ecologist and, in the words of a recent commentator on Västmanland, "we remember him for that and therefore should sing our national anthem more often."[29]

There may indeed be a dearth of dramatic, let alone historical, occasions that call for a rendering of *Du gamla* in a national consensus of Swedish sentiments, in either triumph or defiance. A comparison with other Scandinavian anthems could well single out Sweden in the early 1940s as having been exempt from attack and even challenge by a foreign country. At a time when Denmark and Norway were under the Nazi heel and Finland had recently capitulated to the

Soviet Union, that comparison concluded with the complacent if defensible statement, "a nation that has enjoyed peace and freedom as long as ours can refrain gladly from having even a pearl of a national anthem."[30]

The Swedes of the modern era, by inclination as much as by their geopolitical situation, neither need nor want a national anthem that is displayed only on special occasions like a precious reliquary. They would rather express their feelings through a song marked by the absence of assertiveness, heroics, jingoism, and martialism. Dybeck's simple verses obviously meet that prescription. Thus, they are most often heard nowadays at informal gatherings: in summer camps, at the monthly meetings of senior citizens, or at those of the women's auxiliary service (*Sveriges Rikslatte Förbund*). Invariably, *Du gamla, du fria* is not only referred to as a folk song, but it is used much like one. As yet there has been no known demand to replace it as the informal national anthem.[31]

The continued acceptance of Strandberg's *Hymn*, however, may be more surprising. The author had conjured up a halcyon vision when he created the stanzas. The irrelevance of some of their lines could only increase as a modernized and socialized Sweden made its pioneer appearance before an attentive world. By the same token, the Swedish monarchy evolved from royal absolutism to democratic pluralism. By this evolutionary process Strandberg's key concept of "the people's majesty which is also that of the king" gained a far more concrete meaning and timely ring than when he penned his *Hymn*. And at the centennial of its creation a commentator could justifiably remark, "In these trying times [1944] . . . Strandberg's message and purpose are by no means outmoded but increasingly give expression to the relationship of the Swedish people and their sovereign."[32]

In 1944 the sovereign was King Gustaf V. His reign, which spanned two world wars, had given the country a sense of continuity as well as evolution. He, his equally popular and scholarly son, the tragic death of his grandson in a plane crash, and a youthful great-grandson—the present King Carl XVI Gustaf who married a commoner—all have brought the Bernadotte dynasty closer to the people. The revised constitution of 1974, replacing that of 1809, has merely institutionalized an existing situation in which the monarch is but the crowned representative of the nation.[33]

He and his fellow Swedes now form that entity which Strandberg envisioned. It thus seems that the resolute *kungssången*, still heard when the king is present at national ceremonies, such as the annual Nobel prize award each December, has nowadays more applicability in terms of togetherness than when written a century and a half ago. And while *Du gamla, du fria* and the *Hymn* embody different dimensions of Swedish life, both remain the accepted distillation of national propensities.

NOTES

1. Since the fifteenth century the Swedish peasantry was represented in the *Riksdag* as the fourth estate.

2. See the Bernadotte reference in Chapter 11, n. 3.

3. See Chapter 3.

4. Sven Kjersen, *Svenska Kulturgestalter* (Swedish cultural figures), hereafter cited as Kjersen, *Kulturgestalter*, (Stockholm: Kooperativa Förbundets Bokförlag, 1930), 94.

5. The original verses had been naive and repetitive little rhymes sounding like children's ditties.

6. The Swedish anthem's translation into English provides one more example of the difficulties attending poetry translation. I have used here the English version put out by the Swedish Institute but made a few semantic changes to make it more consistent with the original text. It should be noted that for Dybeck Sweden and North were synonymous terms and that he used the latter term rather than Sweden in the future anthem; nor did the initial version of *Du gamla* carry the word "free" let alone "freeborn" as in the semi-official translation of the Swedish Institute. See also pp. 202–203.

7. Kjersen, *Kulturgestalter*, 96.

8. Sven Kjersen, *Richard Dybeck: Historien om en svensk* (Richard Dybeck: History about a Swede), hereafter cited as Kjersen, *Dybeck* (Stockholm: Wahlström & Widstrand, 1916), 86.

9. *Sohlmans musiklexikon*, 5 vols. (Stockholm: Sohlmans Förlag, 1975–1979), 2:347.

10. Wulff Fürstenberg, "Du gamla, du fria," in *Nordisk Tidskrift för Vetenskap, Konst och Industri, Ny serie* (1939), 15:117.

11. His collections ranged from a tabulation of plant names derived from that of Maria during the sixteenth century through herders' horn melodies to over five hundred folk songs.

12. Franklin D. Scott, *Sweden, the Nation's History* (Minneapolis: University of Minnesota Press, 1988), 321.

13. In a poem written in 1861, Dybeck called Swedes "the freest folk on earth." Such exuberant if also excessive assertion can best be understood in the context of his ethnocentricity. Dybeck is one of the very few anthem authors who never travelled abroad.

14. Carl Mangard, *Richard Dybeck: folksangens skald* (Richard Dybeck: Folksongs' bard), *Västmansland Fornminnesförenings Aarskrift* (1937), 121.

15. For this careful translation I am indebted to Mrs. Eva Dunhem. The popularity of the song, known as the *Orsa March*, has brought about quite a few variations of its lines. The Swedish text used here is taken from Kjersen, *Dybeck*, 55–56.

16. Mangard, 110–11.

17. See Chapter 11 on the evolution of this conflict.

18. Mangard, 109.

19. Like much else in the era of "Scandinavianism" the often used term *North* subsumed Norway as well as Sweden. North as a cultural as well as a political synecdoche is still used in references to all of Scandinavia.

20. Bernhard Tarschys, *Talis Qualis: Studenten poeten* (Stockholm: P. A. Norstedt & Söner, 1949), 5:218 passim.

21. Ibid., 264.

22. This is one of the rare instances of intellectual cross-fertilization among authors of national anthems, always excepting the *Marseillaise*.

23. In preference over available English translations, I again have relied on that prepared by Mrs. Dunhem.

24. Tarschys, 270.

25. See p. 204 of this chapter.

26. The long-smouldering controversy over ultimate authority in policy making came to a head in February 1914 when King Gustaf V repudiated the defense policies of the liberal government, holding back on budget increases. The government resigned under protest, but the resulting crisis passed with the formation of a nonpartisan government, its position strengthened by the outbreak of World War I.

27. Among those called up in the summer of 1941 to guard the frontiers toward Norway, however, *Du gamla* was sung regularly at weekend services. Information was kindly supplied by Mr. Bertil Wedin.

28. Mangard, 157.

29. Bonzo Berggren, *Sällsamheter i Västmanland* (Rarities in Västmanland) (Stockholm: Raben & Sjögren, 1978), 191.

30. Roland Fridholm, "Nordiske nationalsanger" (Nordic national songs) in *Nordisk Tidskrift for Vetenskab, Konst och Industri, Ny serie, Häft* 8 (1942), 581.

31. Fürstenberg has succinctly summed up the characteristics of the Dybeck poem and the reasons for an unchallenged existence as the Swedish anthem to the present day. "That this artless melody with its simple text and almost no empty phrases could become [the national anthem] tells us that the verses talk to the soul of the people." Fürstenberg, 124.

32. Bernhard Tarschys, "Ur svenska hjärtans ju . . . Ett Hundraarsminne" (From out of Swedish hearts . . . a centenary), *Ord och Bild* (1944), 572.

33. The Instrument of Government in 1974 stipulated that the monarch, while formally head of state, would have only ceremonial functions.

15

Luxembourg

Ons Hemeecht
(Michel Lentz)

The Luxembourg anthem is unique, for several reasons, among the anthems presented here. It is the only one written in the vernacular. Its author, competing with himself rather than a rival, wrote another national song which served as a quasi-anthem, especially in times of crisis. Paradoxically, this alternate, known as *De Feierwon* (The Fire Chariot), not only preceded *Ons Hemeecht* (Our Homeland) but held premier rank for nearly a half century. While other anthems were sparked by national crises or visions of national unity, *De Feierwon's* origins related to a local event which immediately acquired national proportions because of the diminutive size of the country.

Lying open in all directions, Luxembourg had been overrun seriatim for centuries by Burgundians, Spaniards, Austrians, French, and Germans. Three major partitions in 1659, 1815, and 1839[1] had reduced Luxembourg's territory and population to less than two-fifths of their original size. Worse still, the steadily diminished country had become little more than an appendage, tossed hither and thither. Once a formidable principality which, in the fourteenth century, had even provided emperors for the Holy Roman Empire, country and people had lacked a native ruler since that time. Not until 1815 did they acquire a titular grand duke; alas, he also was king of the Netherlands. Luxembourg was merely the eighteenth province of his heterogeneous kingdom.[2] Moreover, Prussia was given the right to garrison the rock fortress of Luxembourg City. To make this multiple arrangement still more intricate, the grand duchy was joined to the German Confederation, since the Prussians garrisoned the fortress on behalf of that confederation.

Nor were other claimants to Luxembourg's soil and sovereignty absent for long. The Belgian revolution of 1830 also affected the neighboring grand duchy. Barely in office, the provisional government in Brussels claimed Luxembourg as an integral part of the as yet undefined territory of the new state of Belgium. That claim was not entirely unjustified, in view of the support many Luxembourgers had given to the Belgians in their fight for independence, hoping to perhaps gain their own.

Unfortunately, they were to be badly disappointed. A short campaign by Dutch forces in 1831, though aborted by French intervention, sufficed to bring Great Britain and France, which previously had endorsed Belgian claims, to reconsider their commitment. Under a newly worked-out arrangement, known as the Twenty-Four Articles, only the western parts of Luxembourg would stay with the new kingdom of Belgium. The remainder of the once again truncated grand duchy would revert to the Dutch crown.[3] For good measure the Prussians kept control of the rock fortress, and membership in the German Confederation continued as before. Luxembourg, it might be said without exaggeration, thus belonged to anybody but the Luxembourgers.

True, a new Dutch king gave to his grand duchy a degree of autonomy in 1841. Yet a national identity had to be looked for in directions other than self-government and independence; among them self-respect and self-confidence, a home-grown collective mentality, pride in local attributes and attainments. A tangible sense of localism compensated the pragmatic Luxembourgers for the absence of a more abstract sense of nationalism. Locality and nationality were interchangeable concepts for many a Luxembourger, giving them a blissful feeling of contentment within the compact smallness of the country and the predictable stability of their milieu.

If national independence could not be secured by force of arms—and there never was such an indication in Luxembourg's history—or national union attained by bringing back lost territories and people, or national borders be established only by international consent, there remained one other means to assert a Luxembourg identity: language. It was *Letzeburgesch* which marked most clearly Luxembourg's nationhood and marked off more distinctly than any border that country from its numerous neighbors. This linguistic patriotism, as has been rightly remarked, could only exist in a small country whose idiom had to compete with two major languages—German and French—and which was constantly exposed to the influence of their respective civilizations.[4] In times of crisis in particular *d'Sprooch* (the language) was "the most resolute expression"[5] of the national will, once that will existed.

But even in the linguistic field, foreign influences long dominated in the little country. French has remained the official language for much of the modern era and was spoken by the elite. German served as the primary means of communication for the urban middle class. During the post-Napoleonic era, Dutch was made compulsory in the administration and in schools. *Letzeburgesch* merely lived in the informal and unofficial conversation of the largely rural population.

As in Greece, Hungary, Norway, and Ireland, a linguistic revival movement dovetailed a reformist-minded nationalism. Independence presupposed a native tongue. And *Letzeburgesch*, as the truest expression of a Luxembourg identity, acquired at long last a printed form in 1829. It took another quarter of a century for a native literature to come into being. The beginnings of that literature have been largely credited to Michel Lentz, called not in vain the "national poet." But long before his first collection of poems appeared belatedly in 1873, a number of poems had made his name familiar within the grand duchy. That familiarity was due not just to the responsive chord struck by the author among his generally rather prosaic countrymen, but mainly to the fact that he was the quintessential Luxembourger: content with living in a miniature country, rooted squarely and proudly in it, and unwilling to forego the traditional way of life.

Lentz's first poem to gain public attention and acclaim, never to lose them again, was *De Feierwon*. Engendered neither by the imminence of war nor calls for an uprising to secure independence, this song owed its origins to nothing more dramatic than a departing train. True, it was the first train ever to roll past the grand duchy's borders.[6] Its departure from the new depot in Luxembourg City was watched with fascination by thousands of citizens. Michel Lentz probably stood among them, but unlike the other spectators, he already had poured his emotions and expectations into a poetic mold.

The two-day celebration climaxed in the singing of his new song at a mass gathering in front of city hall. An amateur soloist hardly had finished singing the first of six stanzas when he was joined by the crowd, which picked up the refrain enthusiastically. While rendering it, hats were waved and hurrahs shouted, and within days the song was known throughout the little country whose population resembled, in its compactness, that of an extended family.

The first stanza epitomized the whole poem, glorying in the beauty of the country, its easygoing administration, and the contentment of the citizenry. Small as their land was, it could be shown with pride to any and all of the bigger neighbors.

> Ready stands the Fire-chariot.
> It whistles through the air and off it goes
> Rattling over the iron roads,
> Proudly the neighbors it shows
> That we now, too, found our way
> To the great league of nations.
> Come you here from France, Belgium, Prussia
> We want to show you our homeland
> Go and call all around (you)
> How contented we are.[7]

The following stanzas emphasized the steadiness of the Luxembourgers in holding on to their piece of land, the freedom of the people from oppression and from a heavy tax burden, and their awareness that smallness and snugness made for happiness. All of these advantages, as enumerated in stanza after stanza, built toward the climax of the last line, so popular that it became the national motto: "Mir welle bleiwe wat mir sin" (We want to remain what we are). And it was that line which invariably rose confidently and defiantly in crisis situations.

Welcome as the new iron link with the outside world was, the character of the country and people had to be preserved unimpaired. The halcyon peacefulness, the narrowly circumscribed habits, the moderate well-being, the beautiful countryside, the inimitable pithy language, and blissful cheer were the lasting inheritance of the Luxembourgers as embodied in the *Feierwon*. The eager author not only had furnished the words but also, probably with some help from a friend, the musical score. Nor had he left the distribution to chance. Text and score were distributed at the first presentation. Initially titled *D'Letzeburger*, Lentz had dedicated the poem to "my country" and addressed it to all of its citizens.

Within days, according to a later account, "boys whistled it in the streets; it could be heard around the table of drinking companions and also in workshops [as in] the privacy of households."[8] But Lentz had by no means exhausted his creative drive or his patriotic passion. Within five years another major poem, this one destined to ultimate anthem status, sprang from his active pen. The new creation was triggered by the first national music festival held in the small town of Ettelbrück on June 5, 1864.

Among the selections presented were excerpts from Meyerbeer, Gounod, and Rossini. Number eleven on the program, however, was a novelty: a Lentz poem titled *Ons Hemeecht*, which was set to music by August Zinnen, a professional composer who also acted as the principal conductor at the current music festival. Sung by a male quartet, the new creation met with instant acclaim.[9]

> Where the Alzette meanders through the meadows,
> And the Sauer breaks through the rocks;
> Where the grape spreads its scent along the Moselle,
> Making the Heavens give us wine:
> There is our land, so dear to us
> That we shall give her everything.
> Our homeland that we carry
> So deeply in our hearts.[10]

The next two stanzas reflected Lentz's core conviction that small is beautiful and that there is no better place than his homeland. Its people are blessed by the simple comforts of their lives. An ambiance of *Gemütlichkeit*, that untranslatable word which occurred in other Lentz poetry, made the people feel good and caused cheer and laughter throughout the grand duchy. The final stanza, however, turned thoughts heavenward. In solemn verses made more solemn still by a chorale-like score, the author invoked divine protection to keep the Letze-burger land free from foreign dominance and to let "freedom's sun glow" in perpetuity.

The solemnity of these lines and the idyllic imagery of the whole poem was heightened by Zinnen's composition, much at variance with the marching tempo of the *Feierwon*. But it was not just the music that made the two poems so different. Where the *Feierwon* was assertive, pragmatic, and robust, *Ons He-meecht* was contemplative, pious, and sentimental. And the Luxembourgers soon knew on what occasions and in what situations to have recourse to one or the other song as best expressing their feelings. Thus, a leapfrogging sequence evolved, putting one song ahead at certain times and the other when times had changed.

Whatever the difference between the two poems, they were fuelled by the same unlimited if also unsophisticated patriotism of their author. Born out of a compensatory awareness of the narrow limits of the country, the inability to defend it with an army of three hundred men—as Lentz wistfully observed—and its uncertain existence among a host of stronger neighbors, the author's patriotism was the raison d'être for his poetry, the only artistic medium that he used. Lentz considered the writing of his poems a patriotic duty, and "he sang less from an urge to write poetry than from love for the homeland."[11]

Lentz's visceral attachment to the grand duchy was conditioned as much by his familiarity with the local scene as by the author's homey mentality. Except for one brief sojourn as a student in Brussels, Lentz spent his long life in his beloved little country and that almost entirely in its capital. He was born there into the family of a masterbaker, and there he entered government service as a clerk in 1842. During the next half century, he slowly advanced through the ranks of a bureaucracy as stable as it was staid, until he reached the elevated position of audit councillor.

There were no untoward events in either his personal or professional life, no disappointed hopes, no dramatic changes, no searching reassessments. So regular were his daily activities and habits that the housewives along the way that he took every day to and from the office—weather permitting—set their clocks or schedules, saying in the evenings, "The little man has just passed by. It must be half-past five."[12] Even his diversions followed the same regular pattern: convivial drinking with his boon companions, weekly meetings at the "Gym," the athletic association which he had helped to found, meticulous attention to family affairs, and the writing of yet another poem.

If the routine of his daily life changed so little over the decades and retained its clockwork rotation, it did not follow that his poetry rotated with the same monotonous regularity. The basic themes of happiness, freedom, and pride in Luxembourg remained constant. But beyond these recurrent themes lay others of much variety. There were nature poems, drinking songs, occasional pieces, didactic verses, but none more original, perceptive, and witty than the vignettes of common people in their daily lives. This genre was Lentz's natural poetic habitat, along with his patriotic poetry, and directly related to his own lifestyle within its social and geographic limitations, yet filled with optimism and an earthy humor.

That humor, which on occasion could spill over into satire, was a vital component of Luxembourger mentality. Not by chance had Lentz titled his first collection of poetry *Fun and Earnestness*. He was fifty-three years old when this collection appeared and obviously in no need to make a living from his poetry. Many of the poems, including *Ons Hemeecht* and *De Feierwon*, had already reached the public in some other form. His aim in getting over four hundred pages published now was "to render a modest contribution to German vernacular literature and to counteract the unfortunate prejudice that our language is fit only for jocular, even trivial themes."[13] He modestly added that judgment on the validity of his intentions lay in the future. Yet judgment by his countrymen had already been rendered and found in his favor.

De Feierwon in particular served as the national voice in the troublesome 1860s. The cherished autonomy of the grand duchy over the previous thirty years now appeared at risk on more than one occasion and the fate of its citizens, accustomed to a stable order, much in doubt. Prussia's victory over Austria in 1866 had sounded the death knell of the German Confederation and ended Luxembourg's association with it. Drawn unilaterally into Prussia's orbit, an anxious France very soon tried to exert its counterpull.

The resulting diplomatic tug-of-war between the two big neighbors unnerved the normally placid Luxembourgers. Looking for reassurance that their lives and land would be preserved unchanged, they turned to their nominal sovereign—the Dutch king—and to Lentz's *De Feierwon*. When the king's brother and regent of the grand duchy made his appearance there in September 1866 to quiet anxieties, he met up everywhere with the demonstrative singing of *De Feierwon* and in particular its assertive refrain, "We want to remain what we are."[14] The prince-regent was not slow to respond in the same spirit and words, albeit in French.

But more than reassuring words were needed. Early in 1867, Napoleon III, ever scheming to increase French influence, opened negotiations with the Dutch king to buy the grand duchy lock, stock, and barrel. The deal might have gone through had Prussia's Bismarck not strongly objected to handing Napoleon a "pourboire." Franco-Prussian animosities sharpened to the point of likely war when, in the nick of time, British mediation secured an agreement among the major European powers. The London Treaty of May 1867 not only defused an explosive situation but gave an unexpected bonus to the Luxembourgers: independence. This independence, for which they had made no attempt to fight, fell into their lap and, better still, was guaranteed by the major European powers along with Luxembourg's permanent neutrality. Best of all, both the Prussian garrison and the French purchase offer were withdrawn under the terms of the London Treaty.

Small wonder that Lentz gave quick and succinct expression to the Luxembourgers' jubilance, and hardly surprising that he did so in his familiar terminology: "We are happy, we are free and want to remain so."[15] That pollyannish mood all too soon was overshadowed by yet another Franco-Prussian crisis and one that led to war in 1870. At its very outset, Prussian papers clamored for the annexation of Luxembourg. The local population, in turn, not only intoned *De Feierwon* with emphasis on the bottom line, "We want to remain what we are," but improvised an even more defiant line, "Call out in all directions; we don't want to become Prussians!"

That improvisation attested to the staunch independence sentiments of the Luxembourgers, but for once Lentz found himself at odds with his countrymen. The last thing the friendly and peaceful "little man" wanted was tension with any of the neighbors. And in a poetic retort titled "Sing it as it is," he admonished any singer of the additional lines to mind the peaceable relations with all countries and to sing *De Feierwon* as written by him.

Such admonition, however, failed to succeed as long as a Prussian presence made itself disagreeably felt. Prussia's insistence on controlling the much expanded Luxembourg rail network, whose very opening had brought *De Feierwon* into being, was hardly conducive to mitigating anti-Prussian sentiments. To avoid embarrassing incidents, Luxembourg authorities omitted *De Feierwon* from musical programs honoring visiting royalty of German descent on at least two occasions.[16] But that omission benefitted *Ons Hemeecht,* which gained in prominence during the 1880s.

The generally cheerful author of both national songs was none too happy about the absence of the first of these on certain official occasions. Yet he had the satisfaction of hearing them together in April 1889. At the fortieth anniversary celebrations of the "Gym," the festive gathering honored Lentz as "the national poet" with renditions of both *De Feierwon* and *Ons Hemeecht.* The former was sung by children as he entered the hall, the latter by the active members of the "Gym" as he was about to leave well after midnight. More than once the honoree was about to burst into tears, and in his thank-you address he told the audience that his Muse had laid upon him "the holy duty to sing of freedom, happiness, and contentment."[17]

Such a hyperbolic statement might best be explained not just by the emotions of the moment, but by Lentz's deeply rooted conviction that his verses embodied the essence of Luxembourger mentality. On this special evening he was more aware than ever that he had succeeded in implanting into successive generations of Luxembourgers a lasting awareness of the qualities of their nationhood and country. As he had so often remarked in his poetry, the citizenry did not number in millions; the national territory was minute; no spectacular glory or splendor of achievement attached to Luxembourg's history, but neither did oppression, injustice, or revolution. For these very reasons harmony, moderate well-being, peace, and freedom prevailed, all of them contributing to the ambiance which pervaded the country.

That image of a European Shangri-La stayed with Lentz throughout his life and strongly permeated much of his work. Yet the euphoria of sheltered lives in a milieu of snugness, which he never failed to praise, also carried with it an undiscriminating smugness, and not least so in his two most widely used national songs. He probably had heard them together one last time at the "Gym's" fortieth anniversary celebrations.

In the 1890s, when Luxembourg's relations with the big neighbors east and west were at their most comfortable and peaceable, the need for any defiant reassertion seemed obsolete. As Premier Paul Eyschen, the foremost encomiast of Lentz, explained, the growing preference for *Ons Hemeecht* was due to changed times. "One has become hereabouts calmer and more relaxed than one was in 1866 and 1870. In the maturing life of the state we did get accustomed to situations which formerly would have flushed our cheeks."[18] Not surprisingly, therefore, *Ons Hemeecht* had become, around the turn of the century, albeit informally, Luxembourg's national anthem.

Its author had died in September 1893. Thousands of his countrymen from every part of Luxembourg attended his funeral procession in the capital. The red-white-blue national flag covered his coffin as a symbol that the country embraced him as he had embraced it for so long. Obituaries acclaimed Lentz not only as "the national poet" but as "the embodiment of our national being."[19]

Paul Eyschen once more spoke for Michel Lentz as he had done so eloquently before. His eulogy climaxed in the statement that, if ever needed, the author's voice would resonate throughout the country and that it would be the voice of the Letzeburger people. That collective voice was heard instantly at the close of the burial service when the mourners intoned the final stanza of *Ons Hemeecht*. And all its stanzas rang out again a decade later when a monument for Lentz and a fellow author was unveiled in Luxembourg City.[20]

Yet *De Feierwon,* which in Eyschen's words had been hung on a wall like a shield for the purpose of nostalgic ornamentation, could just as easily be taken down for protection in the hour of emergency. That hour was to come soon enough. In August 1914, the Prussians were back in force along with many other Germans on their way to invade Belgium and France. Resistance of the Luxembourgers was limited to protest notes and the singing of *De Feierwon* together with the *Brabançonne* and the *Marseillaise*.

Four years later it could be heard again. This time around, however, there was no longer a need to voice the rejection of any Prussianization. Now *De Feierwon* was struck up defiantly against another neighbor—Belgium. Rumors persisted that the Belgian government, with French concurrence, planned to press at the Versailles peace conference for the inclusion of Luxembourg into the liberated kingdom of Belgium. *De Feierwon's* line, emphasized anew, was the ever-effective and reassuring "we want to remain what we are."

Whether that line or the song as a whole sufficed to obviate any annexation plans has never been established, but the grand duchy continued its separate existence, except for entering into a customs union with Belgium in 1921. During the interbellum period, *Ons Hemeecht* held sway, since no one threatened the grand duchy's independence. That halcyon situation, however, ended abruptly in 1940. On May 10, the German war machine overran the country within three hours. The only resistance offered at that moment was the renewed mobilization of *De Feierwon*.

The insidious Nazi propaganda to make the Luxembourgers think of themselves as Germans in speech and custom[21] proved abortive. The anti-Prussian improvisation reappeared in renditions of *De Feierwon*, first sung aloud, and after the occupation bore down ever heavier, more stealthily. Yet *De Feierwon's* key phrase continued as the visible and audible motto of Luxembourger resistance.[22] On Liberation Day of Luxembourg City, September 10, 1944, Lentz's two national songs once more could be heard publicly and triumphantly, as the capital's principal paper reported on the following day.

In the half century since, however, *De Feierwon's* function has been mainly that of the escutcheon on the wall, decorative rather than demonstrative. The coal-fire chariot of nearly a century and one-half ago has been replaced by Diesel engines; the sylvan land largely converted to blast furnaces and steel plants. There is no likelihood of invasion, let alone annexation; Prussia does no longer exist, and enviable statistics have made Luxembourger well-being common knowledge, even without being shown around.

Ons Hemeecht, in turn, is as timely in the age of European Union as when first written. The Alzette and Sauer flow unchanged; the Mosel wine is as exquisite as ever in a good year; comfortable living has spread to the last hamlet, and peace and freedom can be taken for granted even without recourse to prayer. This is indeed the era for *Ons Hemeecht* to prevail with its gentle lines of the country's comfort, coziness, and cheer. And those lines continue to ring out on such occasions as the celebrations in 1989 of the 150th anniversary of the grand duchy in its present form.

Yet there are fewer opportunities nowadays to break into the national anthem and hardly any to strike up *De Feierwon*.[23] After all, Luxembourg is in the forefront of European countries eager to give up much of national sovereignty for the sake of a truly supranational and expanding union. Voluntary renunciation of that sovereignty, however, does not imply the abandonment of a national identity. And if that ever were in danger of oblivion, it seems likely that the line would be heard again as affirmatively as ever: "We want to remain what we are."

NOTES

1. In the first of these partitions France had acquired the Thionville area. Prussia took possession of the Bitburg and St. Vith region in 1815. The western half of the grand duchy was allotted, with Dutch consent, to Belgium in 1839.

2. On the composition of that heterogeneous kingdom, see also Chapter 10.

3. This compromise provided for the permanent partition of Luxembourg and re-

placed the Eighteen Articles of June 1830, under which Great Britain and France had concurred to support Belgian claims to Luxembourg.

4. N. Ries, *Le peuple luxembourgeois: essai de psychologie* (The Luxembourg people: a psychological essay), 2d ed. (Diekirch: J. Schroell, 1920), 268.

5. Nicholas Welter, *Mundartliche und hochdeutsche Dichtung in Luxemburg* (Dialect and high German poetry in Luxembourg) (Luxembourg: St. Paulus Gesellschaft, 1928), 9.

6. Two tracks had been laid down in July and September 1859. The new line, Luxembourg-Trier, was opened on October 4, 1859, and was the first to link the grand duchy rails to the outside world.

7. The translation is by Mathias Tresch and has been reprinted in Jul Christophory, *Mir schwätze Letzeburgesch* (We speak Luxemburgisch), *Bilingual Guide to Grammar and Reading* (Luxembourg: Imprimerie Saint-Paul, S.A., n.d.), 131.

8. "Michel Lentz und Staatsminister Paul Eyschen an das Luxemburger Volk" (Lentz and . . . Eyschen to the Luxemburg people), in *Voix d'outre tombe* [1919], 1.

9. Franz Rehm, "Rund um unsere beiden Nationalhymnen" (About our two national anthems), in *Der neue Luxemburger Kalender* (1940), 157.

10. Translation by this author.

11. Welter, 175.

12. Fernand Hoffmann, *Geschichte der Luxemburger Mundartdichtung* (History of Luxemburg dialect poetry), 2 vols. (Luxembourg: Bourg-Bourger, 1964–1967), 1:104.

13. From Lentz's introduction to *Spass an Ierscht* (Fun and earnestness) (Letzeburg: V. Bück, 1873). A second collection of his poetry was published in 1887 under the title *Hierschblumen* (Autumn flowers). A slender third volume of his poetry appeared posthumously in 1920 under the title *Wantergreng* (Wintergreen).

14. *Voix d'outre tombe*, 3.

15. This poem was titled "We are happy" and carried the subtitle "The people's voice from Letzeburger Land."

16. In October 1878, when the grand ducal regent Henry entered Luxembourg City with his wife Marie, a Prussian princess, *De Feierwon* could not be heard from any of the numerous bands and choirs. Again in 1882, it was absent from official musical programs when the Dutch king, William III, and his German-born wife Emma paid a visit to their grand ducal capital.

17. Hoffmann, 1:106.

18. *Voix d'outre tombe*, 8.

19. Obituary in *Haus-und Hand-Kalender auf das Jahr 1894* (Luxemburg: Jos. Bruck, 1893), 21.

20. The monument for Lentz and the dramatist Dicks, pen name for Edmund de la Fontaine, was dedicated in October 1903.

21. In October 1941, German authorities requested Luxembourgers to fill in a questionnaire slanted for propaganda purposes. One category required a reply to the question "mother tongue." In spite of an explanatory note that German had to be substituted for *Letzeburgesch* since that latter was not a "recognized language," most entries read *Letzeburgesch*. The questionnaire was subsequently withdrawn!

22. Posters depicting Grand Duchess Charlotte, the reigning monarch who had fled Nazi occupation, were captioned, "We want to remain what we are." Generals Dwight D. Eisenhower and Omar Bradley, while driving to their advanced headquarters in Luxembourg City on October 14, 1944, noticed numerous banners and placards inscribed

with the same motto. David Eisenhower, *Eisenhower at War: 1943–1945* (New York: Random House, 1986), 489.

23. According to information kindly provided by Dr. Jul Christophory, *De Feierwon* is no longer intoned on official occasions, but the first and last stanzas of *Ons Hemeecht* were declared the official anthem of the grand duchy by the law of June 17, 1993.

Bibliographical Note

One of the major reasons for offering this book is precisely the absence of an up-to-date and comprehensive treatment of the origins and evolution of European national anthems, the characteristics of their authors, and the relationship of author and anthem to their respective national cultures. Numerous collections of national anthems exist in various languages, but none focus on the topics enumerated above and all emphasize music. These collections range from such old standbys as John Philip Sousa, *National, Patriotic and Typical Airs of All Lands* (Philadelphia-New York, 1890) to W. L. Reed and M. J. Bristow, *National Anthems of the World*, 6th ed. (Poole, Dorset, 1985). Yet they all carry only the briefest of references to the history of anthems and their composers and hardly any to the authors.

There are a few compilations that give some background information of a historical nature: Emil Bohn, *Die Nationalhymnen der europäischen Völker* (Breslau, 1908), and Paul Nettl, *National Anthems*, translated from German by Alexander Gode, 2d ed. (New York, 1967), both cited in this book. Bohn's monograph is now badly dated and Nettl's is global in scope. Eloise R. Griffith, *National Anthems and How They Came to be Written* (Boston, 1952), deals with the history of a half dozen European anthems in an impressionistic and superficial way. By contrast, the unpublished master's thesis of Mary Suzanne Campbell, "European National Anthems as a Factor in Modern Nationalism" (Xavier University, Ohio, 1963), presents a thoughtful attempt to relate anthems to both their authors and nations. Unfortunately, she restricted her effort to just a few anthems.

A noteworthy effort at a more comprehensive overview of national anthems, mainly European, was made by the late Erik Ørum, a Danish attorney. His presentation over two Danish broadcasting stations in September 1991 did relate anthems to their historical setting. He also provided some data on the respective authors. Regrettably, further work by him on the subject was cut short by an untimely death.

Encyclopedic articles on national anthems may be found in many of the standard compilations. A brief essay in *The New Grove Dictionary of Music and Musicians*, 20 vols. (London-New York, 1980), 13:46–47, provides an intelligent if sketchy summary on the characteristics of national anthems and a short bibliography, mainly on collections of such anthems. The *Brockhaus Riemann Musiklexikon*, 2 vols. (Wiesbaden, 1971), 2:198, is one of the very few reference works that carry summaries only on European anthems. Paul Nettl has supplied a useful overview, with some reference to both the history of anthems and their authors, in the standard German musicological encyclopedia, *Die Musik in Geschichte und Gegenwart*, ed. Friedrich Blum, 16 vols. (Kassel-Basel: Bärenreiter Verlag, 1949–1973), 9:1274–83. That summary, however, much like all others on the subject of national anthems, is in need of an update.

The meager literature on that subject is augmented by a few articles. The most important among them is Robert Michels, "Elemente einer Soziologie des Nationalliedes," in *Archiv für Sozialwissenschaft und Sozialpolitik*, 4 (1926): 317–61. In this essay the author made a pioneering effort to link national anthems to national cultures. Joseph Zikmund II, "National Anthems as Political Symbols," in *The Australian Journal of Politics and History*, 15 (1969):73–80, sought a similar connection. His short essay correctly maintained that none of the European anthems showed aggressiveness to the point of expansionist war. Theo Stemmler's rather cursory and negative article in *Die Zeit*, October 8, 1993, comes to a rather different conclusion when asserting that some European anthems, among the many others to which he refers, were marked by a gory martialism. Whatever the shortcomings of this kind of quick summation, it does testify to the continued interest in national anthems among the public at large and to the need to explore this subject field further.

Index

About the Author

F. GUNTHER EYCK, Distinguished Adjunct Professor in the School of International Service at The American University, has specialized in modern European history and contemporary foreign policies of West European countries. Professor Eyck's teaching experience spans half a century and has been augmented by 27 years of service with the U.S. government. His books include *The Benelux Countries: A Historical Survey* (1959) and *Loyal Rebels: The Tyrolean Uprising of 1809* (1986). He has also written numerous articles on 19th- and 20th-century European history and current events in Western Europe.

ISBN 0-313-29320-1

90000>

9 780313 293207

HARDCOVER BAR CODE

EAN